Teaching with Creative Dramatics

Teaching with Creative Dramatics

June Cottrell
Western Michigan University

NATIONAL TEXTBOOK COMPANY • Lincolnwood, Illinois U.S.A.

My Turn

I wish to express my gratitude and appreciation to all who helped to make this book possible—my friends and colleagues at Western Michigan University, especially Bill Buys for his invaluable suggestions and photographic work, and Shirley Woodworth who had to fight her way to our shared typewriter through piles of notes and manuscript for several months; all of the children who have made Creative Dramatics come alive and from whom I have learned so much; teachers Janet Green and Kathy Spall and their first graders at Indian Prairie School who were able to involve themselves in their drama so much that they forgot the camera; the many teachers and students who have shared their experiences, especially my friend and former student Bonita Stout for her enthusiasm and useful suggestions about puppetry; and all of the helpful folks at National Textbook.

Above all I wish to thank my wonderful family, my parents and sister, husband Jack and our children, Craig, Laurie, and Chris who have helped me in so many ways to keep alive my own sense of wonder. To them this book is dedicated.

J.S.C.

Contents

Introduction

Creative dramatics is an integrative process in which the child utilizes his whole self in experiences that emphasize imaginative thinking and creative expression. (p. 22)

Those of us committed to a holistic concern for children generally agree that it is the birthright of every child to reach his or her individual potential to be a thinking, feeling, and accomplishing contributor to the human race. Society expects and the future of our world decrees that those entrusted with the education of children provide instruction and experiences that will help each child to be whole; to be mentally, physically, emotionally and socially all that the child can be. Few would challenge the legitimacy of such a philosophical statement of responsibility, but it is in the implementation of our commitments that we often encounter quite disparate views. Those who define the fundamentals of education as reading, writing, and arithmetic (or in contemporary parlance...oracy, literacy, and computation) would relegate the role of the arts to "enrichment" reserved for the few. Such a point of view not only denies human history but also ignores what we know about the mind and the spirit. For though it has been said again and again, it begs repeating: *intelligence without imagination is useless.*

Creative drama is an art for children that has at its core the development and utilization of the imagination. Boys and girls engaged in creative drama are summoned to think in new and more sophisticated ways. To become someone or something else requires the player to imagine how another thinks, feels, moves, communicates, values, and relates to others and to the world. Children involved in drama use their minds to image objects and events not present to their senses. They become creative thinkers who are able to invent solutions to problems through the synthesizing of new ideas from perceptions previously experienced separately and to express those ideas through the drama. Participants draw upon their imaginations to visit the past, to fantasize about the future, and to explore facets of the contemporary scene outside the realm of real and personal experiences.

Creative drama is a group art that encourages children to share the offerings of their imaginations through social interaction. For if intelligence without imagination is useless, we might also add that intelligence without communication is a waste of the greatest magnitude. Communication is, of course, our greatest source of knowledge of self and of others and is basic to social order. Creative drama has come to take an important place within the language arts curricula from early childhood through middle school as such participation provides immense opportunities for children to acquire and enhance a wide range of verbal and nonverbal communication skills.

Creative drama is also a child art not unlike painting and dance, in which each person is encouraged to express his or her unique and individual ideas and feelings. We observe this liberated expression of the self in the spontaneous dramatic play of the very young. Here we see imaginative play unfettered by a concern about what is possible and what is not; it is only required that one can imagine it and communicate what one imagines in some way. Creative drama expands and extends from that creative play of the preschool years; a natural extension of the make believe play of home, yard, sidewalks and vacant lots into new learning experiences in the elementary through middle school classrooms.

The central purpose of this text is to introduce creative drama to all who are committed to holistic learning as essential for developing whole people. In addition, as this is intended as a text to meet the needs of preservice and inservice teachers who may not have much previous work in creative drama, it aims to provide both the theoretical and application guidelines necessary for doing drama with children while reawakening the "child" in the leader as well.

Toward that goal, the first chapter takes a brief look at the value of creative play to the quality of adult life and then a longer look at the play of early childhood as background for a better understanding of creative drama in the classroom. Chapter 1 also examines the role of dramatic play in meeting developmental needs of the very young. The proliferation of early childhood programs provides increased possibilities for engaging preschoolers in planned experiences in dramatic play, and suggestions are included for ways in which adults and young children can work together to assure that preschoolers are supported in developing intelligence with imagination.

With Chapter 2 we turn our attention to the classroom use of creative drama both in terms of what it is and what it is not. By comparing and contrasting creative drama and formal theatre, leaders are provided guidelines for articulationg what creative drama is about as well as how it works to serve children. The crucial role of the teacher and the classroom environment is considered. In Chapter 3 we explore ways of developing cognitive powers, increasing communication skills, nourishing emotional growth, and stimulating imaginative thinking through sensory experiences. Many of the activities in this chapter work especially well as beginning or "warm-up" experiences in preparation for longer or more complex work later on.

Chapter 4 begins by looking at ways to use creative drama to help children learn how people use space to communicate. We also explore ways to organize both space and children to meet or needs. The significance of characterization to the child's understanding of self and others and the use of pantomime in character development is described. This chapter, with an emphasis on movement and pantomime, provides ideas for helping children to become more astute nonverbal communicators.

Oral communication in drama is the primary emphasis in Chapter 5, "Exploring with Words." Ideas for pair work and for creating small group scenes illustrate how role playing and characterization can be used to generate spontaneous dialogue.

Very young children communicate through play; older boys and girls can find new and satisfying ways to express themselves through participation in creative drama. Creative drama in the classroom recognizes a natural way in which children learn. For these reasons many of the drama activities described throughout are, or can be, related to specific content areas or used to explore concepts, attitudes, and skills that are a regular part of elementary education. Chapter 6, "Drama in Curriculum," describes additional uses in language arts, social studies, science and mathematics, and concludes with a sample lesson that integrates creative drama with art activities.

And nothing integates better with drama (and drama with it) than literature. To lead children through adventures in creative drama means also to become a storyteller. Chapter 7 offers suggestions for choosing and using literature as the basis for drama work. A good story can be the teacher's strongest ally in providing a stimulus to the imagination and an impetus to get involved.

Adventures to stimulate the imagination, communication through mime, movement, and spontaneous dialogue, and identification with others through characterization are some of the ways in which we can involve the whole child in experiential learning through creative drama. It is thinking, imagining, feeling and being, but, above all, creative drama is doing. It is a way of learning which can nourish the child...even the "child" of mature years.

1

Play

*Our first great happiness is at
our Mother's breast; but our
second is in the ecstasy of play.*

Will Durant

The Value of Play: Not for Children Only

Not so long ago in our productive Western culture, work was labeled "adult" and play was labeled "child." The admonition, "Stop playing and get to work!" has survived an astonishing number of revolutions—educational, sociological, and technological. We have been told that play is respectable, indeed essential, for psychological health in adults, but we are still suspicious of spontaneous, noncompetitive, childlike play. We even tend to devalue certain kinds of adult activity that seem more like play than work. Many a poet, artist, or craftsman will attest to this. Do not the producers rather than the dreamers and discoverers reap the greatest rewards in most segments of our society?

Yet we need only to look around us to see the sad results of totally work-oriented lives in which play is either a nostalgic memory or a dream of our "golden years." Shortened work weeks, early retirement, and increased good health during the later years are some of the human

---

From *Mansions of Philosophy*.

rewards of our technologically advanced society. But most of us know adults who, upon retirement, feel set adrift, cut off from the mainstream of humanity. Having devoted their lives to their work, they have difficulty in finding suitable satisfying replacements for it. They have lost their ability to play, to be spontaneous, to try things they have never tried before—just for the pure joy of it! Somehow we need to be able to keep alive the sense of wonder with which the infant is endowed at birth and which permeates much of his play. The advent of the Computer Age is forcing us to take a long look at the value and significance of play for "kids of all ages."

Child's Play: What It Is

To define childhood only as preparation for adulthood depreciates what it means to be a child. Childhood has its own unique significance. So too does childhood play. It must first meet the needs of the child; that it later contributes to the quality of adult years does not concern the child.

Children cannot perceive as adults do. They lack the many years of experience that develop adult percepts, concepts, and value systems. They lack, at first, the ability to verbalize perceptions through socialized speech and must utilize nonverbal ways to communicate. That which is perceived through the senses must, of necessity, be responded to and communicated through movement rather than words. Within this context, play is the language of preschool children. Play serves as a primary tool which can contribute to the development of the communication skills of speaking, listening, reading, and writing. How children utilize play as a communication tool is more fully explored and interpreted later in this book in the sections dealing with the needs of young children that are met through dramatic play.

Play is an important communication tool of the child, especially the young child, but it is more. The familiar cliche, "as simple as child's play" seems to suggest that play is something uncomplicated, easy, and undemanding. The statement is simplistic and not true. Play is the work of the young child. Joyce McLellan, Senior Lecturer in Education at The Bishop Otter College in Chichester, England, states, "If you watch a very small child completely absorbed in his play, he is showing all the signs of the very hard worker. He is displaying patience with his material, he is using skill with his hands, giving evidence of reasoning and moving from one conclusion to another. In fact, he is showing the sort of spirit which motivates the most intense kind of work in the adult world."[1] Like the play of the professional athlete, the play of children is not necessarily done during leisure time as a form of recreation. And like adult work that is truly satisfying, the child's play is both enjoyable and satisfying.

What about the child playing just for the sheer joy of it? Among the definitions of play in most dictionaries are: "to have fun; to amuse oneself; to engage in recreation." For the child, play means all of these, and to give other meanings neither contradicts nor depreciates the fun. Whether we describe the play of children as their work or amusement, the potential for learning is there. Children learn through their play, and for kids, learning is fun!

Obviously, for our use, there is no single simple definition of *play*. It has different meanings at different times of our lives; it has different meanings even during one period. Here we concentrate on the significance of play as the language and work of the child, as an important way in which he learns, as a communication tool, and as a problem-solving method for meeting some specific child needs.

How the Young Child Plays

Like all activities relating to human growth, play is developmental. The way in which a child plays is determined by the physical, intellectual, and emotional maturity of the child. Because no two children are exactly alike, the following descriptions of the play of preschoolers at different ages are only broadly characteristic of each age. However, the order of the progression from one type of play to the next is generally similar for all children. Furthermore, the child is constantly in a state of transition from one stage of development to the next, retaining characteristics of earlier development while experimenting with new behaviors.

Pretend play begins at about age two. Two year olds do not have well developed motor or language skills. They lack abilities necessary for constructing things or for verbalizing feelings and ideas through socialized speech, but they do make imaginative use of various materials. A broomstick may become a stallion, an acorn cap a drinking cup for "Teddy," or a length of velvet a king's robe. The two year old may wrap a colorful scarf around her shoulders and tell you that it is her mommy's party cape.

The world opens up for the two year old. His increased mobility allows him to take in almost more than he can assimilate. His world is truly "full of wonderful things." Is it any wonder that he mixes real and fantasy with such lavish abandonment! A brilliant butterfly poised on a blossom suddenly spreads its wings and flits from sight. The sun on the lawn sprinkler creates a child-sized rainbow. Out of a dark grey sky fall bits of lace that disappear on a mitten. With such "magic" all about him, the child does not easily distinguish between these realities and what he can imagine.

The companions of two year olds may also be creations of their imaginations. An imaginary friend may require her own cookie, a place at the table, or inclusion in family outings. A two-year-old child may regale you with wonderful stories about all of the exciting and adventurous things that the imaginary companion is allowed to do that he, of course, cannot. Older children soon discover that their two-year-old brother or sister can be easily frightened by tall tales about goblins and bogeymen. The little child can believe just as strongly in a creation of someone else's imagination as in his own imaginary friend and may cry to have a light left on in his room at night.

Along with the creation of imaginary friends and goblins, two year olds also engage in role-playing through the personification of toys and pets. Peter Slade, in his classic work *Child Drama*, refers to this talking to and through an object as "projected play."[2] "Dolly wants a drink," "Kitty doesn't need a nap now," are examples of the kinds of statements with which parents of older two-year-old children are familiar. Not only does such personification provide the child with companionship, but it also allows him to explore ideas, feelings, and relationships safely. The use of puppets in nursery schools and throughout the growing-up years can continue to provide such "trying-out" in a pleasurable way.

Another significant characteristic of play during this period is the use of pantomime. As an avid imitator of all he surveys, the two year old assumes the posture, walk, and facial expressions of others, both human and animal. The use of body movement compensates for what is lacking in language, and the child often accompanies his talk with a good deal of pantomime. The child also pantomimes to understand things outside himself better. To move like a pony is to understand a pony better; to stride along like Daddy is to understand Daddy better. This acting out—a technique employed by many contemporary therapists working with adults who are seeking understanding of self and others—comes naturally to two year olds.

As the child approaches three, he exhibits early signs of characterization. The little girl with the colorful scarf about her shoulders no longer refers to it as her "Mommy cape;" instead, she is a Mommy. Three year olds may spend hours being someone or something else. Generally the characterizations are familiar homelife characters—Mommy and Daddy, the postman, the man who comes to "fix things," the nurse who gives shots—dogs, cats. Increased competence in language and motor skills allows the child to "become" his character more accurately.

At about three and a half, we see the beginnings of real dramatic play. Communication skills develop rapidly during this period, and children are no longer content simply to personify toys and objects. This early dramatic play is almost totally subjective and idiomatic, that is, the child gives his or her own meanings to all aspects of play—the materials, the constructions, movements and gestures, sound effects, and language. Casual observation of such play by adults cannot accurately and fully reveal the highly personal meanings and significance for the child. Adult interpretations, based as they must be on the intellectual and psychological experiences of the adult, can miss the mark completely. This should not suggest that valuable insights into the child of this age cannot be made by observations of the dramatic play; it does mean that conclusions reached by the adult must take into consideration the subjective and idiomatic nature of each child's play. The adult must accept the child's unique meanings that are signaled by the play activity.

The early stages in the development of a symbolic system—something that is used to stand for something else—can also be seen in the make-believe play of the very young child. For example, in the construction corner of a preschool room we may see some children building "houses" with the large construction blocks while others use the same blocks to ride on or push about as cars and trucks. If we perceive this as the creative and imaginative use of the building blocks for another purpose, we would be right; the assumption that the child using the block as a truck is either ignorant of the intended purpose of the block or being contrary is probably incorrect. The child is making a symbolic use of the material; for him the building block can "stand for" a truck.

The three year old's ability to characterize is also important to the development of a symbolic system. The little child playing a character in his make-believe play uses himself symbolically to stand for someone or something else. He is not using characterization because he thinks it will help him to acquire a symbolic system, yet the very experience of substituting self for another adds to the child's assimilation of the concept. If he can be someone or something else, anything can be something else: words can stand for objects and actions; numbers can stand for quantities of objects; red lights can mean stop; and Golden Arches can mean a place to eat dinner. The building of a symbolic system is fundamental to language acquisition and to the development of communication skills. The symbolic nature of the young child's make-believe play permits him to use it extensively as a communication mode. Later, as he acquires adequate language, he can substitute words for actions and the play is no longer a *primary* mode of communication.

As the young child acquires language, observers of his play notice how the child often accompanies much of what he is doing with words. He talks aloud to himself, naming objects as he handles them and describing his own motor activities as he plays. Our three year old wearing Mommy's colorful scarf may narrate her own play somewhat as follows: "Mommy (meaning herself) puts on her cape." (The child attempts to drape the scarf around her shoulders.) "Beautiful." (She starts to walk.) "Mommy has to go to the store." (She tries to walk without tripping on the scarf.) "Be careful, Mommy, careful of your beautiful cape."

The running narration accompanies her pantomime and makes commentary upon it. The child continues to tell herself, aloud, what to do. The research of L. S. Vigotsky, N. P. Paramonova, A. R. Luria, and F. Ia. Yudovich would explain this use of speech as the young child's means of organizing his motor activity, and is, in fact, representative of a complex and developing process.[3] As early as 1929, Vigotsky reported on the young child's use of external speech not directed to another to help himself solve a problem.[4] The child talks over with himself what he is perceiving and uses his external speech to help direct his own responses to the situation. He will continue to use this kind of discourse with himself but begins to use his words silently so that by the time he is seven or eight he can make complicated mental connections through internal verbalization.

As communication skills develop, young children have a growing need for interaction with other children. From three years old on, they crave social contacts and are ready for group experiences. However, much parallel or egocentric play continues in which the children play along side others without a great deal of interacting with one another. For example, a group of three year olds playing house would appear to be more of a group experience than it actually is. On close observation we would see that each child is talking to himself more than he is talking to others. (Dr. Jean Piaget refers to these behaviors as "collective monologues" and elaborates upon them in *The Language and Thought of the Child*.[5]) However, the presence of the others is tremendously important even when the child is playing, symbolically, within the make-believe situation almost totally independent of his companions. Socialization, like other skills, is also developmental and requires generous opportunities for practice and a suitable environment that will nurture its growth. In the group setting the child's play can develop from the subjective and idiomatic to a communication network with shared meanings. The presence of other children helps to teach not only the nonverbal rules of social order but also facilitates the learning of the "right" language of the social grouping. Whether within the family setting, the neighborhood, or a nursery program, the group experience is important for three and four year olds.

The four year old has come a long way from infancy, and he knows it. He struts and swaggers; he boasts and embellishes. Compared with what he could do earlier, he can now accomplish amazing feats and imagine even more elaborate ones. He has no qualms about blending copious amounts of fantasy into his accounts of real events. Four year olds are explorers and experimenters and will take off in all directions both physically and imaginatively. As a consequence, their make-believe play may sometimes need a subtle suggestion from an understanding adult to redirect it away from catastrophe.

Despite his tremendous need for activity, the four year old cannot resist stories. They stimulate his imagination and involve him in all kinds of vicarious adventures. He loves to look and listen, and with stories he can be involved in the continual process of internalizing the external world through the process of symbolizing the external world. He can also use his own increasing facility with language to make up stories, which is obvious in his dramatic play.

The dramatic play of four year olds takes on broader dimensions. They create make-believe situations in which their characters play out their roles. Make-believe scenarios reflect familiar experiences. Nursery-aged children enjoy playing house, playing doctor, going shopping, playing church—whatever experiences are a part of their routines. The same is true of the toys they enjoy most. Both boys and girls enjoy "housekeeping corners" with sets of toy dishes, mops, and brooms; miniature garden and garage tools; doctor kits; and, of course, dolls to be dressed, fed, rocked, scolded, and loved. All the things that help them identify with adult roles are just right for busy four year olds.

Besides delighting in small replicas of adult equipment, four-year-old children love to create their own "props" for use in their dramatic play. No longer totally dependent on found materials, they can create with paper, paste, crayons, clay, mud, sticks, and so forth. The child of this age is a doer and a builder, and these activities are often incorporated into the dramatic play.

Nursery-aged children incorporate the input of their senses into their play. As a consequence, they naturally integrate the arts. Something constructed may stimulate a particular make-believe situation to be played out. Mud-pie baking may lead into a play episode involving a birthday party or getting ready for company. Or it may happen the other way around; the dramatic play may require some specific props that must be constructed. The drama may stop suddenly while the prop is made, then be resumed. Children engaged in make-believe play may spontaneously add bits of song or dance, often accompanied by their

Imitating movements of humans and animals opens doors to the world of body and movement.

own unique sound effects. It is not unusual to see (and hear) a kind of child opera with the little player giving a melody to the improvised dialogue. In their own spontaneous dramatic play boys and girls use whatever fits to make the experience the most satisfying for them. Educators, who seem to be masters at fragmenting and compartmentalizing learning, might well take note!

Summary

Play is: (1) the language of the child through which he communicates with himself and others; (2) often subjective and idiomatic; (3) developmental in nature, reflecting physical, intellectual, emotional, and social growth and maturation; and (4) a contributor toward meeting physical, intellectual, emotional, and social needs. In describing how children play, we have touched upon why they play as they do. Let us take a closer look at the young child's needs and how play is used to meet them.

Meeting Needs through Play

Physical needs

A child's need to grow physically is first and paramount to all other needs. Active play assures that he is not growing only bigger but also stronger and more coordinated. Opportunities to run, stretch, and climb must be plentiful. He needs an environment in which he may safely develop gross-motor skills. For the preschooler, the home and perhaps a nursery or day care center are the usual facilities. Later the school program provides space, equipment, and guidance for helping him to continue his physical development. Active play for physical growth and fitness is the one kind of play continued throughout the growing-up years. Other kinds of play experiences should be continued as well.

Other physical growth needs can also be met by forms of play. Experiences with materials that involve small-muscle control and hand-eye coordination—crayons, paints, scissors, clay, mud, and sand —not only allow for creative expression but are important for developing fine-motor skills and reading readiness.

Creative movement and pantomime, which the child generously employs in make-believe play, also contribute to his physical development. Imitating the movements of humans and animals can help the child to discover much about his own body and its capabilities. As the child assumes the postures and locomotion of his characters, he is practicing movement control. He also makes discoveries about space in relation to himself. He experiments with tempo, space, and energy and makes some correlations among these three elements of movement. Moving from one character to another as his imagination decrees, he is developing an ability for making his body respond to his mind. He walks like Daddy with long, powerful, and deliberate strides; with quick light movements he becomes a wee mouse hiding from the cat. Using his body symbolically, he is also making mental connections about his experiencing which he can call on another time.

Whether the physical activity is a part of rugged outdoor play or creative make-believe play, it contributes to the child's need to grow bigger and stronger with coordination and grace.

Intellectual needs

We cannot argue with the child's need to grow physically, and during the early weeks of infancy the emphasis is on physical nurturing. This is certainly not because the child has a lesser need to grow intellectually, but rather because a healthy body is essential to both his survival and to his ability to develop intellectually. A good physical start gives added assurance that the child will be able to develop his intellectual and emotional potentials. Even early play experiences must challenge both the body and the mind; as play becomes more complex, the child uses it more and more to meet his need to know. Curiosity appears to be a human drive; thus, much of early play contributes directly toward meeting specific intellectual needs.

Of particular significance to parents and teachers who are interested in the make-believe play of preschoolers is a collection of research by Yale psychologist Jerome L. Singer, Mary Ann Spencer Pulaski of Hofstra University, and others as reported in *The Child's World of Make-Believe: Experimental Studies of Imaginative Play.*[6] This work supports much earlier research by Piaget and others which indicates that the child's ability to daydream and pretend is a cognitive skill that helps him be more creative, a better problem-solver, extend periods of concentration, and even be more patient in terms of expectations of personal gratification.[7] The rewards in terms of the child's intellectual development and emotional health (which is basic to normal intellectual growth), are so significant that increased attention to the stimulation of make-believe and dramatic play must be an important part of his early experiences. This is particularly true for the preschooler, for studies further indicate that in most children the ages of three and four are the most productive for the development of the imagination, that the "fantasy level" is generally set by age five.

Playing house is a favorite activity of young children in our culture.

We see it among children in environments that afford limited experiences as well as among those who have broader opportunities to experience many things. Young children do not play house simply because this is the one experience and environment they know best, but rather because it allows them to explore roles they do not fully understand but with which they feel a need to identify. Playing out adult roles helps a child to understand adults and to fit into a world that is controlled by grown-ups. The child not only imitates adults in his dramatic play; he tests adult behaviors for himself. In doing so he is exploring his own possiblities for becoming an adult. In addition, as he role-plays he can adjust his adult character so that it becomes more compatible to himself; he can adjust the power structure. As Hartley, Frank, and Goldenson have noted in *Understanding Children's Play,* "... the child himself gives the meaning and emotional significance to his play. He makes playthings and activities and people what he personally thinks and feels them to be."[8]

Role-playing of adults within the family structure also permits the child to explore and make significant discoveries about his or her own sex role. Sex-role identification is generally well established by the time children enter school, and much of what has been internalized about a child's own sex role has been acquired through the make-believe play experiences. We see little girls pretending to be mothers and wives, and little boys being fathers and husbands. This sex-role identification is immensely important; little girls do grow up to be women, and little boys do grow up to be men. To understand and accept one's own sex is essential if the child is to know and like herself or himself. However, sex-role identification is one example of how adults, often very subtly and without malice intended, superimpose their biases and value systems on young children. We examine sex-role identification further when we discuss the role of adults as it relates to the dramatic play of preschool children.

Role-playing is not limited to family situations or sex-role identification within the context of the family structure. Children need to identify with and understand many other adults with whom they have real or imagined significant experiences. The themes of children's dramatic play often reflect their particular socioeconomic situations and regional and ethnic differences. Playing school, playing doctors, nurses, "teenagers," shopkeepers, dentists, law enforcement persons—all of these and more may be part of the repertoire. Again we see the twofold nature of "trying out": play provides exploration of a variety of adult occupations and lifestyles and the opportunity to better understand significant adults in relation to self. Both functions, often engaged in simultaneously, relate to the child's need to know and understand self and others.

The child also has intellectual needs that relate to his environment. Anthropologist Margaret Mead states: "... in all cultures, human beings—in order to be human—must understand the nonhuman. They must have some understanding of plants and animals, water and sunshine, earth, the stars, the moon and the sun."[9] The child seeks to know and understand these things through both real and imagined experiences. He learns vicariously through books, films, and television, but much of the real "checking out" that leads to understanding is done through his make-believe play. Indoors and out, he uses his imagination to create whatever climate and terrain he feels his characters require. Being a soldier crawling on his tummy through the mud or a tiger prowling the jungle is fun, but it is also a way to understand such things. If children seem to be closer to nature than adults, it is probably because of their abilities to identify with the nonhuman through their fantasies. The understanding derived from play experiences is significant to the child's development of his own humanity as well.

Emotional needs

The need to know and understand relates not only to intellectual growth but to emotional growth also. To understand how Mommy feels is as important for the child to experience as to know what Mommy does. Make-believe is particularly useful for helping a child better understand his own feelings and those of others. It also offers unique opportunities for him to deal with emotions that place tremendous pressures on him at times. Within the characters and make-believe situations he creates, the child discovers ways for relieving the overwhelming emotions he feels.

Hartley et al. report from their case studies of boys and girls engaged in pretend play that there are three different motifs that occur and recur with consistency. They describe these as "a need for protection (for mothering, babying, being cared for), a need for power (over things and people), and the need to attack and destroy."[10] The better adjusted the child, the better he can play almost any role with ease, moving from one to another with flexibility and willingness. Young children often move in and out of several roles quite casually as it suits their purposes, particularly when playing alone. (This is also true later on in classroom activities in creative drama. Emotionally healthy secure children will generally play any role, large or small, and involving a variety of feelings, with sincerity and good humor.) However, the child with a powerful emotional need, either sustained or temporary, may consistently wish to play only one kind of a role. A familiar example of this is the child who always wants to play the baby, demanding that others cater to him or her as "good" mommies and daddies. Such a need may arise from the presence of a new baby in the family or from adult pressures on the child to mature faster than he seems to be doing. One who is constantly bossed by a domineering parent or sibling may insist upon playing a bossy role, turning any character into a shrill-voiced over-bearing dictator. A child who is the brunt of another's ridicule may delight in name-calling and will find opportunities for doing this in a variety of make-believe situations.

The child with an overwhelming emotional need may handle it by intensifying his real life role. For example, the child who feels a need to be aggressive and violent may become more so in his pretend play. He will create aggressive characters in make-believe situations in which he can display his violent feelings. Even a very young child soon learns that he can attack a toy or an imaginary character without taking the same risks as when his violence is turned on another person. In group make-believe play he rationalizes that the violence directed at another is alright because it is not really his violence but rather the meanness of the character he is playing. Whatever guilt or remorse his angry or jealous character may feel (or not feel) is not entirely his problem. Since much of the young child's play involves little or no interaction with others, the violent and aggressive feelings and behaviors need not be directed at actual others but can be relieved through the fantasy.

The young child may also cope with his feelings by the use of role reversal, particularly when he has feelings of inadequacy. The timid fearful child may create characters who are brave and adventurous. The frail child or one who is less physically mature than his peers may compensate by playing both human and animal characters who are large and strong. The role reversal serves to bolster the self-concept and can make the child feel adequate and equal to others.

The child may consistently take only one approach, either intensify-ing the real-life role and feelings or engaging in role reversal. Whichever form the dramatic play takes, it is in response to some important emo-tional needs and can serve a dual purpose: as a way to explore his own feelings and the feelings of others and to provide an outlet for those feelings so that the child can better cope with them.

The Role of Adults
in the Play of Young Children

Grown-ups who try to interpret or participate in the play of the preschooler without an understanding of the unique and special nature of the play of children often frustrate the child because the big persons do not understand what the play is all about. Many adults cannot resist the temptation to take over, to lead and direct the play. The exploring and trying-out aspects that are so beneficial and necessary for the child can be easily thwarted when adults get into the act. However, parents and others can and should make significant contributions to the play of children, and there are several important ways in which this can be done.

Adults can encourage and support valuable play experiences of all kinds by providing safe and stimulating environments and materials. Whether at home or in a school setting, children engaged in make-believe play need space that can accommodate physical activity of various kinds. Obviously truck drivers taking their rigs cross-country or firefighters rushing to a blaze need more room for maneuvering than a family getting dinner or a dentist filling a tooth. The space for play should encourage both kinds of dramatic play. Of special value is a cozy corner of a room (or some other small private space) that can be used for "family" play since this is such an important aspect of much spontaneous make-believe play. To be most useful, this special place should not be too cluttered, and the furnishings should be lightweight enough so that they can be rearranged by the child for his own purposes. The furnishings are also more conducive to imaginative use if they are not too realistic. Multipurpose boxes and lengths of cloth can be anything —useful for playing house but not limited to that. In addition, children need places that can be private for just thinking—daydreaming places that encourage each child to sit or curl up with his own thoughts and feelings, his own fantasies. This is true at home or in a nursery setting, and the best arrangement of time and space should strike a balance that allows for both planned activities and free time.

Adults affect the quality of a child's play experiences by their attitudes and the expression of those attitudes to the child. Even when we realize the rewards of fantasy and make-believe play, teachers and parents are sometimes prone to alarm when a child creates an imaginary friend or makes up an outlandish tale of his own exploits and adventures. Sometimes we have difficulty accepting the offerings of the child's imagination even when we know, academically, that the development of imaginative thinking is so important. Momentarily overwhelmed by the child's fantasy, we may respond defensively, calling attention to the difference between truth and make-believe. However, responses like, "You have a wonderful imagination, Sarah; I like the stories you make up about your adventures with the purple crocodile," can say three things to the child: (1) the adult values imagination; (2) both the adult and the child are aware that the stories are fantasy, not real, and that both can distinguish between the two; and (3) the adult is interested in the child's use of imagination including the product created by the child. Such an accepting and positive response by the adult can do wonders in terms of the interpersonal relationship as well as the stimulation of learning, while helping the child distinguish between fantasy and reality.

Perhaps the most significant ways in which adults can contribute to the quality of the child's fantasy and make-believe play are by the models they provide. Many of our cultural patterns are ingrained during the preschool period of dramatic play. Values are both overtly and covertly taught, and all play is infused with parental ideas, attitudes, and behaviors. What is modeled may be constructive or destructive in terms of the child's intellectual, social, and emotional development. For example, we earlier spoke of the child's need to identify with his or her own sex role. However, the child's interpretation of what it means to be a man or a woman generally reflects attitudes and behaviors he or she has witnessed in parents and other significant adults. Sexism, like racism and other limiting and detrimental attitudes, can be entrenched during early childhood. "Little ladies don't do that!" "Big boys (meaning men) don't cry!" are adult attitudes we see reflected in dramatic play. How often do we see little girls playing doctor rather than nurse; or how often little boys, being Daddy, pretend to cry?

What we see in the house-playing activities of young children generally reflects parental attitudes that are communicated both verbally and nonverbally. Children role-play adults from what they see and hear, and as a consequence, we see little girls keeping house and little boys going to work and coming home from work. This can be especially frustrating to little boys. They want to play the role with which they seek to identify, but they lack knowledge about how to do it. Parents and teachers can help children have less limited percepts about the roles of men and women. Where and when possible, both boys and girls ought to have some firsthand ideas about the work parents do outside the home. Visits to the place or places of employment are excellent when these can be arranged. The sharing of stories about the work that father or mother does away from home is helpful. This is particularly important when the parent or parents are absent from the home a great deal during the hours when young children are awake. All children can benefit from stories about girls and women who exhibit leadership and problem-solving abilities and stories about boys and men who are concerned and caring about others. Though mother may also work outside the home, her role within the family may be more clearly defined and easily discerned since she is often the parent most involved with the nurturing activities. The father may need to seek special times and ways to relate to the children so that they, particularly little boys,

Adults need not rely on their ability to make-believe; story books of all kinds are there to be shared.

have a male who models for them the human qualities and values that are important to both sexes.

Adults provide other models for children. During early childhood when children are acquiring and developing language, the adult's verbal interaction with the child is of particular significance. The play of the infant is almost totally manipulative in nature. His exploration of objects, for example, is limited to the direct sensory experience. Imaginative creative play requires considerably more complex mental abilities. From his research, Vigotsky concludes that "human mental development has its source in the verbal communication between child and adult."[11] If children are to develop the capabilities required for complex mental activities, they require a language system, which is learned through verbal communication with adults. The relationship of a language system to the higher levels of mental activity, including imaginative thinking, are described by Luria: "Intercommunication with adults is of decisive significance because the acquisition of a language system involves a reorganization of all the child's basic mental processes; the word thus becomes a tremendous factor which forms mental activity, perfecting the reflection of reality and creating new forms of attention, of memory and imagination, of thought and action."[12] The play of children who have had limited verbal communication with adults remains primitive, often confined, like the infant's, to the manipulation of objects. Parents and others contribute in fundamental and extremely valuable ways to the quality of the child's imaginative play when they engage the child in verbal communication.

Verbal interaction between adults and children can also provide opportunities for adults to model an ability to create make-believe. Children are delighted when grown folks share their fantasies with them, and the sharing can provide an experiential way for the adult to communicate his acceptance of the child's imagination. Little boys and girls love to hear about the big person's own childhood, including the fantasies and make-believe play. Stories that begin, "when I was little I had a very favorite spot, and every time I went there I imagined that I was . . ." can be great fun for everyone and successful stimuli for encouraging children to use their own imaginative powers. Of course, the adult need not rely only on his or her own ability to create make-believe; storybooks of every kind are there to be shared. Of all the ways in which the adult can both model the use of the imagination and also stimulate imaginative thinking and make-believe play in children, nothing can beat the well-told story. Storytelling is, in fact, such an important part of early childhood learning experiences that it deserves some special attention. The last chapter of this book deals with storytelling.

Your Turn

1. In pairs or small groups, share your recollections of the make-believe play of your childhood. See what commonalities you can discover and the special ways in which you played because of different environments, locales, family size, family values and interests, and so forth. In retrospect, can you identify some specific needs you met through your play?
2. Visit a nursery school, day care center, or kindergarten. Observe the make-believe play of the children. Write up your observations and share them with the group.
3. Read and report on the research related to early developmental needs and behaviors of children of one of the following: Jean Piaget, L. S. Vigotsky, A. R. Luria and F. Ia. Yudovich, Charles Van Riper and Katherine Butler.
4. Read the last chapter on "Storytelling with Young Children." Follow this with one or more of the following:
    a. *Select a picture book for young children that has little or no written narrative. (Where's Al by Byron Barton listed in the* bibliography of Stories to Dramatize is one example.) Develop your own narrative for telling the story to little boys and girls.
    b. *Develop a short story for young children based on a personal experience. Share it with your class. Evaluate one another's storytelling.*
    c. *Develop a short annotated bibliography of stories to tell to young children. Look especially for books and stories that could be used as a basis for make-believe play.*
    d. *Create an original action story or finger play and teach it to your class (or to a group of young children).*
    e. *Write a short story for preschoolers. See if you can incorporate bits of rhythm, rhyme, or alliteration to increase its child appeal.*
    f. *Select, practice, and share aloud a story or poem for adults.*
5. Spend some time in a one-to-one relationship with a young child. Make a "sense of wonder" discovery together. Respond to your experience in some way—a short paper or oral report, a poem, painting, or short story. Share your response with the class.

2

Creative Drama in the Classroom

Just to be—really be—another person in an undistinguished play is to make one immeasurably free forever.

Hughes Mearns

None of the needs met through play go away just because the child gets older. The need to know who one is, particularly in relation to others, becomes increasingly important and bewildering as relationships are enlarged. The need for opportunities that afford emotional release in constructive ways also grows as life takes on greater complexity. Growth and development engender new needs, particularly in the areas of social behaviors and communication skills. The ways the young child has developed for meeting some specific needs have merit for him as he comes to school and should be considered for use in the classroom learning experiences. Yet we must continually be responsive to how the child has changed and is changing so that the means available to him are appropriate to his new abilities and challenges.

The school-aged child continues to engage in make-believe play, but that play reflects his new maturity, experiences, interests, and lifestyle. As socialized speech increases, pretend play becomes less idiomatic and egocentric in nature, with more real interaction among children engaged in the make-believe play situations. More and more, new abilities with

---

From *Creative Power: The Education of Youth in the Creative Arts.*

language are used for communicating with self and others, and play is no longer the primary communication tool. As children spend more and more time in the classroom and in formal study, there is less time for free spontaneous play. Greater mobility and extended environments allow the elementary school child greater opportunities for real and personal experiencing outside of school time. This time becomes increasingly used for active sports, organized games, and individual interests and hobbies. In all aspects—physical, intellectual, and emotional—the play of the school-aged child is indicative of increased freedom and greater abilities, but play continues to offer significant ways for meeting the child's needs. Consequently, active physical play is a recognized and important part of the elementary school curriculum for the contributions it can make to the child's growth and development. Dramatic play, through the incorporation of creative dramatics into the classroom learning experiences, can also continue to make important contributions.

Like the spontaneous pretend play of early childhood, creative dramatics in the elementary school involves the child in discovering various facets of self through role-playing and characterization and the playing out of imagined situations. Creative dramatics in the classroom allows the child to continue his exploration of other roles, both human and nonhuman, and to create his own relationships with a variety of environments. It is based on a desire to be responsive to the needs of children in ways that are natural and stimulating for them.

That our discussion of creative dramatics in the elementary classroom does not begin with a tidy definition of creative dramatics is not to suggest that it cannot be defined, but rather that it is best understood in terms of its uses with and for children. Ideally, those who anticipate using creative dramatics will have opportunities for observing a successful leader working with boys and girls. This can be tremendously helpful, especially if the observations can extend over a period of time so that growth and development can be seen. In preparation for such firsthand experiences with elementary children and drama, we need to know something of who they are and what creative dramatics can provide for them.

The Elementary Child and Creative Drama

Teachers are certainly aware of the differences that formal education can make in the lives of people. Eager to put their professional skills to work for the benefit of the child, they may inadvertently ignore the sensitivity and understanding with which the child thought, felt, and did before he came to school. Skilled as they are in a variety of "methodologies," they can still overlook some of the ways in which the child naturally and successfully learned before school.

No one, least of all the child, expects life in school to be just like life in the preschool world. If he is ready for school, the child comes eager for new experiences and new ways of learning; he is ready to solve new problems in new and better ways. Children come with varying degrees of maturity and readiness for school. Kindergarten may provide the child's first major experience with an environment beyond his home and immediate neighborhood. Going to school will mean new sights and sounds, new things to explore. He will learn to use his senses in different ways. Greater and greater emphasis will be placed on the distance senses of sight and hearing, as the child works to learn and improve the communication skills of speaking, listening, reading, and writing. Play is no longer his primary communication tool, but it is still a very important secondary one. He will use his body less and less as the basic tool for expressing his feelings and ideas. He learns that to be understood by others, he and they must share some commonalities of meanings through language. In much of his classroom learning he will be accepting another's word for what is real, true, false, right, wrong, beautiful, ugly, kind, cruel, and so on. There is often little time or opportunity for experiential learning. However, when we look at our learning objectives in light of Piaget's goal of education ". . . to create possibilities for the child to invent and discover" to "provide men who are capable of doing new things," we are challenged to do much more than find effective ways of passing on to our children the knowledge, wisdom, attitudes, and critical judgements of others.[1]

Creative dramatics is both an experiential learning method and an art form. As an art form, it lends itself naturally to integration with other art forms, especially dance and music. It offers beginning experiences and background for speech and theatre work. Secondary teachers of the communication arts find creative dramatics useful in their classrooms. It has application in a wide spectrum of communication work: interpersonal communication, public speaking, oral interpretation, and theatre. Boys and girls who have participated in informal drama in the elementary school bring an openness to experience and communication skills to related secondary and college courses. When drama is experienced primarily as an art form and if what happens is skillfully and artfully done the experience is aesthetically valuable. But creative dramatics is more than basic training for the speech and theatre arts. Our emphasis in this text is on its use as an integral part of classroom learning.

Creative dramatics can be used to provide a continuity of experiential learnings remarkably similar to the opportunities in the spontaneous dramatic play the child intuitively uses. It can involve him in exciting explorations of his environment through his senses which nourish and enrich his imagination. He is encouraged to express his ideas and feelings with his body and voice in his own way. He is stimulated to express not only his own thoughts and emotions, but to develop understanding and empathy for others through role-playing and characterization. Like his earlier dramatic play, creative dramatics involves the child in "doing" as a means of learning. Of course, creative dramatics should not be the sole source of experiential learnings in the classroom, but it is one way that is familiar.

One important characteristic of the school-aged child's developing maturity is his ability to sustain an active interest in an activity for longer periods of time. This, plus his continued devotion to learning through play and his new capacities for working cooperatively with others, provides the classroom teacher with the ideal ingredients for integrating dramatic play into the curriculum. Stimulated and guided by the teacher toward specific learning objectives, creative dramatics has potential for language arts, social studies, science, and math.

Creative dramatics is an integrative process in which the child utilizes his whole self in experiences that emphasize imaginative thinking and creative expression. It contributes to the development of his potential as a thinking, feeling, imagining, and doing person. This is the primary objective for creative drama experiences. What, then, are some of the characteristics that indicate that this objective is being met?

For one, the authenticity of the child's involvement is necessary if the experience is truly to benefit the child. Authentic involvement is characterized by spontaneity of movement and speech in response to whatever stimuli are provided. Watch the "dance" of young children as they respond to the first snowfall. Observe the facial expressions and postures in the housekeeping corner when some laborious chores must be performed. Listen to the child's speech as an imaginary villain is subdued. The dancer's feet are not recalling the practiced steps and discipline of the ballet troupe, but sensitivity, naturalness, and sincere response to feelings are there. Similarly, their interpretations of adult behaviors and attitudes may be pantomimed with remarkable skill, though the term *pantomime* is totally outside of their vocabularies. The improvised dialogue of their make-believe play grows honestly out of their perceptions with a vitality that is not possible in formal drama when the language is a stilted reissue of memorized lines composed by adults. Like the spontaneous dramatic play of early childhood, classroom use of creative dramatics should reflect this same sincerity of involvement, with speech and movement emerging from each child's own experiences and perceptions about what is happening. The experiences become part of the learning process and are not performances for the benefit of others. When each child's participation is uniquely individual, authentic, and devoid of exhibition, we can assume that the drama experiences are of value to the child.

The child's openness to new ideas is another indicator that the drama experiences are contributing to growth and development in positive ways. All children need to be encouraged to explore and experiment intellectually, emotionally, aesthetically, and physically. As they do so, they expand their capabilities for problem-solving. The ability to solve problems is intrinsic to learning and requires inventiveness, flexibility, and often a degree of risk. Openness to new experiences and increased problem-solving abilities are also barometers for measuring the value of the drama experiences for the child.

An important aspect of problem-solving, one that is closely related to inventiveness and flexibility, is the ability to think creatively. "Men who are capable of doing new things," says Piaget, "must not only be explorers and discoverers, but inventors and creators." To think creatively requires imagination, for it is through the imagination that a person can hypothesize a result and can bring together old knowledge in new and exciting ways. It is through the imagination that knowledge, experiences, ideas, and hunches can be synthesized. Like other art forms, creative dramatics encourages the child to think, feel, and experience imaginatively. Evidence of imaginative thinking is, therefore, an important and inherent characteristic of creative dramatics. Without it, the drama would be lifeless and of little creative value to the child.

The classroom use of creative dramatics can provide some unique possibilities for helping children develop positive self-concepts. No child can begin to realize his potential as a thinking, feeling, and creating human being unless he feels good about himself. Nor can he handle being a risk-taking problem-solver unless he feels personally adequate. When the emphasis in the classroom is not always on the accumulation of facts, but on increased awareness, understanding, and an ability to solve problems in a variety of ways, every child has a greater opportunity for developing respect for his own ideas, emotions, and abilities. Although children must learn many things that require specific right answers, they also need learning opportunities in which there need not be a single correct response. Teachers sometimes seem surprised to discover that a child who is struggling with spelling or the multiplication tables can create an exciting story or do a remarkable job of characterization. Learning through creative dramatics can offer opportunities in which every child can "solve the problem" correctly in his own way. For example, there is only one correct English spelling for *cat*, but a child can *be* a cat in his own way—a bold adventurous cat; a small, timid, "fraidy" cat; a hungry cat; a tired or hurt cat. Moving as cats through an imagined environment allows each child to explore and express his own conceptions of *cat*. Regardless of how he solves the problem of being a cat, he is right and accepted. Such nonthreatening opportunities for trying out one's own ideas are supportive of the child's need to succeed. When children are successful, they feel good about themselves, and self-concepts are positively reinforced. The child who feels personally adequate enjoys sharing his own ideas and does so with a lack of self-consciousness.

Because he does not feel anxious about his own ability to succeed, the self-accepting child can afford to be more open to the ideas of others and more tolerant of their feelings and behaviors. He will listen to others and work cooperatively in group activities. Beneficial experiences in creative drama are thus characterized by a good deal of lively sharing of ideas among the participants and cooperative behaviors that demonstrate respect and tolerance of thoughts and feelings of others.

As we have emphasized throughout, the classroom use of creative dramatics builds on the children's own use of learning through play. However, to use creative dramatics advantageously for the benefit of children in the elementary school requires more than such a rationale. Let us, therefore, briefly summarize those behaviors in children that indicate that the classroom use of creative dramatics is contributing to each child's growth and development as a thinking, feeling, creative, and achieving human being. (1) Each child's individual and authentic involvement will be indicated by a spontaneity of response to stimuli; (2) because the emphasis is on the learning process rather than on performance, not only is there a spontaneity of movement and speech, but a lack of exhibitionism; (3) each child will demonstrate an openness to new ideas, his own and others; (4) children involved in creative dramatics will show increased abilities to be problem-solvers, displaying inventiveness, flexibility, and risk-taking; (5) children will demonstrate imaginative thinking, which will be reflected in each child's individual and unique participation in the drama activities; (6) children will demonstrate positive self-concepts by their willingness to share individual ideas and feelings. (7) Further, they will demonstrate individual feelings of personal adequacy by displaying tolerant and respectful attitudes toward others; they will listen to one another and work cooperatively together when in group activities.

By identifying behaviors that are characteristic of beneficial classroom experiences in creative dramatics with children, we have defined creative dramatics in terms of its use with and for children. If the response to stimuli is to be authentically the child's own, resulting in

Concentration, spontaneity, and self-acceptance mark an effective creative drama experience.

spontaneous speech and movement, the creative drama requires no memorizing of lines or use of scripts. The emphasis upon participation and the learning process rather than upon performance means that creative dramatics does not require an audience. Similarly, if children are creatively solving problems through drama, relying chiefly upon their own inventiveness and imaginative thinking, they will not be dependent upon costumes, lighting, make-up, and the other technical aids that are characteristic of formal theatre. The emphasis upon successful experiences for all children for building positive self-concepts means that the usual kinds of auditioning and casting are antithetical to our purposes. In creative dramatics all children are encouraged to express their own ideas and feelings and to participate in the experiencing. When the children's own ideas are cooperatively shared so that they may be incorporated into the experiences, opportunities for participating in the planning and evaluation of the experiences are required. The teacher does not serve as a director, but rather as a stimulator, a guide, and a participator in the learning process. Guiding children through a drama experience differs in purpose and function from directing children in a formal play. The role of the teacher as guide serves to keep the emphasis on the value of the process and the quality of the learning experience for the participants. When the goal is not a polished performance for viewing by an audience, the teacher needs an ability to engage children in meaningful learning experiences, not expertise in the theatre arts.

The Role of the Teacher

The role of the adult in the classroom use of creative dramatics is so significant that it must be examined in detail by both preservice and inservice teachers who would incorporate drama into the elementary school program. As discussed in Chapter 1, the drama of early childhood is characterized by such a degree of subjectivity and spontaneity that the adult must be careful not to jeopardize the value of the play by too much involvement in the play itself. The adult usually is neither initiator nor participator in the play. However, the use of creative dramatics in the elementary classroom is usually initiated by the teacher as a way of providing learning opportunities for personal growth and for exploring concepts and information pertinent to the curriculum.

Creative drama, in which the emphasis is on how and what the child thinks, feels, and does, affords a unique format in which children are encouraged to develop and use convergent, divergent, and critical thinking. It can provide the teacher with a particularly useful tool for examining attitudes and values and for teaching concepts as well as facts. When creative drama is used toward such purposes, the role of the classroom teacher becomes one of involvement both initially and throughout the dramatic play activities. The teacher is responsible for the identification of both individual growth needs and needs related to the curriculum, and in this role she identifies the purposes and goals around which the drama activities will be built. The teacher will most often be responsible for providing the stimulation and overall plan that can elicit from the children the kind of sincere involvement that makes the drama process valuable in terms of both human and academic growth.

In the threefold role as stimulator, guide, and participator in the learning process, the teacher must develop attitudes and competencies that will facilitate valuable creative drama experiences. Appropriate attitudes and certain kinds of competencies are both essential in contributing toward the most rewarding drama experiences. Both are interrelated, of course, and reflect the psychological and philosophical orientation of the teacher. However, actions grow out of values and attitudes, and the kinds of skills required and how those skills are used are greatly determined by how a person perceives. Thus the role of the teacher is best understood by first looking at the kind of psychological and philosophical framework out of which beliefs about self, children, and learning are developed before attempting to describe specific competencies that can be used to implement beliefs.

Attitudes and behaviors

Among professionals in the field of education—teachers, counselors, administrators, and researchers—there is a shared awareness that much of what we know about children and learning is not consistently reflected in what happens in many classrooms. We know, for example, that costly and innovative equipment and materials, "ideal" classroom facilities, and community support are not what make classrooms come alive. Similarly equipped facilities in the same building may be dramatically contrasted to one another in terms of the real learning that takes place in each. The differences may also not be related in significant ways to the training and skill of each teacher in terms of academic competencies. Classrooms where both teacher and children are caught up in the shared excitement of learning seem to vibrate with life. Clark Moustakas in *The Authentic Teacher* says, "Life comes from life and the teacher is the living agent in the school. . . . Within the context of personal human attributes, the teacher can engender real life, and significant learning can occur."[2] The teacher's concept of self is basic to this life-engendering process. When the teacher is burdened with feelings of her own inadequacies as a potentially creative person, she may, quite unconsciously, be limiting her openness and responsiveness to the creativity of children. She may even feel competitive with them. If she believes that some people have a gift or talent for creative work and others do not, she may be tempted to categorize her boys and girls in that light. One unfortunate consequence of the labeling process, whether of self or others, is that the person labeled often responds with behaviors that are consistent with the label—what psychologists refer to as the "self-fulfilling prophecy." For a teacher to work successfully with children in drama requires that she anticipates success, her own and the children's. Such expectations to succeed come naturally from the teacher who is self-accepting, secure about her own abilities to create, and confident that she can develop the creative potential in others.

Although the teacher must feel that both she and the children can be successful in creative drama work, she must also be able to accept failure in herself and others. To anticipate success does not mean that only successful experiences will happen or that unsuccessful experiences have no value. Human beings often learn as much from their failures as from their successes. Real value is often discovered in venturing, particularly in learning experiences where the emphasis is on the process rather than on the finished product. Willingness to take a risk is as important to teachers as to children, and it requires that the teacher feel adequate about self and be open to experience. This openness is essential to the success of any creative activity, for such work is open-ended. We do not always know, when we begin, just where we will end or what kinds of things will happen on the way. The elements of exploration and discovery are inherent to creative activity, and the teacher who is open and accepting allows herself and the children to be spontaneous and flexible.

Unfortunately, teachers may feel that they must include creative drama in the class because "good" teachers do those kinds of things. When a teacher is operating out of anxiety and pressure, rather than out of a sincere belief in herself and the children as creative individuals and a real understanding of how children can learn through drama, the product becomes disproportionately important. Performance then becomes the observable proof that the teacher has allowed, even encouraged, creative work by the children—evidence that she is a "good" teacher who can elicit admirable work from her students.

This concern with product may also be evident when a teacher possesses a talent in one of the arts. It can be difficult not to want to "get into the act"—to allow children to fumble about, make mistakes, even

The whole child is personally involved; his product is not something that can be torn up, hidden from sight, or redone by the teacher.

to become frustrated with their attempts. Product is important, but a child can feel successful about his creative work only when he does the creating. A hobby horse built with a crooked mouth, "flounder eyes," and a scraggly mane is beautiful to the child who did it "all by myself." Later he may look at it, see its flaws, and perhaps set about learning some of the ways to make a better product. More probably, if he is a self-accepting child, he will love his creation just as it is and appreciate its originality as something he did when he was "little."

Undue concern with product can be catastrophic in creative drama. Here the whole child is so personally involved; his product is not something that can be torn up, hidden from sight, or redone by the teacher whom he considers to be the expert. His product is an immediate expression of his mind, body, and emotions. Traditionally, creative dramatics has been process-oriented. To approach it otherwise is not to understand it. Brian Way in *Development through Drama* (1967) states ". . . (creative) drama is largely concerned with experience by the participants, irrespective of any function of communication to an audience."[3] Geraldine Brain Siks in *Creative Dramatics: An Art for Children* (1958) writes, "Its [creative dramatics] aim is experience, experience that fosters child growth and development."[4] In 1954 Peter Slade, distinguished pioneer of child drama in Britain wrote, "Those who cannot feel the emotional spell of spontaneity will never understand the beauties of the Child."[5] Paramount concern for product cannot coexist with "the emotional spell of spontaneity." In her role as stimulator, guide, and participator in the learning experience, the teacher must, therefore, be not only accepting of self and the children, but also of their drama, not lamenting its lack of polish, but rejoicing in its honesty and spontaneity.

Writing on the "Meaning of Creativity" in *Creativity in Childhood and Adolescence*, Harold H. Anderson of Michigan State University states, "Creativity is spontaneous behavior, where spontaneity is defined as behavior in the related absence of environmental threat or coercion. Creativity represents a perception, response, action or communication, uncoerced by persons in the environment. . . . Creativity is a spontaneous emergent that can only be elicited; it can be elicited in proportion to the absence of threat from the environment."[6] The elicitor or facilitator of creative dramatics cannot force the child; neither can that person function well as a facilitator of creativity in others if she feels personally threatened by her own feelings of inadequacy or outside pressures in the environment. Ideally the use of creative dramatics in the classroom nurtures the development of the teacher as well as the development of the children.

While we can define appropriate teacher attitudes and behaviors that are necessary for successfully guiding children in creative drama, it is unrealistic to conclude that all teachers should participate in the activities in similar ways. To suggest otherwise would contradict our belief that the teacher ought to be authentically herself. Some adults can naturally and comfortably join in a game of animal tag or become a character in the drama; others cannot. Generally, children are delighted when the teacher joins in. Her participation reinforces theirs and gives them an added assurance of the validity of the experience. The greatest value of the experience for some boys and girls may be the interaction with an understanding adult.

The degree of teacher participation should be carefully considered. It may create anxieties in children who have had little prior experience with adults who can enter in without dominating, and the creativity of some children may be curtailed. Before children have sufficient trust in themselves and the teacher to express their own ideas in their own way, they may look to the adult as a model of how to be and do, thus precluding self-development. Furthermore, the behaviors of a guide should never distract from the experiencing of those being guided. A guide is not a performer, and at no time should the children become so intrigued by watching the teacher's involvement that they forfeit their own participation and become "audience" for the teacher.

Perceptive children are well aware of teachers who feel unnatural and ridiculous performing. Such children may feel embarrassed and unsure about how to respond. The role of the teacher as facilitator is diminished by any behaviors that tend to inhibit the children's confidence and trust.

Although there is no one ideal teacher model or "personality type" who can best lead children in creative dramatics, supportive understanding of children and their growth needs as total human beings is necessary for all learning experiences. The classroom climate must be conducive to creative expression—an atmosphere of mutual trust and respect and an absence of threat and coercion. Let us briefly review some of the attitudes and behaviors that support such a climate. (1) The teacher will be accepting of self as a creative person who anticipates success for herself and children. (2) The teacher will be open to experiences, able to take risks, and to learn from failure as well as from success. (3) She will, therefore, be flexible and spontaneous in her own behaviors when this contributes to the best possible experiences for children. (4) She will be accepting of the ideas, feelings, and creative expression of others and see the value in the experience. (5) The teacher will be appreciative of the special relationship between the child and his product. (6) The teacher will demonstrate an understanding of the creative process by patient encouragement rather than by coercion or threat. (7) The teacher will interact with children in their drama activities in ways that are natural, comfortable, and nonthreatening for herself and the children.

Competencies and techniques

A decision to include drama in the classroom suggests a psychological and philosophical compatibility with it as a valuable approach to learning. Basic to the teacher's role as a participator in the learning experiences with children is her ability to identify and articulate purposes and goals. These competencies are mentioned first for two reasons: (1) The teacher must know specifically what kinds of learning experiences are needed by the children. When these have been adequately identified, she is free to select from a variety of activities those that appear to offer the best potential for achieving her goals. (2) Identifying purposes and goals before the selection of ways for meeting them creates suitable guidelines for evaluating the experiences in terms of overall value and individual growth. When drama is approached in this way, its use contributes to learning in positive identifiable ways. This is in no way antithetical to flexibility, spontaneity, or creativity. The identification of purposes and goals does not limit the exploration of ideas and feelings, nor dictate how those ideas and feelings are expressed by each child. When goals are clearly identified, the teacher is even more free to appreciate the individuality and uniqueness of each child's participation as he works in his own ways to meet both group goals and individual needs.

Because drama is involved with ideas, feelings, and their expression through activity, behavioral goals may deal with cognitive development, affective behavior, and psychomotor skills. The acquisition of understanding can be especially observable because of the emphasis on doing. Learning can be demonstrated through movement and pantomime as well as through verbal expression and written work, thus enlarging the ways by which a child can communicate understanding and knowledge and offering additional opportunities for evaluating learning. For example, boys and girls who have done poorly on a written exam may demonstrate a knowledge and understanding of the same material through pantomime or an improvised drama. For students and teachers who are interested in developing competencies in the writing of instructional and behavioral goals, several excellent aids that deal specifically with these skills are available. Robert F. Mager's book *Preparing Instructional Objectives*[6] and *The Development and Evaluation of Behavioral Objectives* by Armstrong, Cornell, Kraner, and Roberson[7] are two fine examples of the kinds of resources that can be useful to teachers who wish to incorporate the use of drama in the classroom.

STRUCTURE

Closely related to purposes and goals is structure. The teacher must have an underlying understanding of the relationship between structure and creative drama. An open and accepting environment in which creative drama can develop does not mean an absence of structure. Structure, *per se*, is not antithetical to creative work. This is true for all media of expression. There are kinds and degrees of structure, and the creator uses that which best serves his purpose. Structure is primarily a means of organization. It involves a plan—a way of putting interrelated parts of the whole together toward a purpose. The product of that planning becomes the structure, which may be narrowly defined and inflexible or loosely defined with many opportunities for a variety of interpretations. In either case, the planner—generally the classroom teacher—begins with some view of the outcome. We may think of these outcomes as representing the goals and purposes of the planner, and the amount of structuring may be determined by those goals. There are other important variables to consider when deciding how much and what kinds of structure are most suitable for reaching goals in a learning situation. A primary one, of course, is the experience and capability of each of the learners. This requires not only a great deal of awareness and understanding on the part of the teacher, but also an abundance of common sense.

Generally, the less experience a person has in any situation, the more structure he needs to function well. We can see an excellent example of this in our driver education programs. Because admission to the program is contingent upon age rather than understanding of the principles involved or preexistent skills, all students, as a group, begin to acquire a common background of information in the "safe" environment of the classroom. When they have shown a predetermined level of competency with the subject, they practice in the highly structured program of the driving range. As specific goals are met and demonstrated by each student, the learner advances to the more flexible, "creative" activity of surviving on the public highways. We can translate this approach into an early creative drama activity.

Let us imagine that a third grade teacher would like to involve the children in some experiential learning activities as they study the lives and customs of an American Indian tribe. She will initially need to identify the scope of the area of study and the concepts to be learned.

At the onset, she should be able to articulate her purposes as they relate to the area of study and the needs of her children. She will need to identify some specific behaviors she feels will indicate that her expectations for individual learning have been satisfactorily met. Additionally, she will keep in mind individual abilities and interests of the children and will design a structure that will give all children realistic opportunities to succeed. It is accurate to conclude that the teacher has already begun to develop a particular kind of structure at the point where she defined the scope of study, articulated her purposes, and identified her behavioral goals. She is further building a particular structure when she decides where and when in the study the children will be engaged in specific kinds of learning experiences, what individual options will be encouraged, and so forth. Even the availability of various kinds of materials and equipment contribute to the overall structure. Our teacher, perhaps with the children, may decide that it would be more meaningful and exciting to develop and participate in Indian ritual dancing rather than just to read about it or participate vicariously through films. However, the books, films, and other materials will provide initial stimulation and furnish factual information upon which to base creative work. Having provided an ample amount of motivational and background materials, how next might the teacher proceed? In terms of structure, what kinds and amounts will provide the best framework for success?

If the children have had little experience in developing symbolic kinds of creative movement and pantomime, the teacher will need to begin with some simple and highly structured activities. Inexperienced children do not usually respond well to a suggestion like, "When I put some music on the record player, I would like you to listen to it and then become Indians." Some children will begin. Some will remain frozen in their places or copy those who are already moving. Others, put on the spot to produce, may begin running and leaping about in ways that do not relate to either the mood, tempo, or purpose of the music. Probably the result would be a highly stereotyped TV-cartoon version of a war dance!

If only a few of the children demonstrate an ability to successfully "move like Indians" in ways appropriate to the music, obviously most were not sufficiently prepared to handle the loosely structured activity. As a group, they would have benefited from a more highly structured beginning activity—perhaps first listening to the music as they keep time to the beat with their hands. A variety of rhythms and tempos could be introduced. This would be a good time to talk about what the drums are saying: Do they suggest particular meanings and situations? Next the teacher may suggest that the boys and girls move their feet

in place, continuing to clap the beat with their hands, and experimenting with changing levels (high and low body positions). The teacher
may suggest that the children, still in place, add other body parts to the
movement while continuing to keep time to the beat. When there is a
sufficient degree of competency with this activity, the teacher may
want to stop the movement and introduce the idea of symbolic movement—moving in a certain way to represent an idea. This concept will
be new to most children, so sufficient time for both discussion and
experimentation would be allowed before they begin to move about the
room with each child working individually but parallel with the others.
At this point, no one is asked to solo, and no judgements about quality
are made. Gradually, as the children demonstrate more understanding
and creative expression, the amount of teacher direction will be reduced, and additional opportunities for evaluation will be provided.

In our example there is a consistent reshaping of the structure. The
teacher direction diminishes in proportion to the desire and ability of
the children to become self-motivated and self-directing. To illustrate,
we can look at how the teacher might next proceed. The stimulation and
guidance have come primarily from the teacher up to this time, though
there is an increased emphasis on each child's interpretation. Gradually
the teacher introduces new structures that encourage more input from
the children. The group may be ready to decide on the purpose of the
Indian ritual, for examples: rain dance, a ceremony to celebrate a successful hunt or harvest, the death of the chief. The teacher will continue
to lead the discussion and encourage them to give symbolic meanings
to their movements, but the children will be working from their own
ideas. If interest remains high, the teacher may divide the class into
small groups of six or seven, letting each group select a specific purpose
for their ceremony, which the group will develop cooperatively. With
the class working in small groups, the teacher's role may become that
of "visitor" with each group, offering suggestions and encouragement
only when necessary.

The role of the teacher adjusts as different structures are used, generally changing from a high degree of leading to a more supportive role
as the children gain understanding, skill, and confidence. Of course, the
ideas suggested for the Indian activities were not intended to be defini-
tive (or superior), but only illustrative of varying amounts and kinds
of structure suitable for an introductory activity. They incorporated
both highly structured teacher-led activities, and loosely structured
child-developed ones. Such use of structure is designed to be compatible with the growth needs of the children, both those who need a
generous amount of teacher direction in a particular learning experience
and those who do not. This approach is designed to recognize the

developmental nature of learning. It avoids overwhelming pressures on individual initiative and skill until there has been adequate preparation and trying-out; neither does it thwart or limit individual creative expression. Children are encouraged, even challenged, to develop ideas and skills and to use them in their own ways without threat and fear of failure. This kind of organization supports a classroom environment that is both humane and academically responsible, while nurturing imaginative thinking and creative expression.

However the teacher proceeds, she will be the one most responsible for structuring toward optimally successful experiences. Determining the appropriate kinds and amounts of structure is a competency the teacher must develop. It is a skill that grows from an understanding of where children are and how she can best guide them through new learning experiences.

SIDE-COACHING

The teacher may find that in a given activity or experience, the children work best if she guides from the sidelines. This technique is called side-coaching; the teacher makes suggestions and reinforces the children as they work. Generally the more structured the activities, the more explicit the suggestions. For example, in the first Indian rhythm activities, the teacher would have given very concise direct instructions: "Listen to the beat of the drums; now clap the rhythm with your hands, etc." In later freer work she may only offer suggestions from time to time, remind the children of something, and offer supportive commentary. Side-coaching from the teacher can keep the experience moving toward the purposes and goals she has identified. Properly used, this technique motivates, supports, and encourages creative work. Improperly used, it can intrude and inhibit. Threat, ridicule, and coercion are destructive of individual growth and create a climate in which creative drama simply cannot happen. If an activity is not working, if it seems poorly conceived, or if some of the children are exhibiting negative behaviors such as rowdiness or interfering with the majority, it is best to stop the experience and evaluate what is happening. Side-coaching by the teacher produces the best results when it is positive, constructive, and low-key. It is a useful tool when it advances the work without intruding. As a technique, it requires flexibility, sensitivity, patience, and restraint; it works best when not overemployed.

ROLE-PLAYING

Another way in which the teacher may participate in drama experiences is by assuming a role. Role-playing may be used comfortably even by those teachers who think they would feel ridiculous actually joining in the creative drama, for there are options as to the kind of role a teacher creates for self. For example, the teacher need not join in an Indian dance to participate in an Indian ceremony. She might move among the dancers as a visitor, asking questions about the ceremony and the dancers, or as a writer gathering information for a book about Indians and their customs. She could, in fact, side-coach through a role as the voice of an ancestor or the personification of a spirit. The teacher may be fluid in the role-playing, moving from role to role as it advances the drama experience. Her participation should not threaten or dominate, for she is neither the director, in a formal sense, nor "the star." Her purposes and goals *for the children* need to guide her participation when she is role-playing. However, some of the most exciting and rewarding drama experiences for children are those in which the teacher assumes appropriate roles and enters into the adventure. Teachers, too, can grow through drama, and participation through role-playing is a skill that can be developed only through experience. For some it may involve risk-taking, but the values far outweigh the risk.

USE OF QUESTIONS

There is an obvious relationship between the psychological and philosophical orientation of the teacher and the ability to develop the necessary competencies for worthwhile drama experiences. This is particularly so in the kinds of questions she will ask of children in the course of creating the drama. Whether the teacher participates in the drama experiences with side-coaching, role-playing, or a combination of both, she will need to develop skill in asking questions. The quality of the dramatic experiences will greatly depend on the ability of the teacher to ask the kinds of questions that elicit imaginative thinking and promote involvement. Obviously, questions that can be answered "yes" or "no" will do little to simulate creative thinking or expression. Questions that will stimulate, probe, and explore must allow for options. It takes practice with this kind of inquiry to develop it to a high level of expertise; however, even the novice teacher can soon function with a good deal of skill when her interaction with children is based on openness and acceptance. One indication of these attitudes is the way in which she listens to children. When the teacher listens with the desire to understand the perceptual expressions of each child and responds with feedback for his ideas and feelings, she is developing competencies as a stimulator of creative thinking. When she seeks to unify that which seems disparate because she values every child's ideas, she will be increasing her abilities to ask the kinds of questions and make the kinds of commentary that stimulate growth. The way in which the teacher is perceived by a child is strongly related to the way in which the teacher asks questions. Monitoring the kinds of questions and the way they are asked can give the teacher insights into herself and her relation with children. Does she ask many questions that allow options, for which there can be several "right" answers? Do the questions encourage the child to make inferences as well as furnish facts? Are the questions really probing for ideas and feelings or are they, in fact, rhetorical? Do the questions reveal her respect for the ideas and feelings of the children? Do they show that she really listens? Of the several skills and techniques that contribute to the quality of drama experiences for children, the teacher's ability to ask searching questions may be the most important.

Summary

As teacher and children work together in specific drama experiences, the need for other skills and techniques will be discovered. However, we can summarize four broadly useful basic ones: (1) an ability to articulate purposes and goals, to be able to state behaviors that will indicate to the teacher that learning is taking place; (2) competency in structuring, deciding on the kinds and amounts of structure most appropriate in a given situation; (3) the development of the techniques of side-coaching and role-playing as the teacher serves as stimulator, guide, and participator in the drama experiences; and (4) an ability to ask questions that will stimulate imaginative thinking and advance creative expression and involvement by the children.

The teacher who uses creative drama will appreciate adequate space, abundance of source materials, well-functioning equipment, and supportive encouragement from others. She will work to develop the necessary techniques, competencies, and skills. However, an environment for successful drama is built basically through the attitudes and behaviors of the teacher. Life flows from life, and the interaction of the human resources—teacher and children—provides the climate and nurtures creative growth in the classroom.

Creative dramatics in the elementary classroom is an extension of the dramatic play of early childhood. It provides opportunities for children as a creative art form and as a means for experiential learning that can contribute to each child's growth and development as a thinking, feeling, creative, and achieving person. It involves the teacher as a stimulator, guide, and participator in the learning process. Creative drama involves children and teachers alike in unique interactions and personal experiences for the benefit of all.

Your Turn

1. Read from at least two other books or periodicals selected from "Additional Readings for the Creative Teacher" listed in the Appendix. Write a short paper in response to your reading.
2. Think about your own elementary school experiences. See how many very special times you can recall that happened because a teacher initiated something that led to a memorable experience for you. What role did the teacher play? What, if any, special qualities did she or he possess? What kind of classroom climate do you associate with those special experiences?
3. Explain the statement "Form follows function" in terms of structure in the classroom. With your ideas and observations in mind, design an ideal classroom for you, a creative teacher.
4. Read from any of the books on creative drama listed in "Additional Readings in Creative Dramatics" in the Appendix.
5. From your reading and class discussion, write a "Letter to Parents" in which you describe what creative dramatics is and why you plan to incorporate it into your classroom. Try to make your letter both brief and informative.

3

Sensory Adventures

*All learning begins with a
sensory experience—that is, with
perception. Therefore, the
learner has contact by one or
more of his senses with objects,
people, places, or events.*

Barbara Vance

The classroom use of creative drama for experiential learning is unique because of the emphasis on the imagination and concern for the emotional as well as the intellectual development of the child. In her role as stimulator of creative thinking—without which there can be no creative drama—the teacher will be seeking a variety of resources that will serve to capture the imagination of the child intellectually and emotionally. Fortunately, such motivational materials are in ample supply. Anything the child can experience through his eyes, ears, touch, taste, and smell can be used to engage his mind and emotions in response. We know, of course, that we all learn through our senses, but for the child, sensory exploration is an adventure.

Watch a normal healthy infant in the crib. He has come into his environment with his physical, mental, and emotional equipment sufficient to his infant needs, providing his world includes persons of adequate maturity and sensitivity to recognize and respond to them. To

From *Teaching the Prekindergarten Child: Instructional Design and Curriculum.*

survive, an infant must have certain basic needs met. He requires nourishment and warmth and protection from harm; he also requires affectionate contact with other human beings. All of these are basic to his survival. But the child needs more than just to survive. He needs to grow and develop as a unique and worthy individual. A plant that requires sun does not thrive in the shade even when properly fed and watered. It may produce an abundance of foliage but never bloom. So too with the child whose environment does not supply the needed stimulants for the growth of the whole child. A variety of sights, sounds, textures, aromas, and flavors awaken in the child his growth potentials.

Look again at the baby in the crib—wiggly, vocal, inquisitive, exploring his environment through one or more of his senses. His power of concentration is often remarkable, especially when we consider how short his attention span can be when he is forced into some endeavor by an adult. To the very young child, the most entertaining element in his environment is himself. His little fingers and toes are looked at with deep fascination—wiggled, thrust into his mouth and examined orally. Soon he begins to examine other things in his world. He explores his mother's shiny teeth, her eyes, her cheek. The bright plastic rattle is something to know with his eyes, ears, and his sense of touch. He puts into his mouth anything that will fit. Soon he enlarges his experiences as his environment grows. He begins to operate in different kinds and amounts of space. His growth and development are highly related to these opportunities to satisfy his own inherent curiosity.

All children require sensory stimulation. They need opportunities to experience through all of their senses. The learning environment that concentrates on providing mostly eye and ear stimulation cannot be serving all of the needs of all the children. As Margaret Mead reports, "Children also need multisensory stimulation. There are several reasons for this. Because of tremendous individual differences, we do not know whether a particular child will be most dependent on hearing, sight, or touch."[1] We might add that this is true of the other senses as well, and not just because of possible physical disability of one of the senses. Vocational and recreational choices may require unusual development of any of the senses. Surely the fine old art of tea-tasting is not currently threatened by technology. The butcher, the baker, and the ceramics maker rely on a skillful sense of touch. Mead further states, "Children need an environment in which they can learn fine discriminations—in which they can hear small sounds and learn to differentiate between footsteps, learn to hear slight differences in tones of voice, learn to wake and know what time it is."[2]

IMAGINATION

Diddily di—diddily dee
You can be anything
You want to be.

Be a jester
Be a queen
Be the grandest ever seen.

Climb a mountain
Fly a jet
Keep a tiger for a pet!

Higgily hi—higgily ho
You can go anywhere
You want to go.

Cross the ocean
By balloon
Take a spaceship to the moon.

Slide down rainbows
Still a storm
Ride a golden unicorn.

It's a very simple secret
It's as simple as can be.
Anything is possible
With a little help from me!

The Senses and Imaginative Thinking

Ideally, the preschool child's environment provides a wide variety of sights, sounds, tastes, smells, and tactile and spatial experiences. He needs exposure to shapes and colors, a variety of rhythms and pitch, tastes, and textures to expand his sensory experiences just as he needs to enlarge his relationships with other human beings. He does, in fact, learn to know himself and others through his senses. This includes his own body image. He learns the shape of his mother's face, the pitch and rhythm of significant voices, even the touch and smell of those who cuddle and care for him. The child learns to make choices among foods according to taste, texture, and smell. Over and over he is learning by exploring, building on his real and personal sensory experiences. As understanding comes, he does not always need to have the real and personal sensory experience. He can see fire and know that it is hot without experiencing it in a real way. As he learns the symbols that represent people and things, his mother's question of "Where's dolly?" sends him looking for his doll. He can anticipate through his imagination what the cookie and milk will taste and feel like in his mouth before he begins to eat and drink. Birthdays and holidays become exciting and important to the child as he recalls and anticipates the special delights of each.

This ability to imagine and recall sensory experiences becomes an important part of the dramatic play. The little child playing house remembers how mother looks and sounds when she is setting the table, feeding the baby, or scolding the cat. He imagines how cold and sweet and smooth ice cream tastes and feels as he licks his imaginary cone. The high shrill siren of an imaginary fire truck prompts him to cover his ears. Watch and listen to the young child engaged in make-believe play and you can discover a great deal about the sensory experiences he has had and his feelings about them. If his ears are most familiar with harsh, demanding voices, his dramatic play is peopled with imaginary characters with harsh and demanding voices. In his need to understand and identify with adults through his play, he creates adults as he has perceived them through his senses. The child will also create imagined environments for his play from his sensory experiences with the nonhuman. This suggests that the child whose real and personal experiences are limited, threatening, or drab can be cheated twice—once in his real world, and again in his make-believe one.

Out of his innate creativity or through the intervention of others, a child is helped to hypothesize from his real and personal experiences a wide variety of imagined experiences that can enrich and enlarge his perceptions. Multisensory experiences, real and imagined, can make the difference between a limited kind of rote learning, and the development of creative imaginative thinking. Such adventures can help the child value his own sensory capabilities and use them to stretch his horizons —to make valuable inferences from what he knows and feels, to become a creative and imaginative thinker.

Historically, the advance of civilization has resulted from the imaginative thinking of a relatively small percentage of the total human resources. Yet the need for people who are "capable of doing new things" has been and will continue to be a fundamental requirement for the advancement of mankind. If such is indeed the goal of education, what kinds of learning experiences are important? How can we increase the possibilities for more people who can discover new and better solutions to problems and challenges? If to invent and discover is basic to real learning, the child must be more than a recipient of facts, an empty vessel waiting to be filled. Charlotte Selves, in a "Report on Work in Sensory Awareness and Total Functioning," states, "The nature of growth, which may be considered as identical with the learning process, is directly revealed in the developing child, who, when left to himself, lives in a state of incessant exploration which tends to bring him in contact, in one way or another, with all the elements of his environment ... it is between the active process of learning and the largely passive one of being educated that the child actually develops."[3] Knowledge is important and children want to know, but they need to be made active participants in the discovery of knowledge. The active imaginations of young children applied to the process of knowledge acquisition provide early training in creative thinking, an ability highly valued in the adult world. Most children enter school possessing active, vivid, free, and unintimidated imaginations. Unhappily, in the headlong rush to impart facts and develop certain skills, the educational processes actually operate to repress imaginative thinking. Experiential learning that involves a wide-ranging variety of sensory experiences works positively to help children learn facts and concepts, develop skills, and at the same time to develop and strengthen their abilities to think imaginatively and function creatively.

Imaginative thinking is, in fact, the secret missing ingredient in many an otherwise adequate learning environment. The imagination is truly a wondrous thing. Like life itself, in its embryonic state it is invisible to the naked eye—we cannot see it, hear it, or touch it. We often cannot articulate much of anything about it. In the beginning it is often so fragile that undue probing or forcing may warp or destroy it. We do know that from it dreams grow into reality. It is the beginning of the poem, the painting, the melody, the play. It is also the genesis of social and scientific advancements. Through our imaginations we can recreate the past, explore the present, and envision the future. It allows us to create order out of chaos and to find beauty in the ordinary. To stimulate and develop the imagination requires a sense of wonder about ourselves and all of creation. Fortunate are teachers and children who keep alive their senses of wonder through shared sensory adventures.

If learning requires making discoveries, it is necessary to go exploring. Through exploration, exciting discoveries stimulate creative learning.

The Senses and the Emotions

Contemporary children have been armchair participants in one of the great explorations of all times, the probes into outer space. They have seen how the men who have carried out these explorations have involved their total personal resources. These pioneers have been intellectually astute, physically sound, both sensitive and stable emotionally, and aesthetically aware in order to carry out their missions for maximum achievement. Much of the data they have collected could also have been gathered by their tremendously sophisticated equipment without the additional costs and hazards of manned flights. Machines can be programmed to observe, record, compute, analyze, make decisions, and solve problems. But machines cannot be programmed to respond with feelings of suspense, exultation, or awe. No matter how highly developed are the sensors of a machine, they cannot thrill to a single sight or sound, nor be inspired by them. Without the capability of emotional response, machines are limited by the data received.

If learning requires making discoveries, it is necessary to go exploring. School is the environment in which children go exploring. They come outfitted with the most complex equipment we know: the human mind, the human body, and human emotions. What their sensors discover can be recorded, analyzed, and compared. In addition, their discoveries can stimulate the imagination and produce both ideas and feelings, and human superiority over even the most sophisticated technological equipment is revealed in the interaction of a creative intellect with the emotions. Unlike a machine, even the very young child can be intellectually, physically, and psychically excited about his discoveries. When the learning process does not provide opportunities to involve all dimensions of a child, he is being denied part of his human potential.

If we accept Piaget's premise that the goal of education is to create possibilities for children to invent and discover, we dare not presume to limit in what areas and through what facets of self such inventing and discovering shall take place. Experiences for human learning and development should serve the whole child. He needs to know about himself, about others, and about his environment and to recognize his feelings, to value them, and to discover how to integrate them with what he knows intellectually. He needs skills so that he can make discoveries, and so that he can use his discoveries well.

The infant's immediate response to the sensory data he takes in is emotional. Sensory stimuli arouse feelings of pain or pleasure which make the child feel happy, fearful, anxious, angry, and so forth. Sounds startle him, causing him to shudder and cry; bright colors may produce giggles and squirms. His reactions are spontaneous, and immature though they be, they are honestly his own. Even when the child hides his feelings, they are there. As he grows older, he may discover that to reveal himself openly to others takes a great deal of courage, more than he sometimes has. Many children begin school already so conditioned. By contrast, we see adults who continue to react only emotionally to many experiences, remaining immature in those areas of development. Whole people are neither ruled by their emotions, nor do they subjugate their feelings to their intellects so that they become primarily receiving and reporting devices, lacking in essential human qualities. Approaches to learning that polarize rather than integrate a child's total capacities tend to produce adults who are less than whole.

Creative dramatics provides a natural involvement of the total self in the learning process. Drama experiences generally begin with some kind of real or imagined sensory stimulation designed to promote creative thinking and authentic involvement. Sensory experiences are basic to drama because they stimulate the imagination and evoke emotional responses. Drama is man in conflict with himself, with others, with circumstances, with his environment. Creative drama encourages resolution of the conflict, which requires problem-solving; and because conflict involves the emotions, participants must recognize and deal with their feelings. Creative drama can provide the format in which children naturally and securely express feelings that arise from those conflicts they experience. It is never enough to ask ourselves only what we hear, see, touch, taste, smell; machines can gather such data. It is not enough for human beings to draw comparisons, trace relationships, or catalogue information; those are the ways in which we come to understand *things*. It is with the emotions that we can come to understand and deal with the human condition and its eternal struggle.

Summary

Sensory experiences are basic to all learning. They are particularly useful for stimulating the imagination and eliciting emotional response. Creative drama, which emphasizes the total development of children, can be motivated by a multitude of sensory adventures. Even before children are ready to express their ideas and feelings through dramas with characters and plots, sensory activities can be used to give them both real and imagined experiences on which a drama may be built. The inclusion of a variety of sensory activities is fundamental to the development and use of creative drama in the classroom. Sensory input precedes emotional response and ideation, which may be expressed through movement alone, verbalizing, or action and dialogue together.

Creative movement, pantomime, storybuilding, characterization—whatever form the drama activities may take—all are dependent upon imaginative thinking and emotional involvement of the children. Therefore, frequent and generous opportunities for sensory adventures should be provided; for teachers who wish to include creative drama in the classroom, they make a natural, comfortable, and exciting way to begin.

Perhaps the best way to conclude this introduction to sensory experiences is with an illustration.

"What if the little lizard crawling through the ferns and grasses were thousands of times enlarged? Can you picture it in your mind's eye? Can you see the sun glinting on its dark armorlike scales as it laboriously picks its way through a primeval forest? Imagine the thud of its clawlike feet upon the earth and hear the vines snap from the onslaught of the probing neck and grinding teeth. Its eyes blink as the reptilian head breaks through the shade into the light. Smell the rank overpowering greenness of this ancient place. Have you ever before been in such a wild mysterious world or felt so huge and powerful? When you have created your own primeval forest just as you want it, become that prehistoric beast and move like it through your own primitive land."

With such leaps of the imagination, the product of a variety of sensory suggestions, children can go anywhere and become anything. Once the imagination and emotions have been sufficiently stimulated, movement, pantomime, characters, and stories can evolve almost automatically. Not so long ago some visiting elementary children turned a dignified modern university classroom into a prehistoric forest during a Creative Drama Workshop. The room was soon teeming with a wonderful assortment of reptiles, birds, and beasts. When the playing finished, one little lady proudly announced, "I was a Brontosaurus—did you know they are 'distinct'?" She was, indeed, a most "distinctive" dinosaur, transformed by her own beautiful ability to respond with mind, body, and feelings to a sensory adventure.

In the rest of this chapter we deal with each of the senses separately and in combination. Each section begins with some background information included to suggest to teachers possible purposes and objectives that may be met through the various kinds of activities later described. Many of these experiences are in the form of exercises and games. Few will actually deal with characters and plot, though such kinds of creative drama experiences may certainly evolve from them. They are intended to provide sensory-related ideas that can be used to stimulate imaginative thinking, emotional response, and creative expression and which in turn can lead to story development and improvisation. It would be presumptuous to assume that any book on the classroom use of creative dramatics can be a "teacher's *complete* guide to successful creative drama," for this would deny both the creativity and the dynamics of teachers and children actually working together in the classroom. The activities that follow are designed to be useful examples of the kinds of things that work. They include both sensory activities that are real and personal and those that challenge children to create new sensory adventures, the unique products of their own imaginations.

GIVE A LISTEN

I like the song of a gentle shower,
And the hallway clock as it strikes the hour;
The fog horn calling through the rain
To coax the ships home safe again.
I like to hear the doorbell chime
And happy voices of friends of mine;
Soft sounds of summer, the crisp sounds of fall
And sweet sounds of spring—the best of all.
I love the sounds of earth and sea
And I like it when someone listens to me.

Listening Games and Other Adventures

"Oh, Grandma," said Little Red Riding Hood to the wolf disguised in Grandmother's nightclothes, "what big ears you have!"

"The better to hear you with, my dear," replied the wolf.

Unlike poor Red Riding Hood, we know that not only is it really the wily old wolf speaking, but that the size of one's ears has nothing to do with the ability to hear well. More importantly, we also know that the functioning of the senses is only the very first step in their contributions to the growth and development of a human being. We know, for example, that listening involves a great deal more than the physical act of hearing and that it is from the listening rather than the hearing, *per se,* that we learn. Effective listening begins when interpretations and associations with prior experiences are added to the physical function of hearing. Therefore, in the learning process we are concerned primarily with the development of listening abilities.

Some people are intuitively good listeners, very aurally related to the world. It is also true that to listen well requires that a person give his attention to what he hears, that the listener make the effort. Beyond this, there has not traditionally been an emphasis on helping children improve and develop skill in listening as they are helped to read, write, and speak. Courses in listening are a recent addition to education. Growing out of research during and after World War II, we have learned a great deal more about listening. Through a better understanding of the process, we have ascertained that listening, like speaking, can be improved through a variety of experiences. Listening skills can be developed, and many teachers now include specific activities in listening as a regular part of the classroom program. The inclusion of listening in the total language arts program is tremendously important. We do, in fact, listen more than we speak, write, or read. The average adult spends over one-quarter of his waking life listening.

The elementary child listens, or is expected to listen, more than one-half of the ordinary classroom and activity time. He is expected to assimilate information and ideas from listening to his teachers, his peers, and to media materials. He also needs to be listened to by others; the fulfillment of this need is vastly important to the child's general emotional balance and basic to the development of a strong self-concept. This interaction of listening to others and having them listen to us is fundamental to the exploration of self without which meaningful interpersonal relationships cannot be built. Many opportunities for children to practice listening skills, both as receivers and senders, help to build the kind of classroom environment that promotes cognitive development and good mental health and encourages creative thinking and expression.

Just as there are different purposes to our speech (to explore our own ideas, to report information, to share our ideas and feelings with others, for example), there are also different needs that motivate our listening. We listen in different ways for different purposes. At times we all have a need to listen critically in order to compare, evaluate, make judgements; at times we need to listen in order to synthesize ideas—bring things together so that they make sense to us; and at other times we need to listen for accuracy—to get things straight. All of these purposes demand a high degree of aural awareness. Of equal importance to the total development of a person is the ability to listen creatively to stimulate the imagination. Such listening requires not only aural awareness, but also the freedom to explore new ideas.

The use of listening activities in creative dramatics is two-fold. Games and exercises that require careful and accurate listening encourage concentration and awareness, and can stimulate the imagination and provide motivation for both verbal and nonverbal creative expression. Listening games and experiences of all kinds may both prepare children for drama and also furnish the substance from which the creative drama may evolve.

Many drama activities are presented in the form of games to involve children in a way they naturally enjoy and because games require concentration and careful listening to directions. In addition, games often demand interaction and cooperation among the participants, the kind of action/response essential to drama. However, not all listening activities need be in the form of games. Particularly when listening is used to stimulate the imagination, less structured kinds of experiences are generally more appropriate. These more creative experiences also encourage concentration and a high degree of sensory awareness, but the emphasis is on experimentation and the imaginative exploration of many ideas.

Attentive and accurate use of the senses is a good place to begin. In the following listening activities, games and exercises that stress concentration and accuracy are presented first, followed by a variety of experiences to stimulate the imagination and encourage children to make inferences.

Listening Games

A Variation on "Simon Says"

Young children enjoy "Simon Says" for several reasons; there is the element of suspense (wondering what the leader will say next); they are challenged to listen carefully; and everyone plays in a parallel situation which reduces self-consciousness. In this variation, the children are asked specifically to listen to beginning sounds and to respond with their own interpretations of the movement suggested. There is opportunity for individual creative movement and pantomime.

To play the teacher first selects the specific beginning sound and announces it to the group. The teacher may have the group suggest several words that begin with the chosen sound. The first time this game is played, it is wise to let the children have a few "free" tries to be sure all understand. Each "Simon says" will suggest a movement or pantomime to be done by the children, but they are to move *only* when the *last* word of the instruction begins with the specified sound. If the last word does not begin with the proper sound, the children "freeze." Because this is to be a learning experience, there is no special value in having those who miss sit out a round, but rather the teacher simply notes in passing that some people were "caught."

Example: The beginning sound to work with is the *m* sound. The teacher may use statements like the following: "Simon says move like a monster." "Simon says scamper like a mouse." "Simon says hop like a frog" (freeze). "Simon says be a curious monkey." "Simon says drink some milk." "Simon says ride a motorcycle." "Simon says let's go swimming" (freeze). Making a list ahead of time to have a suitable number of words for each sound keeps the game moving well.

As children develop expertise with beginning sounds, they enjoy playing by themselves, taking turns leading the activities. Informal observation by the teacher can continue for evaluation.

Sequential listening games

Sequential listening games are highly structured activities for involving children in listening to one another. Sequential listening games are especially adaptable for introducing or summarizing materials in several academic areas—particularly language arts, social studies, and science.

Because reading abilities are required, this game works best for middle- and upper-elementary grades. The reading vocabulary must be appropriate for the group. This game requires a substantial amount of preparation; however, once a set of cards is prepared, it may be saved and used again and again. The teacher chooses a theme around which to build the game. It may deal with a specific unit of study or some concept to be introduced, reinforced, or reviewed. For her use, the teacher prepares a master list of the statements to be read that cover the specific material selected. These statements are arranged in a logical sequential order so that as each child reads his assigned statements, the rest of the children must listen carefully so that the next reader knows when to read. The master list will contain all of the material in proper sequential order. For the students, individual cards are prepared, each with one piece of material corresponding exactly to the master list. As a convenience for keeping the activity flowing the back of each individual pupil card can be numbered, corresponding to its order on the master sheet. The teacher does not call out the number of the next card unless the child holding that card fails to read his material at the proper time. Each card includes a statement to listen to and a statement to read aloud. If the cards are typed, red and black ribbon may be used to distinguish the two parts. Small and capital letters or two colors of ink pens may also be used to mark this distinction.

To play, each child randomly selects at least one card until all of the cards are distributed. The card to be read first will state. "You begin," followed by the material to be read aloud. After the first card has been read, each succeeding card has the next segment of material to be read aloud, plus that which immediately preceded it. Each child must listen carefully to what is read each time in order to know when to read from his card.

Example: The following is a sequential listening game about the early life of George Washington. It is designed for upper-elementary children. The first three segments are complete as they would appear on each child's card, including the material from the preceding card from which the reader received his cue. From Card 4 on, only the part to be read aloud is given.

1. You begin by reading aloud: *"George Washington was born in Virginia on February 22, 1732. His parents were Augustine and Mary Ball Washington."*

2. After you hear, "George Washington was born in Virginia on February 22, 1732. His parents were Augustine and Mary Ball Washington," you read aloud: *"When George Washington was born there was no country called the United States of America. Virginia was one of 13 colonies which belonged to England and was ruled by the King of England."*

3. After you hear, "When George Washington was born there was no country called the United States of America. Virginia was one of 13 colonies which belonged to England and was ruled by the King of England," you read aloud: *"George Washington's great-grandfather had come to Virginia from England, and he had built a plantation near the seacoast. Away from the seacoast, the land was wilderness where Indian tribes lived."*

4. *"When George was a little boy, his family moved to another plantation on the Rappahonnock River. The plantation was called 'Ferry Farm.' "*

5. *"George Washington had three younger brothers and a sister. He also had two older half-brothers."*

6. *"Life on the plantation was very busy. Besides the main house where the Washington family lived, there were barns and shops of all kinds."*

7. *"Many people lived and worked on the plantation—blacksmiths, carpenters, shoemakers, people who spun yarn and wove cloth, candlemakers, and all of the men, women, and children who worked in the fields."*

8. *"Young George liked to explore the plantation, fish and swim in the river, pitch horseshoes, and watch the barges on the river."*

9. *"Every summer a big ship arrived from England bringing furniture, tools, clothes, and many other things. The ship took back to England the tobacco which was raised on Ferry Farm."*

10. *"George Washington loved to watch the ship unloading and loading. He listened to the captain giving orders, and thought he would like to be a captain on a big ship when he grew up."*

11. *"Young George did not go to a school like children today. His teachers came to the plantation to teach him to read, write, spell, and do arithmetic."*

12. *"There are many stories about George Washington when he was a little boy. The best known one is about George and the cherry tree."*

13. *"Another favorite story is about young George and his mother's favorite colt. The colt was very frisky and hard to ride. One day George decided he would ride the colt and make it behave."*

14. *"The colt began to buck and jump, but George did not fall off. Finally the colt gave a big leap and fell down dead. It had broken a vein. George knew he had done a foolish thing, but he went to the house and told his mother."*

15. *"Even though his mother was sad about the colt, she was glad George had been brave and told her the truth."*

16. *"When George was about ten, his two half-brothers came back from England where they had gone to study. George listened to his brother Lawrence tell of his adventures when he had fought for England in the war with Spain."*

17. *"George especially liked the stories about Lawrence's brave commander, Admiral Vernon."*

18. *"George liked to play that he was a captain in the army. He and his friends played soldiers with cornstalks for muskets. They drilled up and down in a vacant field."*

19. *"When George was 11 his father died. His father left most of his property to his oldest son, Lawrence."*

20. *"Lawrence soon married, and he rebuilt the house on the largest family plantation on the Potomac River. It had been called 'Hunting Creek,' but Lawrence renamed it 'Mount Vernon' after his commander in England."*

21. *"After his father died, George knew he would not be going to England to school like his older brothers. He went to a new school in Virginia and studied hard."*

22. *"When George was 14, he began to plan for his future. He wanted to go to sea and become a naval officer. He was all set to sail for England."*

23. *"Then his mother received a letter from his uncle in England. The uncle wrote that it would not be a good idea for George to join the navy. George was very disappointed, but he did not sail with the ship for England."*

24. *"One day, George found a set of surveyor's instruments that had belonged to his father. There was much land in the new world to be surveyed."*

25. *"Young George helped other surveyors until he learned to be a surveyor. He did such careful work that he soon had many jobs, some for Lord Fairfax, an elderly Englishman who had been a soldier all over the world."*

26. *"Between surveying trips, George learned about military tactics from his brother Lawrence and Lord Fairfax."*

27. *"When his brother Lawrence died, George became the young master of Mount Vernon. If the colonies had not revolted against England and become independent, George Washington might have spent his life as a soldier and farmer."*

28. *"As a young boy, George Washington had a very happy childhood, growing up on the family plantation. As a man, he spent eight long hard years fighting in the Revolutionary War. Then in 1789, he left Mount Vernon to become the first President of our country."*

GETTING TO KNOW YOU

Sensory activities designed to emphasize concentration and accurate use of the senses can combine well with movement and pantomime. In the variation of "Simon Says" listening is combined with body movement or pantomime.

This game for middle- and upper-elementary children combines a concentration on listening with simple movement or pantomime activity, but with a lesser degree of teacher direction. The primary purpose of this game is to get all of the children involved in the sharing activity, but an emphasis on listening and looking is a valuable secondary purpose. If a child has trouble recalling what he has just seen and heard, he may be helped in a casual way and encouraged to share any part that he does recall.

To play, the children will be asked to make a large circle so that all may easily see and hear. The action will move from left to right or right to left as agreed upon beforehand. The teacher may begin by introducing herself: "I am (name), and I like to (names and shows with movement something she likes to do)." The child next to the teacher repeats what has been said and done and adds her own name and something she likes to do. The pantomimes are to be kept simple and done in place. Each person, in turn, begins with the teacher's name and action, adds each successive person in order, and concludes with his own name and movement.

The game is quite difficult, and takes too long with a large group. The teacher may break the class into groups of about 12 to play simultaneously in small circles or first one group then another.

Children may wish to play the game another day substituting some variations; for example, they might follow their names with their favorite foods, sports, story titles, or television shows. These variations may or may not involve the movement or pantomime, but will continue to emphasize listening.

GIVE AND TAKE

For a word or sound to convey a message to the receiver, it must first of all be heard. This activity graphically shows the necessity for being able to hear before we can listen. The first part of the activity can be played with boys and girls of all ages by selecting appropriate themes. The variation is more complicated and is, therefore, more suitable for middle- through upper-elementary grades.

This game is played with children seated in a large circle. To begin, they are asked to tell their favorite food, color, pet (whatever might best interest the group), all at the same time, on signal from the teacher. The teacher may remind them that they should each speak clearly, distinctly, and in an audible voice but not shouting. When the group has done this, the teacher asks several children to repeat one other person's choice, different from their own, which they heard. Few, if any, will be able to do this, and the children may well complain that they could not hear anyone else. After the speaking in unison experiment, the children are each asked to respond to the question, one at a time, going around the circle. The teacher reminds them to speak clearly and listen carefully. Afterwards the entire class shares in reconstructing as many specific answers as they can recall. These may be listed on the board for all to see. This activity should be followed with a discussion of what has happened, emphasizing the importance of speaking clearly, one at a time, and giving attention to each speaker.

In the variation of the activity children are engaged in the give and take of conversation using a game format. Besides requiring careful listening to one another, it also provides excellent preparation for handling improvised dialogue in informal drama.

The most frequently used form of oral communication is at the interpersonal level—what we generally think of as conversation. Almost all dramatic dialogue is of this nature: characters speaking, listening, responding. This give and take is basic to communication.

To play someone begins with a sentence. The sentence may make a statement, ask a question, make a request or declaration. The next child adds a sentence that must relate in some way to the previous statement. Each successive player adds a sentence, always building on what was said by the person just before him. The challenge is to keep the language flowing, without interrupting any speaker, and always responding in some way to what has just been said. To encourage each child to participate, the speaking may pass around a circle. This particular exercise is not aimed at creating a story, but rather to challenge the children to listen to one another as they experience and observe the give and take that is present in everyday oral communication. To stimulate broad participation, this activity may follow some shared experience around which the "conversation" may center, perhaps after a film, play, classroom visitor, or a field trip. This "game," which emphasizes both speaking and listening, might also be useful as a nontechnical approach to an understanding of "discussion" when it is centered around a theme.

More Listening Games

The following are brief descriptions of more listening games that call for accurate listening and concentration. Many of these are old favorites familiar to both teachers and children. Though they are often played "just for fun," they all involve listening skills.

"*Elephants Fly.*" The leader stands in front of the group and says, for example, "Robins fly," while moving the arms like a bird in flight. The others respond by moving their arms up and down. Each time the leader mentions something which does fly, the children respond by moving their arms. If, however, the leader names something which does not fly (elephants, for instance), the leader continues to move arms up and down, but the others "freeze." To add greater opportunity for creative movement, the children may move around the room as the various things that fly, "freezing" when the leader names something which does not. This game is enjoyed by nursery and early elementary children.

"*Can You Ride the Pony, John?*" The leader states a question that asks for both a verbal and pantomime response. The specific child to whom the question is directed is not named until the end of the request so that all are challenged to listen carefully each time. The child to whom the question is directed replies, "Yes, I can ride the pony," and quickly pantomimes the correct activity. Each child is asked to do a different activity. Maturity and interests of the children should be considered by the leader in asking the questions. The game is therefore adaptable for several grade levels.

"Statues." Children move to a beat provided by the leader. The beat may be provided by clapping hands or any one of a number of rhythm instruments. The children must listen carefully to the tempo and pace their movement to it. When the leader calls "freeze," the children stop exactly as they were when they heard the order. The leader may add a further direction to the "freeze," such as "freeze happy," "freeze tired," and so forth. Or the children may be asked to "freeze" as animal characters, circus performers, or as characters from literature. The children remain as statues until they hear the beat resume. This game is also suitable for several grade levels.

"I Packed My Bag." This game is best played in a circle. The first player begins by stating, "I'm going on a trip. I packed my bag, and in it I put *(names an article)."* The next player repeats, "I packed my bag, and in it I put (names article from first player) and *(adds another article)."* Each succeeding player must add all of the articles mentioned previously in proper order, and adds his own. This game works best with middle- and upper-elementary boys and girls.

"The Beat Goes On." This game is similar to "I Packed My Bag," but uses only rhythmic beats rather than words. Children may clap hands, snap fingers, tap feet, etc. to provide their rhythm. Again the action passes around the circle, with each child repeating what has been done by the previous players and adding his own. This game becomes very complicated if the group is too large. However, older boys and girls may enjoy the challenge of recalling a complex pattern. When the activity becomes too difficult, a new sequence may be started.

All of the preceding listening activities follow a game format with directions for playing, a fair amount of structuring by the teacher, and are played toward specific and anticipated goals. Other kinds of listening experiences for use in creative drama encourage more breadth of interpretation by the children and are more open-ended. Such sensory experiences as listening to sounds, words, and music may, like listening games, be used to develop concentration and awareness. They may also be used to stimulate the imagination. In the following sections, which deal with listening to sounds, words, and music, the activities will move from those that emphasize sensory awareness to those that are specifically intended to stimulate the imagination.

Listening to Sounds to Develop Awareness

The use of sounds for developing listening sensitivity offers delightful and unlimited possibilities for children of all ages. Many sources can provide interesting sounds in a classroom. If the room has a sink, the sound of running water is a familiar and distinctive sound with which to begin. Examples of other sounds that can be simply produced in the usual classroom are: the sound of chalk on the board as you write; the opening and closing of a door, a cupboard, or the window blinds; turning the pages of a book; using equipment in the room such as the pencil sharpener, paper cutter, and light switch; and, of course, footsteps and other human sounds. Many elementary rooms also have cages with small animals or aquariums. Such everyday classroom sounds can furnish children with valuable experiences in listening with selectivity and discrimination. They may be asked to listen only to a certain sound, shutting out all other distractions as much as possible. Or they may be asked to listen and identify as many sounds as they can distinguish. Listening with eyes closed will help them to better concentrate on the listening. Whether concentrating on a specific sound or discovering many sounds, there should be ample time for them to listen before sharing their ideas.

This same activity may be repeated while the children listen to sounds outside the room or building and to sounds within their own bodies. Listening to sounds outside of their immediate environment means that they must listen with great discretion, often purposefully ignoring sounds that are nearby and persistent. Such selective listening is challenging, but it is a useful skill to develop. Listening to sounds within their own bodies also calls for concentration and selective listening. Little boys and girls are often surprised to discover that when it is really quiet and they are really listening, they can hear several sounds that are involuntarily produced by their own bodies—breathing, heartbeat ("Can I really hear it or am I feeling it?" they sometimes ask), tummy growls, and swallowing. During this activity some children may discover for the first time that when they are awake there are constant internal noises in their heads—thoughts! An amazed first grader once vividly described her fabulous discovery: "My brains are making a lot of noise!" Children can also be encouraged to listen to silence—which sounds ever so much more intriguing than being told to hush and be still. Children, like adults, need to learn to utilize and enjoy silence, and "listening to silence" can be one way of inviting children to imagine.

In addition to actual sounds generally available in and around the classroom, taped sounds are easily acquired and extremely useful for listening adventures. The teacher may enjoy making her own sound tapes of city traffic; country sounds; the "voices" of nature such as wind, rain, hail, thunder, and surf. Those who have done so have discovered that in the process they have sharpened their listening awareness and challenged their own inventiveness.

A teacher who lived on a large, working farm admitted that she managed to get the whole family involved while making a tape of farm sounds to be used with a group of inner-city kindergartners. She found that it was necessary to walk the horse up and down the front porch to get the kind of clop, clop we associate with a horse. The dirt road did not provide an appropriate surface to produce an "authentic" sound. Her inventiveness was well worth the effort, for her tape was a spellbinder for the children. There are also, of course, excellent commercial tapes and records that can be used for listening activities.

Children may enjoy making their own sound tapes which can be shared with the class. Simple cassette recorders are lightweight and quite easy to use, even for young children. They may work individually or in the small groups making tapes of sounds in and around the school. Older boys and girls can make tapes of special places and events, for example, sounds that are most representative of a shared experience such as a field trip or special project.

After listening to sounds, children may discuss who or what made the sounds, how the sounds were made and for what purposes, the listener's proximity to the sounds, and the moods and feelings the various sounds created in the listener. If sounds are selected because they relate to some subject or concept the class is studying, the discussion and activities may then relate to the broader areas of information. For example, a tape of traffic sounds may be listened to and identified as a part of a unit on the city, or safety, or transportation. Listening to the tick of a wall clock and other types and sizes of timepieces may accompany a unit on telling time or a history of time-telling devices. Listening to sounds within the child's own body may help him to have a greater understanding of his physical self or be an exciting part of a health unit. Eleanor Craig, in her autobiographical book about work with emotionally disturbed children, *P.S. You're Not Listening,* relates how one little boy with a severe inability for self-identification, made some significant strides after listening to his own heart with a stethoscope.[4] For all children, the more the listening activities can be integrated into a larger personalized learning experience, the more meaningful they can be.

Additional work based on stimuli provided through listening to sounds might involve the children in out-of-class listening. The challenge may be to discover a sound they have never noticed before at home or other familiar place. This kind of exploration urges children to practice listening individually and independently in order to make fine discriminations. To later share their own sensory discoveries encourages verbal expression and the use of descriptive language. In another exercise that emphasizes individuality, the children are asked to share favorite sounds and most disliked sounds and to describe them with language or show through movement how each sound makes them feel.

An enlarged experience with favorite sounds may be done as follows: The children are to imagine that they are all to be members of an earth expedition to another planet. Since they will be gone for a long period of time, they will want to take along some of their favorite remembrances of their life on planet earth. Each member of the exploration party may take along as a part of his or her personal gear, only six earth sounds on a memory tape, so they will want to make very careful selections. The children will need sufficient time to make their investigations and narrow their final choices to six. They will need several days to explore. The teacher may suggest that each child keep a record of all of the sounds he considered before the final selections were made. There may be a mid-point report against which each child may later compare his final list. The ultimate choices may be shared orally or as a writing assignment. Depending upon the availability of taping equipment, some or all of the children might actually make a tape of the sounds they selected.

In all of the foregoing activities, the children were invited to give their attention to actual sounds. Such listening calls for careful concentration to determine what is being heard, to discover the source, and perhaps to make individual decisions about the sounds in terms of personal feelings. Real and personal experiences with listening to sounds will also trigger the imagination and stimulate creative thinking. This may be of an investigative nature—the kind required by the physician listening to the patient's chest, the plumber examining the gurgling pipes, or the auto mechanic diagnosing the "hiccups" under the car hood. Or the listening may involve the imagination in some aesthetic response—a nostalgic recollection of another time and place, a fantasy adventure full of new experiences, even the melody of a yet unborn song.

To listen imaginatively to sounds around us invites the listener mentally to explore possibilities with a kind of intrapersonal brainstorming. The listener asks himself such questions as: What do I hear? What else might it be? Where and when have I heard such a sound before? Where else might such a sound be heard? What if this sound were being heard in another time and place? This kind of listening to sounds creates unlimited possibilities by teasing the imagination. In the following exercises, sensory exploration which asks "what if?" is used primarily to stimulate the imagination, arouse emotional response, and provide ideas for creative expression.

Listening to Sounds to Stimulate the Imagination

Several of the preceding exercises may also be used for stimulating the imagination. Listening to actual sounds in and around the classroom, inside oneself, or on record or tape can be the basis for imaginative conjecturing. The following are the kinds of questions that can be used to help children make imaginative inferences from real and personal experiences.

1. What if you were hearing this same sound in another time or place?
2. We know that this is the sound of _____. What else do you suppose it might be?
3. If this sound were many times louder (or softer), what might it be?
4. If this sound were much faster (or slower), what might it be?
5. What if you were someone or something else hearing this sound— perhaps something very small, or very large, or from another time or place? Who or what are you? How would this sound make you feel?
6. If you were (suggest a feeling or emotion such as sleepy, hungry, afraid, or angry), and you were hearing this sound, what would it make you think about? How would it make you feel?

Listening to actual sounds imaginatively can be used as a basis for creative writing and oral storybuilding, with children working either individually or in small groups. Group storybuilding, particularly, may find its ultimate expression in creative drama. In the following activity the children may use sounds in both real and fantasy ways. For example, a drum beat may be incorporated into the story as a drum beat or as some pulsating sound, a heart beat, perhaps.

The class is divided into several small groups. Each group is given three or four actual sounds to which they listen carefully. For example, one group may be given the tick of a clock, a door opening, soft and rapid footsteps, and the bubbling of the aquarium in the classroom. If the same sounds are given to each group, the end result will show how each used the sounds in its own way. If a different set of sounds is given to each a greater variety of story ideas should result. Either way, the object is to have all of the children involved in incorporating their sounds into a story developed by the group. Once each group has its sounds, they work simultaneously for a given period of time, creating a little story built around their sounds. When their stories are finished, they may tell them to the class or share them through pantomime or puppet play, incorporating the sounds at the appropriate times. The stories need not be shared since the greatest value for the participants is in the creative process rather than in the end product.

Each time children are engaged in storybuilding, individually or in small groups, orally or written, the teacher has an opportunity to reaffirm with them the basic components of a good story—characters, plot, conflict, climax, and ending. Who or what makes each sound suggests the need for characters; sound in itself suggests movement and therefore action and possible conflict. The teacher may suggest that one or more of the sounds be used to build toward the climax and strengthen the ending. Polished stories are generally not the goal, and in beginning work especially, the purpose is to involve as many children as possible in imaginative use of the senses in ways that result in imaginative thinking and creative expression. A certain lack of originality and inventiveness will probably be present at first. The sounds may make the children think of familiar stories and situations. As they gain experience and develop trust in their own abilities to create, storybuilding will become more creative, both in the development of ideas and in their expression through drama.

Producing their own sound tapes is another activity that can involve children in listening to actual sounds with both fine discrimination and imagination. They may wish to make their own sound tapes to accompany the playing out of a story in a manner similar to the creation of a sound track for radio or film. Such technical work requires a great deal of accurate listening and inventiveness. It also demands purposeful experimentation with sound production and reproduction. For example, some fifth graders were eager to make a tape to accompany a dramatization that required the sound of a fog horn and the creaking of a heavy door. The children found a creaking door in the building, but discovered that on tape it did not produce the prolonged or mysterious creak they required. Ultimately, they created the sound they wanted with some large blocks of styrofoam. They decided that they would have to produce the moan of the fog horn with their own vocal equipment and ended with everyone auditioning their own mournful notes. Careful listening, experimentation with properties, inventiveness, and a good deal of hilarious sharing were all part of this learning experience.

Though it is more fun for teachers and children to discover their own ways of creating interesting and intriguing sounds for listening and drama activities, the following are a few suggestions that others have found useful.

1. Crumpling brittle plastic containers in which some cookies and fresh produce are packed are excellent for creating fire sounds; everything from a little spark to a crackling forest fire may be suggested depending on the weight of the material and how rapidly it is crumpled. This same material may also be used to suggest walking through fallen leaves, ice cracking on a pond, twigs snapping, the shattering of glass, and a variety of fantasy ideas that come from the children's own imaginations.

2. Large plastic bottles such as household bleach containers partially filled with water are quite satisfactory for a variety of water sounds, especially the gentle sounds of waves lapping against the shore or against the side of an anchored or slowly moving boat.

3. Wind sounds are best made vocally but are hard to sustain for a very long period of time without help. The teacher may begin the sound and involve the children in sustaining it for as long as needed.

4. Footsteps approaching and fading are easily made with the palm of the hands flat against a desk top or on the hard cover of a large book. This is much easier to control for volume and rate than to use actual footsteps.

5. Two substantial blocks of styrofoam, the kind molded for packing around small appliances, can be rubbed together to produce beautiful creaks—just right for castle doors and creaky stairs.

6. Flexible cookie sheets can be manipulated to create thunder, and fingernails lightly tapping on a metal surface may be combined to create the sounds of a rainstorm.

Manipulated by the teacher, while the children listen with eyes closed, commonplace odds and ends may be used to tantalize imaginations. Sound-making materials are generally free for the discovering, and the possibilities which are virtually unlimited, may be discovered by the children using their imaginations to solve specific problems.

Listening to Imagined Sounds

Children may also listen to sounds that are totally created by their imaginations. This kind of imaginative listening works best when they have had many, many opportunities to listen and work with actual sounds. From this wealth of real and personal experiences they are enabled to discover and invent entirely with the imagination.

The teacher plays an important role in stimulating totally imagined sensory experiences. With descriptive language, and provocative suggestions and questions, she may guide children in creating sounds entirely within their minds. The sharing aloud of poems and stories that suggest sounds is excellent. The teacher may create her own materials or use the abundance of such materials in literature. Either way, the most satisfying and exciting experiences happen when the "stage" is properly set.

The following is an example of a teacher-led activity with night sounds. The teacher may guide the children in establishing an appropriate mood and environment by softening the light in the room or suggesting that the children listen with closed eyes. A soft confidential tone of voice and the use of the first person also helps to create a feeling of a shared experience. The teacher may suggest that they are all lying in bed listening to the sounds around them—a common and familiar bedtime activity.

"Sometimes, just before I fall asleep, I like to lie very still and listen to the wee small sounds that are hidden by the big busy sounds of the daytime world. The night brings soft sounds, gentle sounds, tiny mysterious sounds I did not hear when the world was full of the important sounds of work and play. It is nice to snuggle down in my bed, and nestled in the velvety darkness, I can see with my ears and with my mind. I listen and wonder.

"Scratch, scratch, scratch. Is that the sound of the bare twigs of the maple tree tickling the side of the house? Or elves playing a game of hide and seek in the moonlight? Can you hear them? Listen. I can almost hear one whispering, 'Here I come, ready or not.' Or maybe it is a little spaceman in a silver suit skipping about on my window ledge, trying to peek in at me. I try to lie very still and quiet so that I do not frighten him away.

"I listen. There is a new sound. Do you hear it too? Now I remember —under the eaves a small, brown bird has built a nest of twigs and grasses. The little bird makes a very little sound. Sometimes people and puppies make funny sounds when they are dreaming. I wonder, do birds dream? If I were a little brown bird, I would dream of climbing high into the blue sky on a summer day and soar like an eagle above a golden cliff, catching the wind with my wings.

"The wind! I know it was blowing when I walked to school today, for it tossed my hair and crept inside my coat, but I didn't hear it above the traffic noise. There it is now, blowing down the rainspout and sending up a spooky tune like a pipe organ with only two notes. Or maybe it's a giant blowing in a huge empty pop bottle.

With descriptive language, suggestions, and questions, the teacher guides the children in creating sounds entirely within their minds.

"Swish, swish, swish. It feels so nice to stretch my arms and legs between the smooth sheets. Like walking through a field of tall ripe grass. Someone else is moving through my meadow. I can hear him breathing—such low quiet breathing. I wonder who it can be. Listen, do you hear someone nearby? (Pause and allow children to listen to the silence.)

"My eyes are still asleep, but my ears know it is morning. I hear the little bird singing his wake-up song. The daytime world is stretching and yawning. The night sounds are quietly slipping away. I open my eyes for my ears hear the sounds of the new day. Do you hear them too?"

After this kind of imagined experience, there should be ample time for the sharing of ideas and feelings. The discussion should not be rushed; it is a vitally important part of the total creative process. Sensory experiences of this kind may conclude with the discussion or may lead into further dramatic activity. They may be used primarily to stimulate the imagination by concentrating on the creative use of one or more of the senses, or they may become motivational material that develops into one or more story ideas.

Stories and poems that suggest sounds to be imagined may also be used to encourage the children to make the sounds aloud. Younger children, especially, enjoy making sounds as a story is being told, and since each child makes each sound in his or her own way, everyone can be successful. The following themes are favorites for sound stories with elementary children: *Animals*—usual and unusual pets, farm animals, zoo and wild animals, fantasy creatures; *mechanical things*—household appliances, tools and equipment used on farms, tools and gadgets used in the yard or garage, construction equipment, machines used in business and industry to make things, laboratory equipment, fantastic machines that do fantastic things; *transportation*—cars, trucks, buses, motorcycles, boats, planes, space ships; *life in different cultures and environments*—city, country, seas and seaports, forests and jungles, other lands and peoples; *the elements*—storms, fire, floods; *special events*—fairs, circuses, sports and games, picnics and parties.

In all of the foregoing activities, children would be listening to sounds or to words that suggest sounds either to encourage careful accurate listening, to stimulate the imagination, or both. Especially with early elementary children, the use of sounds and simple words that suggest familiar sounds allows for a variety of listening experiences that do not require an advanced degree of language development. As children become more language oriented, the meanings and interpretations of words become more and more useful as stimuli to the imagination. As language develops and children come to have richer and more varied experiences with words, there is probably nothing that does more to trigger the imagination. The uniqueness of word meaning is apparent in both written and spoken communication. Though there is a certain validity to Gertrude Stein's "A rose is a rose, is a rose," for each of us it is our very own rose of that moment when we see or hear the word. The use of words as a sensory experience for stimulating the imagination can play an important role in the language arts program as children come to understand and identify with a word as well as to recognize it.

The very young child is fascinated by his own ability to repeat sounds and syllables. This repetition, or echolalia, may become a chant accompanied by various amounts of body movement. As the child immerses his whole self into his sound and movement activity, he makes it his own invention quite apart from any recognition of its imitative nature. Dr. Piaget and others have reported on this behavior in young children.[5] In his egocentric way the little child displays all the rights and privileges of ownership when dealing with language—he plays with it, has fun with it, experiments with it. Making discoveries about sounds, syllables, and words can continue to be exciting for children. Rhyming games require careful listening and allow children to experiment with language as they solve each specific rhyming problem. Such games may ask for all of the words that the children can list that rhyme with a given word. The list may include nonsense words for which children can invent their own meanings. They may be asked to find a specific word that not only rhymes with the given word but correctly answers a question. For example, supplying the last word of a couplet with a word that rhymes with the last word of the first phrase and also makes sense, such as:

> Our kitten with her coat like silk
> Enjoyed her lunch of fish and _____.

Rhyming riddles are also fun. The leader asks for a word that rhymes with a given word, plus a clue.

> "I know a word that rhymes with fleas;
> A mouse likes to eat it, the word is _____?"

In rhyming games the children must mentally play with the sounds of words as they create them in their minds. Words and simple phrases may also be used to stimulate the imagination by suggesting mental pictures as well. The following activity is designed to do just that. The teacher begins by saying a word or short phrase. Each child is asked to describe the mental image the word spontaneously produced. Their responses may be shared orally or jotted down. The way in which the words are said may be chosen to influence the kinds of responses given; voice pitch, rate, and volume may be varied for the same word on different occasions, and the different responses, if any, may be discussed. The idea is not for the listeners to give definitions for the words, but rather to let the words trigger mental images, other ideas, and feelings. Each child's responses will reflect his own orientation and experiences.

The elementary school child, like the preschooler, may enjoy immersing his whole self in his imaginative involvement with sounds, syllables, and words. Integrating creative movement and pantomime with oral response can reinforce the nonverbal as well as verbal aspects of speech. It can further illustrate the individuality of each child's imaginative response to aural stimulation. And of no lesser value to children, the physical activity may make a variety of language work continue to be exciting and fun.

Listening to Music

The distinction between listening to sounds and listening to music is made for the benefit of adults and not as clarification for children. To a little child, a dog barking is a noise, but the racket he himself makes by beating a cake tin with a wooden spoon is music (though to be truthful, the barking of the dog may be more melodious)! The distinction for the child seems to lie in the intent rather than with any technical or aesthetic criteria. It is interesting to observe how very early a child may become interested in and responsive to that which he defines as music. Eclectic in his tastes, his creativity may be stimulated by everything from the "song" of the electric mixer to the repetitious tune of a TV commercial to a Bach fugue. Music as stimuli may literally "wind him up" or "wind him down"—send him prancing and galloping as a wild mustang over the prairie or floating weightlessly above the earth without ever moving from his special listening spot. Of all of the possible means a teacher can use to stimulate a child's imagination to lead to dramatic expression, involvement with music seems universally reliable.

Music is so important to creative drama that it is difficult to imagine any serious involvement with its many aspects without some way to provide music, not only to accompany creative movement and pantomime, but also to tantalize the imagination and to create moods and stir emotions. The most advantageous kind of music for use in almost all creative drama activities is instrumental—live or recorded. All of the many rhythm instruments as well as string instruments such as guitar and banjo are useful. The piano is particularly useful because of its large range, harmonics, and so forth. Taped and recorded music of all kinds is generally available to classroom teachers from the school library or media center. When using taped or recorded music, the teacher will want to preview what is available. Recordings with words tend to limit the child's own imaginative response to the music. This may be evident when children are listening to a selection done only instrumentally but where many know words to that music. For example, children who recognize "Up, Up and Away" will often visualize a balloon ride though there is nothing inherent in the melody or tempo that suggests only this one response. This is not to imply that such music should not be used, but it does illustrate how easily a truly free use of the imagination can be stifled.

The teacher may sometimes wish to direct the imagination toward some special purpose. For example, she may select pieces of music that are representative of a particular culture. The children may listen to become acquainted with this special music and also to help them to visualize a particular environment, peoples, historical period, or lifestyle. They may be asked to imagine themselves in that environment or to think and feel as a member of that culture. And though the range of creative exploration is more narrowly defined, the experience for each child remains subjective and unique.

Generally when music is being used as a sensory stimulus to the imagination, short passages are more satisfactory than entire pieces or multiple movements. Children do not respond to music (sound) intellectually but with their emotions. They seldom have the training or skill to evaluate the worth of a composition or the degree of artistry with which it is being performed. Listening to music is a sensory experience which makes the child feel a certain way, thereby creating certain images in his mind. The music makes him feel happy, sad, lonely, frightened, and so forth. Based on his own feelings, he may assume that the music is "telling" about something cheerful, mysterious, funny, or scary. The teacher may encourage each child to think about how the music makes him feel and what it might be about. When he does this he begins to relate some of his own experiences to what he is hearing, and his emotional involvement and intellectual curiosity work together to stimulate imagination. To handle this kind of involvement requires concentration, the synthesizing of ideas, and the finding of the necessary language to articulate his response. Particularly for the young child, this is a big order and makes the use of brief passages of music highly preferable to entire pieces or longer passages.

Many of the prior sound activities discussed may be done with music, with particular emphasis on the child's own personal feelings.

Music, unlike the dripping faucet or creaking door, is inherently concerned with emotional expression. Listening to music, even when the focus is on aural awareness and sensitivity, tends to create a mood and stir the emotions. Movement is a response to rhythm and tempo as well as a manifestation of the listener's emotional involvement to the total experience—rhythm, tempo, harmonics, melody, dynamics. Music for movement or dance generally requires an obvious rhythm; that used purely for sensory stimulation may include music that is not suitable for movement, but which strongly suggests moods, feelings, and ideas.

Your Turn

1. Monitor your own listening habits for a week. Keep your observations in a journal to be shared in class.
2. Recall a sound (other than words) that has been significant in your life. See how many things the recollection of that sound can stimulate in your imagination. Choose one idea and develop a story idea from it.
3. Create an original listening game to use with children to stimulate imaginative listening. You may need to collect or develop some materials for use with your game.
4. Listen to a piece of instrumental music. As soon as the music ends, jot down all of the images, thoughts, and feelings it stimulated in you.
5. Make a tape of sounds to use with children. Decide how you would use your tape to stimulate aural awareness or creative listening.
6. Develop a list of poems and stories that can give children sensory experiences with listening.
7. Write a "sound poem"—no words, only letters in combination that can be sounded out orally. Share your poems aloud in class. Share your interpretations based only on the aural experiences.

WHAT DO YOU SEE, DEAR TEACHER?

What do you see, dear teacher, when you see a
   child?

The matador
Swaggering so brashly
Flourishing the illusory cape of courage
To detract the funnel-eyed and shallow-sighted?

A Darwin
Behind the dreamer's eyes
Secretly plotting a course
For some high adventure to places
As yet unchartered by the curriculum guide?

An embryonic Churchill
Exhorting his comrades
To gallant victory against unrelenting foes
Learning how it is to win and lose?

A Pavlova
In muddy sox
Pirouetting through todays, looking for tomorrows
When even the most secret wishes become reality?

Look again, dear teacher, and help them to truly
    see.

Looking Games and Other "Insighting" Ideas

"I see my father. . . . In my mind's eye," said Hamlet, and the reader
knows at once that the Prince of Denmark is speaking of his ability to
create in his mind an image of his father. Hamlet's "eye" is, of course,
not a sensory organ, but rather his imagination. However, the poetic
expression is particularly significant when we realize how richly the eye
can supply the mind with endless nourishment with which to feed the
imagination. We are limited only by preoccupation and insensitivity to
the world around us.

This is generally not true for the young child. Little boys and girls
rely heavily upon what they see to furnish them with much needed
information. They also take an aesthetic delight in what they see. The
infant watches with fascination the gay mobile above the crib; the
toddler visually devours the colorful picture book. The young child
takes in everything from the jet silhouetted against the sky to the
intricacies of a ladybug. Even the everyday and mundane sights around
him can be sources of joyous discovery.

Adults who have been privileged to share in moments of spontaneous discovery with a child know the almost spiritual quality of such occasions—a kind of melding of self with his environment which produces an almost inexplicable joy! Fortunate are those adults who can vividly recall those occasions from their own childhoods. Such pristine moments are possible because of what Rachael Carson referred to as the child's inborn "sense of wonder." In the beautiful pictorial book published after her death, *The Sense of Wonder,* Miss Carson states, "If a child is to keep alive his inborn sense of wonder without any such gift from the fairies, he needs the companionship of at least one adult who can share it, rediscovering with him the joy, excitement and mystery of the world we live in."[6] Beautiful moments of shared discovery ought to happen within every adult-child relationship—for the growth of the child and the nourishment of the adult as well. Frank Barron, who has done years of research in the area of creativity and the creative individual, reports, "Creative individuals retain qualities of freshness, spontaneity and joy, as well as a certain lack of cautious reality-testing —openness to the nonrational, if you will. They are in that sense childlike.... They bring their childhood along instead of leaving it behind."[7] Adults may need those shared moments of discovery with children just as much as children need adult companionship. The world needs people of vision (pun intended) of all ages.

In the English language the phrase "I see" may, more often than not, mean "I understand." In this sense we think of schools as places where children are helped to "see better." But understanding can only follow awareness, and in this sense also schools need to help boys and girls "see better." Children, like adults, may "have eyes and see not" even by the time they enter school. In fact, in some informal experiments with five and six year olds, we have discovered that many kindergartners are not so visually observant of the world around them as we had assumed. We may suppose that several children have not had in their preschool years an adult companion who assisted the child in keeping his inborn sense of wonder alive. For those children and all others, the teacher may become that privileged partner in exploring and discovering the world.

For a variety of reasons the teacher may wish to discover several things about the visual awareness of a child or of a group of children. For example, accurate and imaginative observation is critical to all areas of scientific inquiry, and the teacher may need to know just how aware the children are of what there is to see in a specific environment or situation. What things do they tend to notice most—how accurately and in what detail? Does the visual stimulus and observation elicit critical inquiry and divergent thinking? Do the children (or some children) tend to notice some things most and ignore other things of significance? If so, why? (Some boys and girls may be purposely shutting out certain sights which they view as threatening or ugly.) These kinds of questions and others, may be answered with the playing of some simple games and activities.

There are many old favorites children enjoy that involve visual concentration such as "I Spy," "Concentration," and one that appeals to a wide range of ages—"Black Magic." The latter is especially fun since it includes an element of "magic." Directions for playing this game, and some other looking games are included here. As in the preceding section on listening, looking activities follow the same format beginning with real and personal experiences designed to increase awareness and concentration, then experiences that are intended primarily to stimulate imaginative thinking and response, and finally looking activities done solely with the "mind's eye."

Looking Games

BLACK MAGIC

This game may be played by first or second graders and up. It is a variation on "I Spy," with a pinch of magic thrown in.

Directions: One child is chosen by the teacher to be "it." The child who is "it" and the teacher step out of the room while the teacher shares the magic secret with him. He remains out of the room while the rest of the class decides on something he must guess on his return. The magic clue given by the teacher is that, just before the object chosen by the class is asked, the teacher will ask about something that is black. Therefore, the teacher must always be the one to ask him to name the object chosen by the class. Of course, once all of the children know the magic secret, the game is no longer "magic." The fun is not only in trying to discover how the magic works, but in discovering things in the room that few have noticed before so as to properly challenge "it."

Example: "It" is chosen and steps out of the room while the teacher briefly shares the "magic" clue. The teacher returns to the room while the children decide on the secret object he must guess. The teacher notices that Bobby is wearing black shoes so that she can use those as her clue to "it." The children decide on the pencil sharpener as the secret object. When "it" returns to the room, the teacher asks, "Is it the waste basket?" or "Is it the hamster cage?" Just before she names the pencil sharpener, she asks, "Is it Bobby's shoes?" "It" will know that the chosen object will be the item just after Bobby's shoes because they are black.

Another time the game is played, the teacher may select another color. A fun variation just before St. Patrick's Day is "Green Magic," or "Red Magic" on Valentine's Day. The teacher must be careful to name only one object of the magic color, and that just before she asks about the secret object chosen by the class. Otherwise she gives a false clue and destroys the "magic."

Second Look

This is a game enjoyed by early elementary boys and girls. It involves them in visual concentration and is especially useful early in the school year when young children are getting acquainted (or reacquainted) with one another.

Directions: Depending upon the size of the group, three or four children are chosen to start the game by standing for a few moments in front of the rest of the group. Those observing are told to look very carefully at each of those in front. The teacher then takes those children apart from the group and very quickly changes one thing on each child. (Older boys and girls may quickly change one thing on themselves or each other without the teacher's help.) When the chosen children return, the rest of the group tries to discover each of the changes. Each child from the first group chooses another person to take his place, selecting from among those who have not yet had a turn. Play continues until everyone has had a time being in front. If the group is getting acquainted for the first time, be sure every child is identified by name to the class. This game is a variation of several familiar looking games but has the plus of involving boys and girls in looking at one another rather than at things.

Detective

Enjoyed by first graders and up, this game is sometimes called Indian Chief or Indian Scout.

Directions: The children all stand or sit in a circle. (Standing allows for more body movement.) The entire class can play at one time. One person is chosen by the teacher to leave the group. Another child, who remains in the circle, is asked to be the leader. Staying in place, the leader initiates a movement. Everyone tries to follow the leader's movement without giving away who the leader is. The "detective" returns and stands in the center of the circle. The leader changes motions as slyly as possible while the detective has three guesses to name the leader. If the detective successfully names the leader, he may select the next detective; otherwise the teacher names a new detective.

This game makes a good "warm-up" activity which may lead into improvisation because it engages children in observation, concentration, and creative movement as part of a problem solving experience.

Looking to develop awareness

We need not limit looking activities to games with "rules" to lead children through interesting and valuable experiences in careful, accurate, or creative observation. The teacher may ask each child to try to recall as accurately as possible something the whole class has seen. Each child may compile his own list, or the group may collectively reconstruct orally the details of something shared by the group. This is an especially worthwhile activity to do before and after a field trip. Careful observation before the trip may be practiced by using a common area in or near the school—the media center, nurse's station, or the playground. Encourage the children to try for accuracy and details—the little things that make a place unique. Describing their own classroom while out-of-doors on the playground may be fun for younger boys and girls. The teacher may serve as recorder so that the children may check the accuracy of their own recollections when they are back in the room. After a field trip, again either individually or as a group, the children are encouraged to reconstruct as much of the trip as they can. Of course they should be reminded beforehand that there will be a sharing of what was seen after they return to school.

Another observation activity is one that is fun to do in pairs. Each child is given a picture and a specified amount of time to look carefully at it. Then, by turns, each one shares his recollections with his partner. As with many looking activities, other skills besides visual concentration are required, particularly the development of verbalization and the use of descriptive language.

Obvious benefits can be derived from developing such skills in observation, certainly in academic areas such as spelling, laboratory work in the various branches of science, and the important communication skills of reading and writing. In addition, helping children to understand the significance of the nonverbal acts in oral communication can be tremendously important in the development of their total communication skills. Indeed, ways of communication other than through socialized speech are primary communication tools of the infant. Through creative dramatics we can continue to develop the nonverbal aspects of the oral communication process. As we get more involved in pantomime and character development, we stress the sending of nonverbal messages through facial expression, posture, and body movement.

Children seem to be helped to be better senders of messages through pantomime and creative movement if we spend some time first exploring, analyzing, and evaluating nonverbal messages received; for communication is a process involving both the sending and receiving of messages, both verbally and nonverbally. The infant's lack of socialized speech influences the means through which he receives messages, forcing him to rely upon such things as rate and pitch of voice and his visual observations. The infant smiles in response to a smile, is warned by a cross look, and soon becomes sensitive to a whole range of nonverbal messages sent by others. He, in turn, imitates the nonverbal until he develops a "vocabulary" of expressions and gestures through which he participates in common communication with others. (Waving bye-bye, playing peek-a-boo and pat-a-cake are familiar examples.) Even the older child may trust more in the nonverbal message than in the spoken word because of his early reliance on his observations of the nonverbal. He may also have discovered that the nonverbal message is often more accurate. "She didn't really like my picture," says the child, "I could tell by her looks." However, some important concepts to be understood are that communication generally involves both verbal and nonverbal components that are interwoven in the communication act, that neither aspect should contradict the other, and that the whole is a dynamic process in which the participants are simultaneously sending and receiving messages. Unfortunately in much classroom work in the language arts, the development of skill as receivers of the nonverbal aspect of oral communication is often overlooked. The following are some simple, yet effective, ways for challenging children as receivers and perceivers of nonverbal communication.

SLIDES, FILMSTRIPS, MOVIES

Because most of our children are very media oriented, the use of slides, filmstrips, and movies can provide a familiar base for the observation of nonverbal messages. Slides and filmstrips are naturals, for they do not usually have built-in audio portions, though the teacher may have to manipulate the projector to cover written captions until after the children have had an opportunity to discuss what a frame is "telling." This is a good time to tell children about the reporter's five "W's"—who, what, where, when, and why. Answering these important questions will improve their interpretations. As children gain experience in informal drama, they may enjoy creating tableaus of selected frames from a filmstrip. A series of significant scenes may come to life with each picture group playing out their scene in sequential order. To keep the emphasis on the nonverbal, pantomime works well.

A similar use may be made of silent movies. For older boys and girls, track down one or more of the classics of silent film days. Charlie Chaplin or Harold Lloyd films are excellent. The movie may be stopped at any point while the children decide what is happening, what is being said, what the relationships are among the characters as told through the nonverbal communication. A sound film with the audio turned off has the advantage that after seeing and discussing the film without sound, the audio may be added and the film viewed again. During the silent showing emphasize that we are not trying to read the lips of the characters but rather are attempting to discover what is happening from all of the nonverbal cues. When the film is then repeated with the sound track, the viewers can compare their interpretations based solely on the nonverbal with their perceptions with the audio.

Games

Children whose reading level is sufficiently developed to play sequential games may also enjoy looking games similar to the listening game previously described. The format is the same and requires that the teacher prepare separate cards, at least one for each child, that correspond to her master list. A sample sequential looking game follows.

This game was designed for fourth and fifth graders. It does not require special skill in pantomime; the movements have been kept simple so that the activity can be used early in the school year as part of the class observance of Columbus Day. The directions are purposely quite explicit, though they do allow for individual interpretation to show feelings and actions. The children's cards are not numbered, so they are challenged to pick up their cues only from observation. This particular set of cards was designed for a maximum class size of 30, though fewer may play by giving those children who so desire a second card. When this is done, the teacher must be careful to give those with additional cards a second card that is not the same as the first nor one that requires interaction with the first card. Several of the activities are designed for small groups of children; the number in italic is a suggested number who may take part.

Columbus Discovers a New World

1—*3*:   You begin. You are a sailor on the Santa Maria. You are scrubbing the deck with a big mop. The sea is very rough, and it is hard to do your job. Empty your mop pail over the side of the rolling ship. Return to your seat.

2—1:   After you see sailors mopping the deck of the ship, you are the cook. You are stirring a big pot of fish soup. Wait for others to join you, then give each of them a bowl of the soup. Return to your seat.

3—3:   You are a sailor. When you see the cook stirring a big pot of fish soup, join the cook. He will give you a bowl of soup. It is not very good. Show that you do not like it very much. Return to your seat.

4—1:   You are Christopher Columbus. When you see sailors eating their fish soup, go to the deck and look for land through your spy glass. Show that you do not see land and walk slowly back to your seat.

5—1:   After you see Columbus look for land through his spy glass and return to his seat, you are a sailor looking over the side of the ship. You see something in the water. You are very excited. Motion to others to come to see what you have found. Wait for others to join you and show them what you have found. Go back to your seat with them.

6—5:   When you see someone looking over the side of the ship and motioning to other sailors to come and see, be a sailor and go and see what was found. Crowd around the sailor who found something. Show how happy and excited you feel. Go back to your seat with the others.

7—5:   After several sailors have looked at something over the side of the ship, run out on deck and begin working the lines on the sails. Others will help you. Pull hard on the ropes. Go back to your seat with the others.

8—1:   You are a sailor. After you have seen other sailors pulling hard on the ropes that work the sails, go on deck and look through your spy glass. You see land. Show the others what you have discovered. Wait for others to join you. When they have, show them the land, then go back to your seat with them.

9—4:   You are a sailor. When you see someone point to land, run on deck. Show how excited and happy you are. Look toward the land and show others where it is. Return to your seat.

10—1:   After the sailors who were looking and pointing toward land have returned to their seats, be Christopher Columbus. Step out of your landing boat. Kneel down on the shore. Stay until you are joined by your sailors. After someone shows a sign to the class, go back to your seat.

11—4:   You are a sailor. When you see Columbus step out of a landing boat and kneel down on the shore, join him and kneel down also. Stay until someone shows a sign to the class. Then go back to your seat.

12—1:   When you see Columbus and the sailors kneel down on the shore; while they are still kneeling, show the entire class your sign. Then return to your seat. Sign says:

October 12, 1492
Columbus Reaches the New World
and
You Were There!

PICTURES

Teachers who plan to incorporate creative dramatics into the classroom program will want to compile a good collection of well-mounted pictures. Newspapers and magazines are often good sources of provocative pictures. They can be used for encouraging children to be careful and accurate observers; pictures of people and animals have another excellent use as a resource for studying nonverbal messages. Close-up pictures of faces and candid shots of people and animals caught in the midst of an event can be looked at and discussed in terms of each viewer's individual perceptions. This can lead to useful discussions of how each of us, out of our own past experiences and personalities, gives our own unique meaning to what we see.

Any serious discussion of nonverbal messages must deal with feelings and emotions. (Please pardon the redundancy, but children sometimes separate feelings and emotions in a perfectly legitimate way—for example; "My teacher feels tired [a feeling], and when she is tired she is very crabby [an intense feeling, an emotion.]") For this reason, close-ups of faces are particularly advantageous because the children must go beyond a simple conjecture about what the person (or animal) in the picture is doing. That is often impossible to tell when only the upper part of the body is visible and little or no background is showing. Of course we cannot be certain the observer "accurately" reads the real feelings behind the face in a picture—that is not important. What is important is that children develop an awareness of how feelings are communicated through all of the nonverbal cues, particularly facial expression and "body language" and that they continue to develop their ability to identify the feelings correctly that certain cues represent. Activities that involve them in developing such awareness and skill can also lead, quite naturally and sensitively, into discussions about feelings, especially their own. When this happens, the teacher can again best serve as a gentle facilitator and an accepting listener. The following actual classroom experience illustrates how one teacher uses pictures to help children identify feelings based on their sensitive observations. The discussion that developed is representative of the kind of response the activity may elicit from a very normal group of upper elementary children.

During a demonstration workshop in creative dramatics with a group of fourth graders, the children were looking at close-up pictures of faces. The teacher was using a series of teaching pictures that showed children expressing a wide range of feelings. They were asked to study each picture carefully and to decide individually what feelings were being shown on the faces. No attempt was made to arrive at a group consensus, and for some a number of related but different views were expressed. The teacher was quietly accepting of all responses, but regularly encouraged the children to explain, if they could, why they had decided on their answers. For some of the pictures, several of the children either could not decide or they were not firm in their decisions. They had looked at and discussed several when they were shown a boy about their own age. A little girl opened the discussion by saying that she thought that the boy in the picture looked mad. Immediately one of the boys announced, with great conviction, that the boy in the photograph was afraid. Most of the children, especially the boys, nodded their heads in agreement. Even before another child could respond, the child repeated his comment with even more feeling and added, "That boy is afraid because he has to go to the dentist." Soon there was a lively but thoughtful discussion about being afraid, initially dominated by the boys. Independent of any special urging from the teacher (though she continued to be accepting of the children's ideas and became a part of the group by describing a fear of her own), the children

Looking activities lead naturally into creative thinking and excursions into the realm of the young imagination; even the floor can become a stage.

became deeply involved in a sharing of their own fears and even began to catagorize some as "silly" and some as "real" fears. Several of them showed a depth of understanding and concern for others that they had not revealed before. An unusually large number of the children spontaneously participated in the discussion. Some told of specific situations in which they had felt very much afraid, including instances when they had felt ashamed about their feelings. They were supportive of one another in ways that showed a maturity not generally expected from nine and ten year olds.

Several days later, when this same class began doing group pantomimes, they showed an especially high degree of involvement and sincerity in their work. Much of the self-consciousness that is often evident among children of this age, who have had little or no prior work in drama, was lacking. Apparently the sharing of their personal fears had made them less fearful of one another. They seemed to have established, as a group, an acceptance of all kinds of feelings and that it was "okay" to show them to others without feeling guilty or silly. In addition, they seemed particularly capable of expressing their imagined feelings nonverbally.

Another good activity for upper-elementary children is to study a scene in a picture, assume the roles of "witnesses" and compare their individual perceptions. As each witness has a chance to tell what he saw, the children can experience what can happen at the scene of an accident or in a courtroom as several observers testify. This activity encourages awareness, careful observation, creative thinking, and self-expression. Obviously there need not be only one set of right or wrong answers.

Looking to stimulate the imagination

Classroom experiences in looking may be provided primarily for the purpose of stimulating the imagination rather than to challenge the beholder's awareness and acuity of observation. Looking activities lead naturally into creative thinking and excursions into the realm of the imagination. When we speak of looking accurately or critically or imaginatively, we are making some arbitrary and artificial delineations that really don't seem to mean too much except to help us establish goals in response to purpose. What we see is motivated, to a large extent, by what we are looking for and why. For example, we grow roses in our garden, and generally roses are grown to be enjoyed because they are so lovely to look at. However, we may look at a rose in different ways for different reasons. We may look to see if a new variety of rose is growing and producing the kinds of blossoms described by the nursery or so that it may be accurately described to a fellow rose tender. We may examine it critically for signs of distress or disease. A particular blossom may be looked at in terms of how it will look as part of a floral arrangement in a specific setting. We may even look at the dormant plant early in the year and imagine it leafed and blooming, beaded with morning dew, with a velvety bumble bee in the depths of a blossom. Most often we look at a rose only to appreciate its beauty as it fulfills its own purpose. Of no less value, we may look at a rose because it stimulates in us thoughts and feelings. The immediate pleasure in the rose may be secondary to other ideas and feelings apart from the flower itself which it stimulates within us. Like all sensory experiences, our involvement with the rose may nurture our own unique creativity. Anything that can be explored visually can often stimulate an abundance of creative ideas. Paintings and poems, stories and symphonies— all kinds of art have been brought into being because the creator was responding to some visual stimulation. In addition to the sure knowledge that the use of visual stimuli is so effective in producing imaginative responses from children, the compilation of a box of materials to look at and speculate about can be a great deal of fun. Some of the most effective and creative teachers we know are selective "pack rats" who are constantly on the prowl for bits and pieces of this and that to be used in creative work of one kind or another. A special box of items for use in creative dramatics can be almost, but not quite, as much pleasure to collect as to use. The materials may serve in two very useful ways: to stimulate the imagination and, sometimes but not always, to be incorporated into a scene or story as it is dramatized.

For those who are just beginning to organize materials for use in creative dramatics the following list of suggestions may be helpful, but every community will have unique and easily available things that may be exciting and special to use. Things that are indigenous to the locale (natural materials such as pine cones, sea shells, mosses, and driftwood), scraps from local industry, and attic "treasures" of the area's past can provide special materials that are often free for the carting. Only space and the teacher's ingenuity need limit the collections. Many of the materials in the following list may be available in and around the classroom.

Visual Media to Stimulate Imaginative Thinking

Pictures. The best pictures encourage a variety of interpretations and challenge the viewer to speculate further about what he is seeing.

Picture blocks. These can be made by covering all sides of a cube with a variety of pictures, perhaps faces only of people of several ages. The children are urged to use their imaginations to relate two or more pictures in a story idea.

Children's drawings. Developing a story idea from one or more children's pictures gives young artists additional pride in what they have created. Pictures are easier to handle and have a longer life expectancy if they are mounted and laminated. Clear plastic, the kind with an adhesive back from which the protective backing is peeled, can be used as a simple substitute for laminating.

Films, slides, and filmstrips. Additional scenes and further adventures can be created from materials created by others.

OTHER MATERIALS AND OBJECTS
TO STIMULATE IMAGINATIVE IDEAS

Jewelry. Flamboyant or outlandish pieces—the kind left over from rummage and garage sales—are often just right.

Fabric. Look for unusual patterns, color combinations, and textures. Laces, velvets, and tapestries that appear old, elegant, and suggest an interesting past are particularly useful. A few special pieces are better than lots of "run of the mill" remnants.

Unusual boxes, vases, and other containers. Rummage and garage sales are a dependable source for these items.

Parts and pieces of equipment. In their fragmented condition, these things have become unrelated to the original item.

Natural materials that are abstract in design—driftwood, dried weeds and grasses, rocks, shells, seed pods.

Articles from other times, places, and cultures. Household and farm equipment from earlier times are often totally outside of the experience of contemporary children.

Unusual buttons, old or foreign coins, and other small memorabilia that can be passed among the children, looked at up close, handled and about which the group can wonder.

Collection of hats. Even if your school does not allow children to dress-up in hats for sanitary reasons, unusual hats and those which suggest interesting or unusual occupations and other cultures can be looked at and talked about. Hats are especially useful for helping children to develop characters, and, if allowed, may be worn by the characters as children create the roles.

Toys and stuffed animals. Children often bring favorite toys and other "treasures" to share with the group. They are delighted to have their special possessions used to motivate a story idea. Items brought for Show and Tell can take on a special significance for the entire class when they can lead into a drama activity.

Colors as Visual Stimuli for Imaginative Ideas

Music has a very special place in aural experiences; color plays a comparable role in visual experiences. It adds the "melody" to what we see, creating moods and eliciting emotions. Our response to color is usually individual and often capricious—seldom do we arrive at our preferences through any kind of logic. Among grown-ups color preferences are often related to some past or present associations. We become psychologically involved with colors. Certain ones make us feel certain ways but in highly individualized and personal ways, depending upon our experiences with those colors.

Since young boys and girls do not have such a wealth of associations, they can respond more freely to a color in and of itself. They are also not burdened by what adults call "good taste" or by convention. Why not a girl with green hair who always wins at hide and seek by just crouching quietly in the tall grass! In their art work children often use colors in different and daring ways, and art activities have traditionally provided them with opportunities to experiment with self-expression through color. Creative drama can also bring children and colors together in stimulating ways.

Drama activities with colors take some special equipment and planning, but the results can be tremendously exciting. The choice of lighting is an important part of the dramatic illusion in children's theatre because the audience responds to the moods created by the play of light, shadow, and color upon the scene. If there is access to an area in the building with even simple stage lighting, it is great fun to let the children explore an environment bathed in different colors. Personally experiencing such an environment can transport them beyond the ordinary and into new dimensions of consciousness. An excellent example of the use of such lighting to create a special environment for drama is shown in a film produced at Northwestern University entitled, *Creative Drama: The First Steps,* narrated by Rita Crist. In one activity the children move through a purple world, and the intensity of involvement is beautiful to see.

When suitable equipment is not already available in the building, the teacher may enjoy using her own innovativeness to create special lighting effects. Deeply tinted colored gelatins, the kind used on theatre lights, can be used to cover the light on such readily available equipment as filmstrip and slide projectors producing beams of colored light through which the children may move. A couple of small spotlights with colored gels may be available through the media center or from a secondary drama department. The small revolving spots that are used to illuminate artificial Christmas trees work well. To turn a classroom from its everyday look into a place of mystery and enchantment with the use of colored lighting is well worth the time and effort involved in obtaining the necessary equipment.

In the beginning the teacher may want to use the colored environment only as a means for providing a unique visual experience. The children may simply move around the room observing how everything and everybody looks flooded with the colored light, later discussing how they felt in and about their special world. Combined with appropriate music to reinforce a mood, this can lead into individual and group pantomimes or dance drama. For the teacher who wishes to further integrate the art forms, the experience may also be used to motivate creative writing. The use of poetry with drama provides a natural alliance because both drama and poetry involve moods and feelings. Delightful five-line poems (cinquain) have been written by elementary children following a movement or pantomime activity in a colored setting. The cinquain format is especially fun with colors because it allows for a personification of the color, thus giving a concreteness to something abstract. It also includes a line of action words. The formula for five-line poetry is:

Line 1: one word title (noun)
Line 2: two words describing title (adjectives)
Line 3: three words expressing an action
Line 4: four words expressing feelings
Line 5: one word synonym for title

The following are samples of cinquain poetry written by three fourth graders after exploring a green world.

Green
Lively, vibrant
Striving and growing
Always gay as springtime
Fresh

Green
Cool, soft
Calming and soothing
Makes me feel sleepy
Shade

Green
Mysterious, dense
Closing around me
Makes my heart pound
Jungle

Each child had experienced green in a quite different way, and in the movement activity had moved according to his own sensory impressions. Later each child became a character other than himself and moved through the green environment as that character. Most of the children became insects or animals, moving through grass or forests. Some of the children imagined that their green environment was the result of some mad scientist's fiendish experiments. Several made up brief stories of some adventure involving their character which might have become the basis for a longer piece of dramatization or creative writing.

We have often begun with a green environment because many children can relate to several natural green environments—gardens, parks, woods, jungles, meadows, or even the grass under a shady tree. But other colors may stimulate even greater creativity because their associations with environments are not so apparent. Blue often produces a variety of undersea or space adventures; red is often conducive to ideas about flames, fires, and mighty conflicts.

A converse approach using colored environments involves the entire group in a specific agreed-upon locale. For example, if the class were studying the nomadic peoples of the desert and wished to experience a world of dazzling brightness and golden sands, the area for playing would be bathed in amber light. Music of the near east would also enhance the sensory impact.

In the preceding activities, the emphasis would be on responses to questions such as: When you were exploring the (name color) world, where were you? What was it like there? What would you do there? Whom or what might you be there? The teacher may wish to stress the emotional response to the environment with questions like: Did you enjoy that place? How did you feel there? Why do you think you felt as you did about it? Have you ever been in a real place that made you feel very much the same way? If you explored this special environment again, what would you do the next time? Do you think you would feel the same way again? If the children have explored several colored environments, they may also make comparisons about their own feelings in each. Teachers and children will undoubtedly find additional ways to use these special experiences, particularly when individual discovery is encouraged.

Little boys and girls enjoy working with colored scarves. (If enough scarves are not available, crepe paper streamers may be used equally well.) The best scarves are the inexpensive, plain sheer ones in bright and pastel colors. They are made of a variety of synthetic fabrics, and the ones with a fair amount of crispness are the most fun since they float and flutter easily during movement activities. Generally scarves are used to help stimulate creative movement, but the colors of the scarves may also be the basis for an activity. The color of each scarf may suggest specific kinds of movement—for example, green trees swaying and tossing in the wind, yellow butterflies darting and hovering in the sunshine, blue waves or rainshowers. The color may also suggest certain kinds of movement response related to how the color makes the child feel.

A variety of approaches are valuable for young children who are learning color concepts. Color activities can be especially intriguing since a child must come to know and understand the concept of each color totally through the sense of sight. Color cannot be touched, tasted, smelled, or heard. It is generally a property of an object that possesses other properties as well. An apple and red are not the same thing, although they appear so to the child until he comes to understand the concept of "redness." The more ways children can experience colors, the more reinforcements they have to understand color concepts. Nursery children, kindergartners, and first graders who are still developing an understanding of color concepts have great fun spending a day or more to "celebrate" each color. As a part of the celebration, each child is given a scarf or paper streamer of the special color of the day for creating his own interpretative movement in response to the color. If these activities are to be the most creative, the teacher must be very careful not to impose her own interpretations upon the children in any way. A child moving dreamily with a red streamer may be unconsciously recalling the red glow of his bedroom night light, while all about him his classmates gleefully twirl and leap about as bonfires or fire engines.

Given a variety of experiences with colors, each child builds his own associations; and he learns more about himself and his world as he builds them. A charming incident with colored scarves illustrates one five-year-old boy's individual response to colors. The teacher passed out a variety of scarves to the children. Each child had a moment to investigate each scarf; then they all moved about the room using their scarves in their own ways. Periodically the teacher stopped the music and the children exchanged colors until they had all worked with several colors. This little fellow, like the others, moved about in a variety of ways with the different colors until he was given a scarf of a soft brown color. While the others began to move with their scarves, he knelt down and carefully folded the brown scarf neatly into a square, then holding it close to himself, he walked slowly and quietly around the room among the dancing and skipping children. For whatever reason, the brown scarf was special and different to him. On the next exchange, he took his new color and once again held it high above his head and joined the others in active movement.

Looking with the Mind's Eye

Imaginative thinking stimulated by what is seen is not useful only to the writer, the painter, and others in the arts; it is of equal value to the scientists, engineers, builders, inventors, and indeed to anyone who has a need to picture mentally not only what has been seen before but what *might* be seen. The ability to invent and create "in the mind's eye" is essential to human progress.

Generous opportunities to exercise such mental picturing ought to be part of classroom learning. Disciplined daydreaming is fundamental to most creative productivity. The young child begins to do this in his dramatic play as he moves beyond the need for materials to create characters and make-believe situations. Creative dramatics for older boys and girls can continue to develop this kind of imaginative thinking and help children to channel it toward meaningful ends. Using pictures, props, and other materials to stimulate imaginative thinking lays a foundation for imaginative thinking without the need for such materials. Creative drama, with its emphasis on the use of the imagination for developing roles and ideas for improvisations and its lack of emphasis on the technical aspects of formal theatre, requires copious amounts of mental visualizing. Without props, make-up, costumes, sets, and lighting, the players must create these appurtenances in their minds. Lots of actual (real and personal) visual experiences provide children with a wealth of ideas and stimulation when they have a need to see something only with the imagination. Beyond their very significant value as motivators, real materials may begin to encroach upon the child's use of imagination. The following classroom experience illustrates the point.

Some upper-elementary children were working in pairs in which one of each team was to be a shoe salesperson and the other the customer. Because the children had been involved in some movement activities earlier, they had removed their shoes and placed them in a corner of the room. One eager salesman decided to take advantage of such a magnificent supply of props and immediately ran and brought back to his partner as many shoes as he could carry. All of the other children continued working totally with imaginary shoes and were having a grand time. The pair working with the real props soon decided that the

"Winifred the Wonderful Genie looked at the staircase with wonder. It went up and up, higher and higher, into the sky above her castle."

activity was not much fun after all. The salesman had a hard time describing his shoes other than as they actually looked, or if he embellished them with superior qualities, the astute customer was quick to call him to task for misrepresentation. He could not interest his fastidious customer in assorted well-worn and ill-fitting sneakers, loafers, and school shoes. When the suggestion was made that the real shoes be returned to their corner and the salesman create his own line of goods, the buyer soon had a fantastic variety of footwear from which to choose. The children imagined shoes, slippers, and boots from around the world and an impressive number of very original creations as well.

Imagination and mental health

To "see with the mind" can be important to our good mental health. Anticipation of good things in life, progress and change for the betterment of the individual and society are all tied to this ability to picture an ideal, a goal, or a fond memory in the mind. Prisoners of war have kept alive their hopes and their sanity by mentally visualizing their homes and families. The old and infirm who have the capacity to picture happy times in the past can relive those "good old days" over and over again. For little boys and girls, the anticipation of a birthday or special treat based on their recollections of a previous experience may be more enjoyable than the event itself. Of special importance to older children and young people can be the ability to see themselves sometime in the future as successful men and women. If for these reasons only, regular opportunities for stimulating awareness with looking activities and many many experiences with building mental pictures through the imagination should be included in all learning programs. Daydreaming and fantasizing by children in the classroom should be more than just tolerated; it should be encouraged and generously integrated into curriculum.

Your Turn

1. Read Rachael Carson's book, *The Sense of Wonder*. When you have finished, take a "sense of wonder" walk with another person, preferably a child. If the walk is over a familiar route, see if you can discover something you have not noticed before. Find a "treasure" and take it home with you—but only in your mind.
2. For a week, keep a journal about your visual discoveries. See if you can preserve them through the use of descriptive language.
3. Make up a story, write a poem, or create a song or dance about something you wrote about in your journal.

4. Watch a segment of a television program (drama, news report, sport event, wild life, or travel shows) with the audio turned off. See if you can describe what is happening and supply the dialogue. (Don't try to read lips; that's cheating!)

5. In class, work in two groups—movers and watchers. The movers explore a designated part of the room using appropriate senses (for example, looking, listening, touching, smelling—whatever best allows for investigation of specific things in the environment). When the music stops, the movers "freeze." Each watcher surveys the statues as a group of characters in a tableau and gives a one-line title to the total scene. For example, movers frozen at different levels may suggest "Wildflowers, Ferns and Toadstools in the Spring Woods;" a closely bunched group of statues might suggest "Holiday Shoppers Boarding a Bus." Play several times, then reverse roles. Periodically take some time to share perceptions and ideas.

6. Close your eyes and take a fantasy journey to your ideal vacation spot. First create the scene in black and white—if you can—then as a color print. Now put yourself in the scene doing something you would like to do there. Add other characters if you like. Bring the scene to life, see yourself moving about in the scene. In pairs, describe your fantasy journey to your partner.

7. Read "A Tall Tale Told Under the Woofle Tree" in the appendix. Write a short story for children of the age level of your special interest. Let your imagination fly! Base the story on some different way of perceiving (topsy-turvy, backwards, inside-out, mirror images, shadows, little as big and big as little, atypical colorations).

8. Incorporate your story into a lesson plan for children of appropriate maturity. Include purpose(s) and objectives. Your lesson may deal with concepts such as perception, individuality, acceptance of others, and so forth. In the lesson, include a "doing" activity for children that involves them in some visual experience.

9. Create a sequential looking game for children. Relate it to some area of curriculum or some concept to be developed (for example, a visit to a pond in early spring as part of a unit on pond life or ecology).

10. Begin collecting a variety of small "props" to use with children for stimulating imaginations through visual exploration.

11. Compile a short annotated bibliography of poems and short stories that may be used to stimulate imaginations through real or imagined visual experiences. Include titles of suitable films and filmstrips in your list.

12. Collect and mount a starter set of pictures to be used for creative work with children.

Getting the Feel of Things

There are lots of things that I like to touch
And other things I don't like much—but I like
The smoothness of a wind-dried sheet
And dew-damp grass beneath my feet
The silky coats of pups and kittens
And the coziness of fur-lined mittens
The polished gold of mother's locket
A handful of shiny coins in my pocket
The mother-of-pearl inside a shell
A velvety rose that's nice to smell.
There are lots of things that I like to touch
And other things I don't like much—for
    instance—
A wad of bubble-gum stuck to my sole
Or reaching inside a cob-webby hole
Walking bare-foot on hot concrete
Facing the force of wind-blown sleet
And though I've but felt it in my mind,
The business end of a porcupine.
Sometimes I can tell with just a glance
If touching something is taking a chance,
But what is lovelier just to see
Than a star jelly-fish or a bumble bee?

Keeping in Touch

The title for this section dealing with the sense of touch was not chosen capriciously or with an attempt at cleverness, but rather because it described our rationale for including tactile experiences as part of classroom learning. Recall that the infant begins life relying greatly upon what we call the proximity senses—touch, taste, and smell. They are the important senses for his physical and emotional well-being. The little child continues to use his proximity senses in special ways, partic-

The sense of touch can provide instant communication. Tenderness, understanding, excitement, or fright can be sensed at your fingertips.

ularly his sense of touch. Nothing has been truly explored until it has been investigated with the fingers, hands, and often with other body parts as well, including the mouth where it is as important to feel something as it is to taste it.

As the child develops the senses of sight and hearing and as he uses them more and more for improving his communication skills, he depends less on the other senses. Particularly in cultures such as ours, where body contact between adults plays a small part in most of our interpersonal communication, we often begin very early to condition children away from a dependence on the sense of touch. "Who are you, and what are you to me?" inquires the infant with hands and fingers exploring the adult face hovering above his own. Later the child develops more sophisticated and "polite" ways of making his discoveries. He also uses his sense of touch to discover and explore things until "Don't touch!" becomes a familiar admonition conveyed through scolding words, cross looks, and slapped hands. Of course children should not touch everything in sight or put foreign objects in their mouths, but we are not talking about the things that are inherently out of bounds. Children not only need the sensory experience of exploring with touch, they need to learn how to touch, how to handle with gentleness and confidence. They need to develop responsibility in handling and touching as well as in other skills. The more ways we can know something or someone, the better we can understand. A child cannot really know a lovely china cup, or a puppy, or a baby until he can touch and hold and fondle all of those beautiful things. His sense of wonder needs the stimulation of touching.

Margaret Mead's observations about our inability to know in advance just which of our senses may be unusually important to us in the future, either personally or vocationally, ought to inspire us to include a multitude of sensory experiences involving all of the senses in classroom activities. Sighted children are often amazed that blind boys and girls of just their own age can read Braille, touching the raised symbols with such sensitivity that they can read with their fingertips. Share with them Mary O'Neill's poem, "Mimi's Fingers: Fingers are always bringing me news." If touching experiences are being introduced (or more accurately, reintroduced) to older boys and girls, this may provide an excellent way to begin. Children have always used their sense of touch instinctively to explore and discover new things. It is interesting that many of our new spelling and reading aids are now incorporating tactile experiences.

The sense of touch has three distinct uses in creative dramatics, all of which are of value to the child in addition to whatever skills he may develop in drama. Like the other senses, touching can be a means of stimulating the imagination. Touch can become important to improving interpersonal relationships through the communication process. And the actual touching of shapes, sizes, and textures as preparation for developing skills in pantomime can be one more way of increasing awareness of self and the environment. Furthermore, touch activities, like listening and looking, can be easily done in the classroom and its environs as an integral part of other learning experiences. For example, five properties of an object can be discovered by touching—size, shape, weight, texture, and temperature. Such an array of data may have almost unlimited use in several subject areas in addition to stimulating creative thinking—the kind needed for analyzing and solving problems as well as for artistic purposes.

As with the other sensory experiences, touch activities are best introduced by first working with actual materials. The following are some suggestions for involving children in simple tactile experiences.

Developing Awareness through Touch

Perhaps the simplest and most common way to introduce tactile experiences to young children is with a bag or box of items into which the children thrust their hands and feel one or more items. They may be asked to see if they can identify each item or to describe out loud as many properties of one item as they can determine by using touch alone or to express how the various items in the box make them feel. Such "Touchy-Feely" boxes are simple and inexpensive to construct and have great child appeal. The contents may be orientated toward something of special and immediate interest to the children, and there is always the element of mystery and suspense when we explore the unknown.

Sometimes items are simply passed while the children examine them with closed eyes, again placing a greater emphasis on the sense of touch by keeping the items from sight. Older boys and girls enjoy passing articles behind their backs while seated or standing in a circle. This way they may keep their eyes open and they enjoy trying to read the non-verbal cues as each classmate handles an item and passes it on. All of these tactile explorations are easy to provide, fun to do, and useful for developing awareness and stimulating creative ideas.

There are other ways of providing touch experiences that are a bit more unusual. Exploring the classroom to discover the variety of shapes, textures, and temperatures may be done with eyes open or as a part of a trust walk. Middle- and upper-elementary pupils enjoy leading each other on a blind walk as a way of giving and receiving trust. Because this may cause some children anxiety or some leaders may be less than careful, a few guidelines for blind walks are helpful. Younger children should not use blindfolds because of the possibility of transmitting eye infections and because, if a child becomes momentarily frightened while his eyes are closed, he may take a peek, reorient himself, and continue without feeling like a failure. We have also found the entire experience more enjoyable, better controlled, and safer if the children can do something besides lead and follow. For example, the leader will look around to discover a variety of shapes, textures, and perhaps temperatures; he will then guide the follower to explore the same objects with the sense of touch only. Later each pair can discuss, compare their perceptions, exchange roles, and investigate another area.

Outdoor touch walks are great. There are so many different kinds of things to examine with fingers and hands and several kinds of surfaces to walk upon—grass, sand, asphalt, cement, fallen leaves, wet pavement or grass, snow and ice. How about a touch walk during each season as a way of collecting data for comparison?

When we speak of touching something, most of the time we think in terms of touching with the fingers and hands, but we need not limit our touching to hands and fingers. Children quite naturally explore with other body parts as well. Feeling mud with the fingers is not nearly the same as feeling it between the toes! Although we must be very selective, lips and tongues are especially useful for touching. To know a snowflake on the tongue is to know it in an intimate way. Cheeks and knees and arms and elbows can all be used for touching and may produce different ideas and feelings than those that follow exploration with fingers and hands. A silky spider web provides a very different sensation when felt by cheek or forehead than with the hands. Touching a familiar object as though it had never been felt before, doing so with a number of body parts, can also be an intriguing activity. Each child may explore something of his choice, touching it with fingers, hands, arms, cheek, forehead, and so forth. Within the group, the discovery of each person's unique feelings as well as those shared in common may stimulate a discussion or become the basis for individual writing or expression through art or movement.

Just as scenes and stories can be built around sights and sounds, they may also be inspired by and incorporate a variety of tactile experiences. Be prepared for a number of thrillers and chillers, especially from the older boys and girls. They delight in making relationships between the weird and spooky and the experience of touching. (A snake may be looked at with admiration, but touching it is something else, even though it doesn't really feel as one might imagine.) Walking over a variety of surfaces may contribute to some unusual settings; textures may suggest characters, particularly nonhuman characters; temperatures experienced with a variety of body parts may suggest something special, even bizarre, about the elements. Children may focus on sizes and shapes as the basis for story ideas. Stories with round, square, and triangle characters can be an excellent means for becoming more familiar with geometric shapes. The immediacy and physical involvement of tactile experiences contribute measureably to their worth for spontaneous stimulation for oral storybuilding.

All of the senses can be involved either actively or passively. I can see, hear, touch, taste and smell; I can also be seen, heard, touched, smelled, and even tasted by something or someone else. When someone or something touches me, I generally know it. It is the touching that makes me aware that the mosquito has landed to take a bite!

The sense of touch can provide instant communication whether it is the crack of the ruler across the knuckles or a gentle touch of a hand on the shoulder. The message conveyed through body contact is generally swift and clear. We are so aware of this with violence but may overlook the possibilities when searching for ways to establish understanding and empathy with one another. In our culture we do not engage in a great deal of casual body contact with persons with whom we do not have a familial or sexual relationship. Many persons in our society have never shaken the hand of a person of another race or, beyond early childhood, embraced another person of their own sex. It is not unusual to have children who come from homes where they are seldom, if ever, hugged and fondled. Though these children particularly need physical contact with other human beings in gentle and affectionate ways, they may be inhibited, self-conscious or even frightened if expected to participate in activities where they touch and are touched by others. Sometimes these deprived children react in an opposite manner and want to be constantly touching or being touched by the teacher. These little clinging vines are seeking ways to meet their needs, the "touch-me-not" children are not. The one exception is often seen when these same children are involved in sports and games. The children who backed off from touching others in a dramatization, may enthusiastically play leapfrog, football, or participate in gymnastics with others. They will often, in fact, engage in physical contact when it is rough and tumble, but not when it is part of an expression of kindness, friendship, or concern.

Initiating or accepting physical contact can lead to penetrating barriers that have been erected out of anxieties born of a lack of understanding. We recognize this so clearly when a young child retreats from petting a friendly puppy. We understand that the child, for his own reasons, is irrationally afraid of the dog and that if the child can overcome the fear enough to touch the animal, the fear often dissipates. The child's fears must not be ridiculed, nor should he ever be forced to pet or handle something that frightens him. He needs nonthreatening rein-forcement, and above all he needs a model, whom he can trust, to emulate. Touching another person can be just as frightening as petting a puppy, often more so. Given a choice between a warm, tail-wagging dog and pruned-faced Auntie Agatha, the child may instinctively em-brace the dog. Children need to see big people communicate with warmth and acceptance of others, and the instant and clear message of touching is an easy one for children to understand. Touch activities in the classroom involving both things and people, with the teacher par-ticipating with the children, can provide all of the children with at least one model.

A simple activity involving communication through touch is walking to a beat, stopping when the rhythm stops, and greeting a person nearby with a handclasp and a greeting. This can be fun to do as people from another time and place (for example, people at a royal ball or at a reception during Colonial times, when men bowed and ladies curtsied, or greeting one another with traditional oriental courtesy). However, moving about as ourselves is more important for helping children to understand and appreciate the use of touch in their own communica-tion. The following game is one that works well with children of all ages.

See How Many Ways You Can Say Hello!

If there is adequate space, all the children in a class may participate at one time and as one group. The teacher provides a variety of beats to which the children move, stopping to greet a person nearby when the rhythm stops. The teacher calls out the body part or parts to be used in the greeting. When the rhythm resumes, the children again move to the beat within the playing space.

Example: The first time the rhythm stops, the teacher calls out, "Hands," and everyone shakes hands with a person nearby. The next time the teacher stops the beat she names another body part to "shake" with a neighbor—elbows, knees, and so forth. She may name two body parts such as "Hands and elbows." Sometimes she calls, "Your choice."

Variations: A piece of music with a lively beat may be used in place of a rhythm provided with drum or tambourine. "Spooks in Space" from *The In Sound from Way Out!* (Vanguard label), "March of the Cue Balls" from *The Best of Mancini* (RCA Victor), or "Sweet Georgia Brown" from *Al Hirt Swingin' Dixie*, Vol. 3 (Audio Fidelity) are all very different in mood and tempo but work equally well.

The children may also move as something other than themselves, particularly as animal characters. "Baby Elephant Walk" from the Mancini album suggests moving as little elephants and is especially enjoyed by primary children. However played, this activity creates an atmosphere of fun and good humor and has been successfully used with mentally handicapped and emotionally impaired children with excellent results.

Even the simple activity of passing objects around a circle can give children opportunities in touching both objects and people with awareness and care. The teacher may initiate the activity and serve as a model, reminding the children to be careful and considerate both giving and receiving the items being passed. The group may also pass and handle objects as persons other than themselves, perhaps who have never touched such things before. A child might imagine how it would feel to be a peasant child or a pioneer whose clothing was always rough and homespun, touching a piece of velvet, silk, or one of the modern fabrics that even a royal person of another age might have envied. The children might examine a piece of polished steel or aluminum as people from a Stone Age culture. Putting such remarkable materials into the hands of another will require deliberate and careful physical contact with one another.

Another game that breaks down inhibitions about touching another child is a variation on the mirror game. Generally done as a creative movement to music activity, the children work in pairs with palms together, one leading and the other following as in the mirror game, making large and small movements in time to the music. The fact that the children are touching one another in a nonsport activity may be only a secondary reason for the experience, but for those who are squeamish about some kinds of physical contact with another child, such experiences can provide successful breakthroughs. Music such as "Windmills of Your Mind" from *The World of Mantovani* (London label) can help to create a dreamy mood conducive to feelings of awareness and sensitivity.

Touch experiences to stimulate the imagination

Touch activities increase awareness, and they can also engage the imagination. Objects examined during a blind walk, passed around the group behind backs or with closed eyes, or discovered in a touch box may stimulate imaginative thinking. As with other sensory activities, provocative questions may lead into fantasizing about what else the various discoveries might be, where else they might be found, what other uses might be made of the objects, and to whom the items may have belonged in another time or place. Touching and handling things as someone or something else requires imaginative thinking both in the creation of the imagined feelings and in the conjecturing from another's perspective. For example, touching warm sand on the playground or at the sand table, a child might imagine how an Eskimo boy or girl would feel walking for the first time on a hot sandy beach. Handling a piece of smoothly polished driftwood, a child might imagine what it would be like to live in the sea constantly moved by the unceasing currents.

After viewing the film *I Have an Egg*, in which blind children learn about an egg by feeling it in its variant forms (the yolk, the white, boiled, and finally as an egg hatched into a newborn chick), the children may examine a familiar object as the blind child would, trying to imagine not only the object but also the feelings of the blind child. Trying to imagine someone else's sense of wonder can nurture the development and enrichment of one's own.

Group sharing of individual perceptions based on each person's sensory exploration may furnish additional creative ideas for scenes and stories. A familiar story is based on a Hindu fable about six blind men who investigate an elephant using only their sense of touch. Each man investigated only a part of the beast (the trunk, tusk, tail, a leg, and so forth) and came to some very wrong and humorous conclusions about the nature of an elephant. The story is fun to dramatize and can be used as motivational material for individual and group activities. Though the moral of the story points out how misleading only limited investigation may be, it also illustrates how different perceptions can be when based on each person's special and unique experiences and how the *shared* perceptions of several people may be more accurate than the fragmented experiences of each one. The fable also shows children how exploring something through the sense of touch only may be used to stir the imagination, even though their conclusions may be inaccurate and humorous.

Touching with the imagination only

Because in creative drama props and equipment are generally created solely with the imagination, children rely on previous experiences with objects to help them use and handle imaginary properties well. Touch experiences that help them to develop skill in pantomiming with imagined objects may begin with actually handling, carrying, lifting, and using a variety of common objects. Simple, at-the-desk exercises may be done as follows: Each child begins by actually picking up and handling a familiar object such as a book, pencil, or cup. The item is examined as though the experience were entirely new, as though the child has never handled the object before. When the child feels that he knows just how it feels in terms of texture, weight, size, and shape, he tries to imagine handling the object. The real object is put away and the child pretends to handle the object using only his recollection of the actual item to aid in his pantomime. At any point that he wishes, he may reinforce the sensory memory and clarify his imagined awareness by once again examining the actual object.

Though the handling of objects is generally done with fingers and hands, the same kind of activity may be done with other body parts. The child may give special attention to how the feet feel against the floor, how the legs and buttocks feel against the seat of the chair, how a sweater feels against the neck and arms. When he is ready to work with his imagination only, he no longer uses actual equipment. Keep in mind that at this stage the emphasis remains upon the sensory experience to stimulate the imagination rather than on the quality of the pantomime.

A follow-up activity may be particularly useful as a part of a science activity—observing with the other senses such things as stones, fossils, plants or other living things before touching them, trying to imagine how each thing will feel when it is finally examined with touch. They may even pantomime picking up and handling the item before and after they actually do handle it. This is a good activity for pairs of children, encouraging them to share their perceptions both verbally and through pantomime.

Work with actual objects should be followed by work with imaginary objects. Passing imaginary objects around a circle is a good way to begin. The teacher or one of the children starts by giving something fragile, perhaps a tiny furry kitten to the child seated next in the circle. The kitten is then passed around the group, and each child is reminded to concentrate on the size, shape, texture, and warmth of the kitten. The teacher may again remind the group of the importance of giving and receiving carefully. Anything relatively fragile that appeals to the age and interests of the group can be passed. The fragile quality is important because each child must give and receive with concern for what is being passed and for the person to whom it is being given. Often it is necessary to put the object directly into the other's hand or to place it gently in the next child's arms or lap. Eggs, flowers, snowflakes, and baby animals are suitable for little children; older boys and girls may relate to a priceless scroll from the pyramids, an ancient treasure map, valuable works of art or bits of antiquity, or something in nature such as a Luna moth, a dandelion seed puff, or the last remaining dinosaur egg.

Though the teacher may begin this activity, the children need to have opportunities to decide what is to be passed, to "create" it, and to initiate the movement of the object around the circle. At any point where the children seem to be losing interest in what is being passed (or become silly and careless in the handling), the teacher can suggest that something new be created or that the original object has changed in some special way. For example, a fuzzy caterpillar may change into a cocoon from which a moth or butterfly may ultimately emerge. Of course not all items to be passed need to be fragile. Hot potatoes, ice cubes, and things that slither and shake are all fun to hand around, but at any point where concentration on the giving and receiving lags, something that must be carefully handled should be introduced. Sharing time at the end of the exercise is an important part of a creative experience. "How did the caterpillar feel in your hands? Have some of you held a garden snail before? Do you think the robin's egg would be lighter or heavier than a chicken egg?" This kind of follow-up questions can lead to meaningful discussion of the experience.

Sensory experiences generally invite sharing, and sharing with children through the sense of touch enriches their possibilities for inventing and discovering. It may also be a means by which an adult keeps in touch with both self and environment in the rediscovering of an appreciation for the sense of touch. Within these experiences are beautiful opportunities for adults to literally and figuratively touch the lives of children in positive and creative ways, which is one of the most special things that can happen to any grown-up.

Your Turn

1. With a partner, investigate an area of the room through the sense of touch. Select a surface or object in your area and brainstorm all of the ideas, feelings, and experiences that come to your minds from the tactile experiences with your choices.
2. Build a collage of shapes, sizes, and textures with different materials which can be used with children to stimulate awareness and imaginative thinking.
3. Bring something that has an interesting shape or texture to class. Divide into small groups and share your contributions. As a group, create a story idea that incorporates all of the shapes and textures shared by the group. (The actual object need not be incorporated into the story. For example, a flat pebble may suggest the shape of a footprint; a scrap of burlap may suggest the hide of an animal; something metal that feels cool to the touch may suggest a cold and frozen place.)

4. Develop a lesson plan to use with children in which you side-coach them through a special environment full of interesting textures over or through which they must travel. Decide on grade level. Find an appropriate poem to incorporate into the lesson.

5. From a large carton build an environment box to be explored by children primarily through the sense of touch. (An appliance box with openings at both ends allows children to crawl in, feel the shapes and textures of materials you have placed inside, and leave through the other end.)

6. Close your eyes and explore something, using only your sense of touch. List all of the words you can think of to describe the object. You may also do this exercise with a partner, with each of you investigating the same object; then each write your own list of descriptive terms and words. When both are finished, share your words with one another.

7. Read the story in the appendix, "How the Touch-Me-Nots Got Their Name." Design a game to involve children in getting acquainted which includes some physical contact with one another. Keep in mind that the game should not make anyone feel embarrassed and that adequate controls are built-in to reduce silly or rowdy behaviors.

Exploring with Taste and Smell

Many stories enjoyed by children involve tasting and smelling, especially tasting. In everything from "Little Miss Muffet" to Dickens' "A Christmas Carol," food and eating play an important role. Goldilocks would never have had her adventure in the home of the three bears if the porridge had not been too hot to eat when the bears sat down to breakfast; without the poisoned apple, Snow White might have died of old age; and, Jack Sprat and his wife are remembered only because of their unique eating habits. What could be a more natural theme for children's stories? Early life is almost totally involved with eating and sleeping. Love and affection and being fed are so integrated in the child's mind that even as adults many of us take refuge in food when we are lonely or troubled. Many of the children's own stories, growing out of playing house, involve being hungry and preparing and eating a meal. Improvisational dramas created by college students are often built around some aspect of eating, though adults are more apt to use the gathering of people for a meal as a means of bringing characters into interacting relationships.

Classroom activities involving the senses of taste and smell are generally entered into in a spirit of camaraderie. Food means fun, and a group of people tasting even "pretend" food creates an atmosphere of party time. Furthermore, children have had a great deal of real and personal experience in tasting and may have experienced an astonishingly wide variety of tastes. Working with tastes also reinforces to the child, in a positive way, his own uniqueness. There is perhaps no area in our private self where we are more individual than in our food preferences. Except in cases of religious or cultural taboos, there are no right or wrong preferences. (This is not to ignore health and nutritional factors but only to emphasis individual prerogatives to like or dislike.) Again, we are involving children in looking at themselves nonjudgmentally so as to better understand just who they are. Like many sensory activities, imaginary taste experiences provide opportunity to relate to a common, shared experience while allowing each child to be "right" yet different.

An interesting hypothetical situation that combines an opportunity to share commonalities while encouraging individuality may be done as follows: Instead of all of the many kinds of things to eat that most members of our society enjoy, if we were each limited to only one kind of food (as are many living things in the nonhuman world), what would you choose and why? Any students who choose the same food may work as groups; the others will work individually in preparing and presenting their "cases." Sometimes one commonality, such as a shared favorite food, can bring children together who have not been previously attracted to one another. At the same time a child who makes a "different" or unusual choice may be as "right" as the others.

Trying to imagine what unfamiliar foods taste like is interesting, particularly if none of the children have tasted them. I recall a group of kindergartners who wanted to dramatize "Little Miss Muffet." Everyone had a chance to play Miss Muffet, packing a picnic of curds and whey and happily skipping off to sit upon their tuffets and eat their lunches, and the spider, frightening imaginary Miss Muffets. Then one of the children wanted to know about curds and whey. After the explanation, they all decided that such fare would not make a very good picnic and set about packing decent lunches of fried chicken and peanut butter sandwiches. The first time through with the curds and whey, the eating had been less than enthusiastic. In the final playing, the lunches were eaten with great gusto, sincere emotional response, and quite good pantomime.

To realize how much simpler people ate in the past is sometimes difficult for our contemporary children. Those who are well nourished cannot fully understand hunger or existing on the monotonous diets of the poor. We could encourage them to imagine what it would be like to be very hungry, and then to be offered something they have never eaten before.

Another taste experience that can stimulate the imagination and help develop greater understanding and awareness of others, is the participation in an imaginary festival of another time or place. Preparing and eating the first Thanksgiving dinner is fun because of the great characterizations it suggests and the sensory experiences involved. Celebrating national fêtes of other countries, including traditional foods enjoyed only through their imaginations, can help children break their own mindsets about certain foods and flavors. As they are eating unfamiliar foods as the peoples who enjoy them, they are stretching their own range of possible experiences. Perhaps such imaginary excursions into the lifestyles of other cultures will help to prepare our children to be more sophisticated, less provincial, and more compassionate.

Tasting imaginary foods may also be used to elicit sincere emotional response. Children are often surprised to discover how accurately their salivary glands respond to biting into an imaginary lemon or a crisp juicy apple. The idea of savoring a favorite food may produce genuine expressions of pleasure, and swallowing the nasty medicine may make some children shudder if they have had such a real experience. Both tasting and smelling activities are easily and conveniently done while seated and are excellent to do in limited space where small movement is more appropriate then large motor response. No classroom can possibly lack adequate facilities for this kind of creative work.

In designing sensory activities for the classroom involving sight, hearing, and touch, we began with real and personal experiences. It is a simple thing to provide actual sounds, sights, textures, shapes, and sizes within the school environment. Real and personal tasting and smelling experiences can be somewhat more complicated to arrange because of factors that may curtail realism. Food and respiratory allergies are considerations as well as the obvious problems of handling things to taste with even a nod toward hygienic conditions. Imaginary experiences are probably better when exploring the use of these senses for creative purposes. The one exception may be certain kinds of things to smell. After all, a discriminating sense of smell is essential to many science experiments, and guided by some common sense, the teacher may also provide the boys and girls with experiences that stimulate aesthetic discoveries as well.

Some children are totally unfamiliar with many odors in this day of convenience foods and plastic flowers. Children who have eaten dozens of vanilla ice cream cones may not know the aroma of vanilla extract. No wonder they continue to get mixed up between vanilla and manila long after they have conquered the beginning sounds involved; they do not relate the flavor to a bean or a bottle on the pantry shelf that can fill the kitchen with its distinctive perfume. Other familiar fragrances such as dill, clove, and ginger may be ones that many of the children do not recognize apart from pickles, chewing gum, and a story about a runaway cookie. These kinds of pantry odors and such things as lavender, balsam, and pine are easy to supply to introduce children to greater olfactory awareness. For some, raised on TV dinners, aluminum Christmas trees, and drip-dry house plants, smelling a freshly cut lemon or a sprig of mint can be a delightful moment of discovery.

If the boys and girls have already been increasing their sensory awareness through hearing, seeing, and touching experiences, they will be able to taste imaginary food and smell imaginary odors.

We have primarily been discussing the sense of taste, realizing that taste and smell are physiologically related in tasting. Many odors not related to food can extend sensory awareness and stimulate the imagination. There are odors in and around schools despite efforts to create environments which are "odor free." Classrooms, libraries, nurses' stations, cafeterias, and gyms often have their own distinctive aromas that may or may not be noticed by many of the people who spend time in them. A "scent" walk around the school neighborhood may turn up a variety of pleasant and unpleasant odors. Local residents may become so used to the odors in the environment that they are casually tolerant of pollution which might be controlled. Letting the sense of smell become dormant may not only deprive us of certain pleasures and

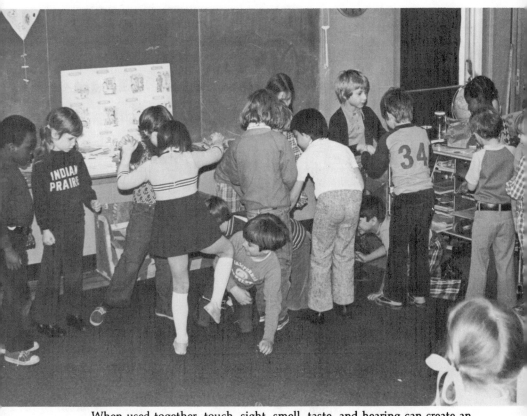

When used together, touch, sight, smell, taste, and hearing can create an exciting stimulus for exploring new and different environments.

creative stimulation, but also reduce our involvement in our surroundings and lower our social consciousness. Children need to be challenged to become aware of odors in their neighborhoods. This awareness may be the beginning of concerned adult attitudes about clean air, better housing, and other societal problems. Because children generally relate unpleasant odors to horrid, even bizarre, happenings, stories stimulated by "stinky" odors are often peopled with witches, monsters, and violence. Suggestions of pleasant exotic odors may lend a balance, of course.

As children mature, the distance senses of sight and hearing become more and more important to their growth and development. Much of what they learn will come through listening and looking, but some continued experiencing with the proximity senses of taste and smell can also nourish their sense of wonder and enhance their sensitivity to their total environment. Conscious awareness of flavors and odors can be added stimuli to imaginative thinking and creative living. Even an imagined taste or smell can conjure up such emotions in children that stories as old as "The Gingerbread Man" and as contemporary as Roald Dahl's *Charlie and the Chocolate Factory* can produce the kind of child involvement that is necessary to creative drama.

All Together: Multisensory Experiences

Emphasis on the senses ultimately leads to integrated, or multisensory, experiences in which we explore any given material or situation with all or most of the senses. This kind of cross-referencing is essential to understanding. It can also be the basis for the kind of innovative thinking that is essential to creativity. A simple experiment will illustrate the need to explore and challenge with a multisensory approach.

Let the children begin by examining an unfamiliar object with only one sense, perhaps sight. Based on what can be discovered with the one sense, the group brainstorms all possible uses for the object. Record their ideas. Allow a second group to examine the object in all possible ways, using as many senses as can be useful. Again brainstorm for ideas and record. The entire group may then compare the two lists. See if they can determine which ideas of the second group came about through the multisensory examination.

If you wish to extend the creative involvement with the object beyond the basic experiment, let each group use the object to stimulate the imagination and create a story based on their ideas. The first group may only look at the object; the second group may touch it, handle it, smell it, explore any sounds it can make, and so on. Look at the stories from the point of originality and imaginative thinking. See if there is a correlation between the creativity shown and the number of senses involved in examining the object used for stimulation. The Hindu fable about the blind men and the elephant might well be used in conjunction with these activities.

Many of the exercises described for one sense can also be done using the senses in combination. Exploring the classroom and the school environs utilizing several senses is excellent preparation for a field trip in which the children hope to come back with a comprehensive understanding of their experience. For younger boys and girls, an imaginary trip in the classroom as a follow-up to a real experience challenges them to recall what they have already seen, heard, touched, and smelled (and perhaps tasted), and it allows them to recreate the experience in their own ways. For example, the child who was apprehensive about one of the animals at the zoo may, during the pretend trip, imagine himself bravely feeding the animal or even petting it.

Such creative experiences involving multisensory exploration, at least at first, should be side-coached by the teacher, using narrative to guide, but not impose. This works best when the teacher discreetly limits the narration to some descriptive comments, provocative questions, and occasional reminders to investigate with a particular sense. It is difficult for a child to listen with his imagination if the narrative is too constant and overwhelming. The adventure may actually involve movement in space (as further developed in the section on movement and pantomime), or the children may sit with eyes closed, experiencing only with the imagination. Such multisensory creative experiences allow children to make "field trips" to any place and in any time. It allows them to go as themselves or as someone or something else. The format is familiar to them, building as it does on the make-believe situations they created as preschoolers, but it is also dependent on new ideas, information, feelings, and perceptions related to their new levels of maturity.

Multisensory explorations of their environment, real or imagined including the human and nonhuman elements, give them increased emotional data as well as additional cognitive information. To experience something through only one of the senses may evoke quite different feelings than to know it through another sense or through several senses. A large fire, viewed from a distance, may elicit feelings of excitement and fascination. Experienced up close where one can also feel the heat, smell the fumes, and hear the roar of the flames, the scene becomes one of horror.

Sensory input spontaneously produces emotional response, and the more comprehensive the sensory experience can be, the deeper the emotional involvement. The depth of emotional involvement is what sets us in motion, both physically and intellectually. The interaction of sensory data with emotional, physical, and intellectual response creates conflict both within the self and within all of our relationships with both the human and nonhuman in our worlds. This element of conflict is basic to drama. Sensory experiences are, therefore, fundamental to drama because they trigger the emotional responses that in turn produce the physical and intellectual actions that are the visible manifestations of conflict.

Your Turn

1. Working in groups of six, one person in each group will suggest a sight, one a sound, one an odor, one a taste, one a texture, and one a weight. As a group, see if you can create a ministory that incorporates all of the suggested sensory impressions. (Example: sight—the color red; sound—water slowly dripping; odor—a dusty road; texture—soft fur; taste—lemonade; weight—light as a feather. The sensory ideas are decided independently and then shared. The group works cooperatively to develop the very short story incorporating the impressions.)
2. Develop a game in which children must use two or more senses in a creative way. Relate your activity to a concept to be taught in some area of curriculum. State your purposes, objectives, a short warm-up activity, the main activity which involves two or more of the senses, and a quieting activity for the conclusion. Also specify grade level for which you feel your activity would be most suitable.
3. Find a short story or poem in which two or more of the senses play an important role. Create a series of questions to be used related to the poem or story which would encourage children to think and respond imaginatively.
4. Write a short narration you could use with children to "talk them through" a movement activity in which they would respond to the imaginative use of two or more senses. Example: exploring a dark cave, giving special attention to textures and sounds.

4

Creating with Pantomime

> *Nature has so constituted us that movement is the medium in which we live our lives, not only in our internal physiological mechanisms but in our outward conduct as well.*
>
> John Martin's Book
> of the Dance

The very young child explores through the senses, responds to those discoveries with his emotions, and expresses those feelings through movement. The child moves because he must; even before his first breath, his internal organs were moving as they functioned, and arms and legs moved him about inside his mother's body. After birth, his movement is a general indicator of his development; rolling over, sitting up, crawling, and walking show that the child is becoming physically stronger and that his neurological system is maturing. When his senses evoke emotional responses, the nervous system is triggered, sending impulses to the muscles, stimulating them to move. Even the mature nervous systems of adults often send messages so rapidly to our muscles that we respond spontaneously to certain stimuli without waiting for our intellects to intercept and logically plan our reactions. The spontaneous movements of adults in response to certain sensory stimuli is very much like that of children similarly aroused, showing a consistency between the emotional response and the kinds of spontaneous movement triggered. We may even see similarities in response between humans and other mammals. Puppies and children wiggle their bodies and race around when they are happy and excited; the anxious lion in the cage paces back and forth looking amazingly like a politician on election night. Such movements are not necessarily representational of the emotions, but somehow the nature of the feelings and the intuitive reactions are tremendously consistent.

The preschool child who is moving from primarily psychomotor to cognitive behaviors makes extensive use of movement as a communication tool. Even as language develops, he continues to emphasize his new use of symbols with accompanying movement. Movement is his natural language, and for a long time he will continue to communicate through a combination of words and movements, much as the person who is learning a second language continues to use his native speech for emphasis or when he lacks vocabulary in the new language. The teacher or parent who asks a young child to "stand still and *tell* me what happened" may be asking the child to do the impossible.

The emphasis in the early years on language acquisition and the development of oral and written communication often neglects the child's need to express himself through movement. His ability to do so deteriorates from lack of continued use and development. This ability, which was so natural in the two year old, becomes an art form that relatively few adults do well, and so we marvel at the expertise of the Marcel Marceaus, the Chaplins, the Martha Grahams, and the Gene Kellys.

When he is involved in movement activities, the child is exercising his body, building coordination, developing grace, discovering how his body moves, becoming attuned to his own inner pulse and rhythm, relating to others and their movement, and discovering and utilizing space. All of these are excellent growth experiences, and all of them relate, either directly or indirectly, to how he communicates with himself and with others. Movement can continue to be an important and exciting aspect of communication for everyone, though only some will continue to develop it to an artistic level. The inclusion of such activities in the classroom can actually assist children in their oral and written language development.

Movement work in the classroom requires an understanding of how children learn and grow, and how their motor skills and neurological systems develop and mature. They need involvement in all kinds of movement, large and small, utilizing all of the body parts that can move. Discoveries of what moves (and how) occupies a great deal of the infant's time and concentration. He seems to watch his own body movements objectively; through exploration and observation he actually discovers his own body image, which is the beginning of his self-identity. "Hey, those are a part of me out there," discovers the baby as he watches his own little fingers reach for the bottle or toy. He begins to orient himself in space—to perceive distances between himself and someone or something else. Space is as necessary to movement as sound is to listening, and the young child spends a good deal of his energies in extending his own space and in discovering relationships between himself and whatever else is sharing space with him. He does not need language to express his delight with himself when he finally succeeds in propelling himself through even a small amount of space.

Part of the young child's egocentricity is his obvious fascination with himself and what he can do. We have observed this same kind of wonder when older boys and girls discover that they can do something with the body which they did not know they could do. A fifth-grade girl who was working to express the feelings of Jonathan Livingston Seagull as he perfected his flying became so involved with her own graceful hand and arm movement that she momentarily forgot her original purpose. Children also reveal many things about themselves to others when they are working individually in movement activities. When the other members of a boy's club discovered that one of them could "run a race in slow motion" so that he looked like the instant replay on television, the child was so enthralled that he continued to work very hard developing his ability to pantomime. He was not a very verbal child, but the other children's admiration for his skill in pantomime encouraged him to open up more with them.

Teachers and educational programs do not "introduce" children to movement, but perceptive adults who understand a child's need to continue learning about the physical self and to express ideas and feelings through movement can incorporate many kinds of movement activities into the curriculum. Drama is doing, and as such it is inherently involved with many kinds of movement—creative movement and child dance, pantomime, the development of roles and characters and their nonverbal behaviors, and all kinds of movement that are intended primarily to free children so that they may overcome self-consciousness while developing a clearer consciousness of self.

Obviously, movement requires space, and one of the first questions teachers ask when contemplating drama as part of the classroom experience is "What do I do about space?" Solving spatial problems and understanding spatial relationships is important to both children and teachers and is a basic consideration in designing any kind of learning environment.

SPACE SUITS

Try these on for size—

A crack in the sidewalk is plenty of space
For the ants to build their new home,
But the tiger would surely laugh at that place;
He needs a jungle to roam.

Hundreds of honey bees live in a hive,
And the squirrel is content in his trees.
But the eagle requires a piece of the sky,
And the dolphin a part of the seas.

Our pussy is happy to curl up at night,
In a ball, at the foot of my bed.
And the puppy's warm basket fits him just right
From the tip of his tail to his head.

The leopard, the cougar, the fox and the bear
Need their freedom to range through the wild.
But I know a cozy nook under the stair
That is just the right size for a child.

The Space Age

More and more we are becoming a people with an increased awareness of space—outer space, inner space, the conservation and use of
space, the societal demands upon space, and so on. Several years ago
when introducing spatial concepts to a group of college students, it
would be necessary to put the word on the board—it was not com-
monly a part of everyone's vocabulary. Today our space scientists and
engineers, sociologists, environmentalists, and others have caused us to
have new concerns about space. All of our elementary children are
expected to become involved, within the school curriculum, with some
aspects of space travel, the planets in our solar system, and even some
concepts about the space beyond. In the areas of social studies and
ecology, children are learning about the uses of space in our cities, in
our wilderness areas, and in our global approaches to the use of our
planet to support both man and the wild kingdom. Spatial concepts
have become an important part of the curriculum.

For the young child, the concepts of space and its use begin to have meaning as his understanding of his own body image grows. Space is a challenge to the infant as he strives to extend his space through increased mobility. Space is to be conquered so that he may put himself where he wants to be. Generally this is encouraged, and he is reinforced in his efforts to sit, stand, crawl, and walk. Once he is actively exploring space, he also discovers that there are restrictions on how he uses space and on what space he may use. "Keep your hands to yourself." "Stay put!" "Please remain in your own places." Such statements remind the child that space, like other commodities, has size and shape and, sometimes, ownership. Understanding spatial concepts is inherent in understanding the concepts of privacy, sharing, and cooperation. The best utilization of space depends on an understanding of the finite nature of space. The space available at any time and in any place is limited by laws. Yet movement requires space whether it is required to play a game; dramatize a story; walk as a group to the cafeteria; or live together in the home, classroom, neighborhood, and community. Because of the basic relationships that exist between space and movement, movement activities with children may logically begin with an exploration of a variety of spaces.

School-aged children are still exploring their capacities for movement, still building on the three basic movements from which all other movement skills are developed—bending, twisting, and stretching. The form of these basic movements (and the many variations on them) is, at least partially, controlled by the size and shape and population of the space in which the movements take place. The following suggestions for exploring space may be used with both younger and older elementary boys and girls. With the little ones, the emphasis may be upon what body parts move and how and ways to use space; with older children, the emphasis may be on discovering the relationships between space and mass, the social consequences of crowding, and how we can improve our shared use of space.

For the first activity, each child finds a place on the floor, just enough space to be able to extend arms and legs in all directions without actually taking any steps and without "trespassing" into someone else's space. To give the idea of a definite and finite space, suggest that each person be inside a container of some kind. An egg is good because children can relate to something alive actually being contained within an egg shell. It is a very private and safe place—we cannot see into it nor look out from it. Each child is free to explore all of the space in his or her own egg shell, feeling the sides with all body parts until the size and shape is determined. The egg shell fits its occupant, and each child may be as active or inactive as he wishes to be. Always allow for a discussion of how each one explored the space, what limitations the size and shape of the space placed upon activity, and how each child felt about the experience.

Other interesting containers to explore are ketchup bottles and jelly jars. Bottles are transparent, so, unlike the egg, an occupant of such a container can both see out and be seen as he moves about within the space. Ketchup bottles are usually tall and narrow, especially at the top so that the most natural movements within involve stretching, squatting, and turning in place. Jelly jars, the kind used for home canning, are generally narrow at the bottom, not so tall, but wide at the top and allow for more freedom of movement with the upper parts of the body, especially horizontal movement with the arms. Once each child has determined the size and shape of his particular bottle or jar—one that fits him and does not collide with others nearby—the entire group may begin working with various body parts, moving fingers, hands, shoulders, heads, waists, hips, knees, feet, toes, even facial features within the space identified through movement exploration.

After children have explored solid containers, they may wish to create other kinds of imaginary containers. Being inside of balloons gives them a very different kind of environment, with different colored opaque walls that are not so rigid as glass but are also fragile. Balloons are fun because they come in a variety of shapes and they float aloft if not restrained. Soap bubbles are transparent, iridescent, and extremely fragile; so movements inside must be very controlled and gentle. Such a place might be best investigated in slow motion. Older boys and girls may wish to be inside objects related to things which they have been studying, reading about, or using at school or in leisure-time activities. Test tubes, various kinds of flasks used in science experiments, space capsules, diving bells, and a variety of balls used in sports are all examples of environments that might be used for private explorations.

After children have had several experiences exploring varieties of personal space, let them combine and work in pairs to utilize their double space. They may continue to be in bottles or balloons, but ones of just sufficient size to accommodate two people. Let them discover the new things they can do in twice as much space and the problems to be solved when the space must be shared. The human problems may become the more challenging ones. Such experiments in exploring and sharing space may be expanded to combining space and sharing with four or eight people in a group. While only two are sharing, each occupant may simply watch and move to accommodate the other person with little verbal communication. The nonverbal communication between two people generally works very well. Some of the children may even discover that two people within the shared space "solve" movement problems by mirroring one another. This, of course, reduces traffic problems but also reduces individual freedom to create, at least half of the time.

With four or more in the group, especially among upper-elementary children, they find it necessary to organize through discussion. Leaders often emerge; rules are made; relationship problems may develop and may or may not be solved. If the group solves their problems in a way that is satisfactory to all, the space will probably be used well, and the occupants will enjoy the interaction. If not, they may not make the best use of the space available and feel that their group was not allotted enough space for so many. Many concepts may be explored and discussed during and after these experiments—for example, sharing, cooperation, awareness, and communication.

Another interesting experiment with combined personal space is to put four people into the space originally shared by two. Suggest that each person see how active he can be in the space, observing how he must limit and control his movement in order to coexist in such a crowded environment. Half of each group may also try to engage in less active pursuits while the other half is very active. Such situations can provide real experiential learning when studying societal problems such as urbanization, the population crisis, and ecological problems concerning the use of space.

Comparing the experiences, particularly their emotional responses, is an important part of all of these activities; it encourages children to verbalize their ideas and feelings and to express them through movement; again and again we can emphasize the total communication process incorporating both the verbal and nonverbal behaviors.

Having begun with movement within small, defined spaces, children should have a better understanding of space as a finite commodity to be valued and used well. This is important before they will make the best use of the larger space required for most creative movement and drama activities. Ideally the space available for those experiences should be neither too large or too small. Too much space often results in either part of the space not being used at all or in movement that is neither socially nor aesthetically sensitive. Initially, a large gymnasium is too much space for little boys and girls; it overwhelms them and encourages some to tear about and others to withdraw from participation. Furthermore, the acoustics in such places are generally dreadful; voices, rhythm instruments, and music are garbled. However, ample space should be provided for large movements and to challenge the group to share and utilize the entire space available in the best possible ways. Insufficient space curtails development of motor skills and restricts communication.

Music for Movement and Pantomime

One of the wonderful things about creative drama is that it requires so little in terms of equipment and supplies. With children, a leader, some space, the world around to inspire, beautiful drama experiences are possible. However, creative drama without music is difficult to imagine, for music can stimulate the imagination, create moods, intensify emotions, and provide both the stimulus and the accompaniment for movement and pantomime. The teacher will want to acquire a small, selective music library for use in drama, and if carefully chosen, it need not involve a large expenditure of money. An excellent basic collection may consist of only a few pieces and albums but should include music to provide a variety of moods, rhythms, and tempos.

Music with movement and pantomime activities can provide the common experience that gives the work a cohesiveness when all of the children work parallel but independent of one another. Music can set the tempo for warm-up activities and provide additional control by establishing the desired mood and atmosphere. It can heighten a feeling of conflict and help to build a climax. It can strengthen endings so that a sense of resolution and conclusion is established. An appropriate musical accompaniment can help children to identify with characters and to express them with the whole body. During pantomime sequences, music may literally "speak" for the characters being portrayed.

The kinds of music the teacher leading creative drama will find useful are quiet, contemplative music to inspire feelings of well-being, solitude, introspection, and exploration of places, ideas, and emotions; flowing music for exotic modes of travel such as sailing aloft in a balloon or riding on a cloud or magic carpet; sinister music to accompany clandestine activities, the creeping about of those who are bent on villainous plotting; mysterious music to accompany adventures into the unknown such as space travel, exploration beneath the sea, haunted houses, and old castles; exciting exhilarating music to use in encounters with the elements and forces in nature such as wild animals and visitors from outer space or to build toward the climax of a battle; majestic music for scenes of pagentry and ritual; and rhythmic music to accompany everyday kinds of activities such as building things and working at various occupations.

Many children come to enjoy and appreciate the classics and good contemporary music by hearing it often in creative drama. It is not at all unusual for them to ask the name of a piece with which they have enjoyed working. In addition, children enjoy the several kinds of contemporary music including rock, soul, and modern folk. Boys and girls sometimes bring favorite records to school to share with the class. When the teacher can find a suitable way to use their contributions in the drama, she communicates her acceptance and pleasure in something important to them.

The following list is representative of the kinds of music that are useful in drama experiences. Many of the compositions are available on a number of labels and performed by various artists. Teachers and children may base their selections on personal preference and availability. The school media center or the record room of the public library is often a good source, particularly for the classics. Where a specific album is listed, the producer's name is included. To simplify selection, music is grouped according to at least one use in creative drama.

MARCHES

"March" from *The Nutcracker Suite* by Tchaikovsky

"March" from *The Love of Three Oranges* by Prokofiev

"Trumpet Voluntary" by Jeremiah Clark (regal processional)

"Entry of the Gladiators" from *Merle Evans Directs the Ringling Bros. Barnum and Bailey Circus Band.* (Decca label) (real circus music!)

"Bridal Chorus" from *Lohengrin* by Wagner

"March of the Cue Balls" and "Baby Elephant Walk" by Mancini from *The Best of Mancini* (RCA Victor) (slow walking march tempo)

"Stars and Stripes Forever" and "Washington Post March" by Sousa (martial band music)

"Soldiers March" by Schumann

MUSIC FOR FLOWING MOVEMENT

"Visa to the Stars," electronic music by Perrey and Kingsley from *The In Sound from Way Out* (Vanguard)

"Theme from Elvira Madigan," arranged by Milner from a composition by Mozart on *The World of Mantovani* (London). Also on the same album: "Windmills of your Mind," and "Theme from *Romeo and Juliet.*" (all hauntingly beautiful)

"Rhapsody in Blue" (in part) by Gershwin

MUSIC FOR MYSTERY AND ADVENTURE

"Night on Bald Mountain" by Moussorgsky (music for weird and mysterious happenings)

"Catacombs" and "The Great Gate at Kiev" from *Pictures at an Exhibition* by Moussorgsky ("Catacombs" is mysterious and somber; "Kiev" suggests a great procession passing through the massive gate at Kiev—heavy, powerful.) "Scheherazade" by Rimsky-Korsakoff (harems and dancing girls and the mysteries of the Near East)

"Firebird Suite" by Stravinsky (exciting, with good climax)

"Storm" from *Peter Grimes* by Britten (a storm at sea)

"Experiment in Terror" by Mancini from *The Best of Mancini*

"The Miraculous Mandarin Suite" by Bartok (suggests stealthy movement)

Music for Contemplation and Other Quiet Times

"Lullaby" and "Little Sandman" by Brahms

"Berceuse" from *The Firebird* by Stravinsky

"Evening Prayer" from *Hansel and Gretel* by Humperdinck

"Morning" from *The Hall of the Mountain King* by Grieg (pastoral music)

"Il Vecchio Castello" from *Pictures at an Exhibition* by Moussorgsky

"Claire de Lune" by Debussy

"Poisson D'or" by Debussy (Water sounds)

"Summer Idyl" (Folkways label) (electronic music, early morning sounds in summer including a fog horn)

Special Music for Special Uses

"Sorcerer"'s Apprentice" by Dukas (a "must" when pantomiming the story)

"Carnival of the Animals" by Saint-Saens (for animal stories and activities)

"Barnyard in Orbit" and "Jungle Blues from Jupiter" from Perrey-Kingsley album, *The In Sound from Way Out* (Animal sounds)

"Ballet of the Unhatched Chicks" from *Pictures at an Exhibition* by Moussorgsky

"The Pines," "Fountains of Rome," and "The Birds" by Respighi (musical impressions that suggest sun and shade, water and bird songs to create special environments and moods)

"The Planets" by Holst

"Appalachian Spring" by Copland (moves from very slow tempo, builds to sudden bursts of sound, and ends with soft tender mood)

"Billy the Kid" by Copland (creates the feeling of the prairie and the important incidents in the life of Billy the Kid)

Several bands from *Leroy Anderson Conducts Leroy Anderson,* particularly "The Typewriter Song," "The Waltzing Cat," "Sleigh Ride," and the fast moving "Fiddle Faddle"

"Spooks in Space" and "Unidentified Flying Object" from *The In Sound from Way Out* (good to use with mechanical and machine-type movements)

"Grand Canyon Suite" by Grofé (The "On the Trail" movement invites participation.)

"Theme from *A Summer Place*" by Steiner from the *Hawaii Five-O* album by The Ventures (Liberty) (Perfect tempo for slow-motion activities)

"Coltrane Jazz" by John Coltrane (London)

"Jazz Impressions of New York" by Brubeck (CBS label) (The progressive nature of Dave Brubeck's music makes it especially useful in drama.)

In-Space Movement

Movement activities will be more successful when children understand how to work cooperatively in a given space. Beginning individual movement activities generally start with children working in their own spaces, interacting only occasionally. Even after children are functioning well in the entire space, using it wisely and creatively and showing respect for one another, movement in self-space is always useful for warm-up activities. These are designed to free the children and stimulate their involvement in the activities that follow. They are often stimulated by some kind of sensory experience, real or imagined, and the use of a time beat to motivate the movement and lend a cohesiveness to the activity.

Before the movement activities begin, everyone finds his own space. (Little children may enjoy the use of imaginative labels such as "your own igloos, space ships, tepees, nests," usually something that specifically ties in with the rest of the lesson.) The warm-up activities should relate as closely as possible to the purpose and theme of the lesson. Getting every part of the body moving is always a good way to begin. Children start by moving just one part and add others as side-coached by the teacher until everything is in motion (fingers, then hands, etc.). This simple activity can be done with different sequencing (beginning with toes, for example, especially if done to the tune of "Dry Bones"), or sitting or lying down rather than standing, or expending different amounts of energy, or changing the tempo.

The following suggestions are intended to stimulate the teacher's

In our self-space we can each begin to explore ideas in our own way and learn how to express, learn what and why we feel as we do.

(and children's) own ideas, but are representative of individual in-place movements that can be built from tion.

Listening

1. You are visiting a friend who lives in the country (or city). When you get into bed it seems very quiet. Listen to the quiet, then begin to hear all kinds of sounds that are new to you. How do you feel?
2. You are talking on the telephone, but the person on the other end is doing most of the talking. You have something important and exciting to tell.
3. You are a photographer for the International Wildlife Society. You understand that you are camping in lion country. You have never had to set up your camp alone before, but at the last minute your assistant had to leave on an emergency. ("Jungle Blues on Jupiter" from *The In Sound from Way Out* album may help to set the stage for this.)
4. You are sound asleep. You awaken to hear the fire sirens coming closer and closer.
5. You are a little mouse asleep in your nest. The family where you live has company who brought their large cat with them. (May be a warm-up activity for dramatizing "Merlin the Curious Mouse" in the appendix.)

Looking

1. You are sewing a hole in your sock and drop the needle.
2. You need a warm sweater which you usually keep in your chest. You can't seem to find it. Your friends are waiting for you to go skating.
3. You want to read a book at the library. Find one and begin to read it. (Good warm-up before doing other activities with *Andy and the Lion.*)
4. There is a bee buzzing around your head while you are eating an apple out doors.
5. There is a ladybug crawling up the back of the person who sits in front of you.

Touching

1. The hamster has escaped from the cage and is hiding behind some supplies in the cupboard.

You are sitting in the darkened movie theatre and drop your bus pass. It is your only way to get home.

3. You are making something with clay for your father for his birthday.
4. You are climbing a very tall tree.
5. You are a pirate burying some treasure.

Tasting

1. At a birthday party you are given an ice cream cone of a flavor you have never tried before.
2. You are eating a taffy apple.
3. You come in from the cold, and mother gives you a cup of very hot cocoa.
4. You come in from play and pour yourself a large glass of milk. It has soured.
5. You are making oatmeal for the family for breakfast. You get too much salt in the water. (Good warm-up to use with Lucretia Hale's funny story, "Mrs. Peterkin Puts Salt in Her Coffee.")

Smelling

1. You are riding over a very bumpy road with your Dad or Mother. Suddenly there is a strange odor inside the car.
2. You wake up in the morning and Mother has fixed something special for breakfast.
3. You are on a picnic. Just as you are spreading out your lunch you notice a peculiar odor.
4. You are watching a good television show. Your dog comes in from outdoors and climbs on your lap. It is raining hard outside.
5. Your class is taking a test, but the class next door is making popcorn.

In each of the preceding, one sense was emphasized. In the following, the children will base their perceptions and activity on whatever recalled sensory experiences come to mind. Again the list is only representative of the kinds of ideas that work.

Seasonal activities

1. Preparing the soil, planting seeds, weeding and caring for the growing plants. The child may become the plant and grow in whatever way his plant grows, perhaps as a vine or a very erect and tall plant.

2. A bird building a nest, sitting on the eggs, becoming the young bird who carefully tries to stand and stretch his wings. (Fun to do as a warm-up with many poems and stories, *Horton Hatches an Egg* by Dr. Seuss, for example.)
3. Cleaning and painting (remember the whitewash scene from *Tom Sawyer?*), washing and polishing a bicycle or car.
4. Making and packing a picnic lunch.
5. Exploring and having fun at the seashore—digging clams, building things with sand.
6. Climbing way up in a tree and then coming down again.
7. Playing a game in your own space—imaginary jump rope, marbles, checkers or chess, for example.
8. Watching your favorite act at the circus. If this follows a discussion with the children of the sights, sounds, tastes, and smells at the circus, they can become more involved. Many children have never seen a live circus so they may need help in making associations.
9. Watching your favorite team play whatever sport or game the child best enjoys watching. Each child decides how his team fares.
10. Raking leaves, playing in the pile, and building a bonfire or putting the leaves into bags.
11. Selecting and cleaning a pumpkin and making a jack o'lantern.
12. Building a snowman or snowfort. The child may become the snowman.
13. Decorating a room for a festive occasion (holiday, party, special event).
14. Boxing and wrapping a gift.
15. Practicing a difficult trick on ice.

In all of the preceding, the children will need to recall sensory experiences and their own feelings about them to help them to show those perceptions, ideas, and emotions through movement. The teacher should avoid suggesting to the children how to think, how to show feelings, or how to move. For example, before the planting experience begins, the group may talk about preparing a garden and planting seeds. They may watch a film in which a garden is planted and cared for. They will share some of their own experiences with plants and gardens—or just digging in the dirt.

In the discussion the teacher encourages the children to imagine a variety of sensory experiences related to the activity. However, once the children are in their own spaces and ready to begin, the teacher's questions and comments should aim to stimulate a wide range of individual ideas. "You will need to decide how big your garden is to be and what kind of soil you have in your garden" allows for more individual and creative response than to ask, "Is your soil wet and heavy or warm and sandy?" Sufficient preparation before the movement activity would suggest many different ideas about the soil, the kinds of seeds to plant, and so forth.

Though we have referred to all of these as movement activities, the teacher and children may prefer to call them exercises in pantomime. Children enjoy learning this term, and the teacher may find it convenient to differentiate between the kind of creative movement just described and that which is more abstract and interpretive as in dance. If the term *pantomime* suggests a level of expertise children can rarely develop or implies a concern that there be no verbal accompaniment, the word should be avoided. Drama activities are intended to stimulate language development and facilitate speech. If children spontaneously add sounds and language to their movement, suppressing the speech would seem antithetical to one of the important purposes for using drama in the classroom.

However, children should be encouraged to develop skill in their movement activities just as in the other aspects of communication. Three simple suggestions that may help them to do so are: (1) Simplify the movement whenever possible. It is not, for example, necessary to include all of the details involved with making a cake to suggest that process. Too many details often clutter the picture, and they can impair the communication. (2) Just as pauses are important and necessary in speaking, pause in movement can help to clarify meaning and emphasize what is important. Children are often relieved to discover that when they are doing movement activities they do not have to become perpetual motion machines. Pauses make the movement more effective rather than less so. The teacher's use of "freeze" can help the children discover the value of pause in movement. (3) Movement and pantomime work can often be improved by occasional reminders to the children to keep a mental picture of what they want to show. This requires concentration. Though these suggestions sound easy, they are not. Simplifying the movement, for example, means that the child knows which details to eliminate and which to keep to communicate his ideas and feelings. This presupposes that he has identified his ideas and feelings with some degree of clarity and that he has been sufficiently motivated to do so. While the children are working primarily in their own spaces is a good time to introduce suggestions for quality work and to encourage each child to work as best he can. The better beginnings they can make, the more fun they will have doing more complex group work later on.

Many of the activities suggested for movement in self-space are suitable for doing at or beside the desk. At-the-desk activities may be desirable because of a lack of space in the classroom. Small space to be shared by a number of children makes drama activities more difficult, but not impossible, to plan. The children may need to work basically in the space around each seat. The teacher may have to divide the class into small groups, with only some of the children working in drama at a time. This is often the way children in open classrooms work best because there is much individualizing and self-selection of activities.

Movement activities at or beside seats are more easily controlled. Very active boys and girls may need the more confining space to help them develop their own responsibility in the use and sharing of space. Children who are not used to working cooperatively in large areas may be overwhelmed by it or have a hard time controlling their behaviors. Indeed, all movement activities from simple in-space movement to more involved group activities require both self-control and some kind of external control with which the teacher can quickly communicate with the children.

Movement Control

The use of space may be one way in which the teacher helps the children to control their behaviors during movement activities. In addition, she will want to develop some kind of signal with which she can get their attention, begin and end activities, and generally serve as a means for instant communication with the group. Some teachers use the light switch for such control, flicking it on and off to get total group attention. One advantage of the light control is that it is quiet and does not break into creative endeavors as much as some kinds of signals. A disadvantage is that it eliminates the use of the room lights for other purposes in drama—sensory effect and to heighten certain dramatic situations.

Holding up the arm or showing a "quiet" sign of some kind is also unobtrusive, but may not work when children are very deeply involved in their activity. A simple easy-to-remember signal with a rhythm instrument works well for most teachers and children. A couple of beats on a drum or a few shakes of a tambourine gets attention. If any actual drum or tambour (drum with head on one side only) is not available, a perfectly adequate one may be made from an empty coffee can that has a replaceable plastic lid. Because many movement activities also require a beat to which the children move, the use of the drum or tambourine to signal "stop," "quiet," and "attention, please" fits into

The tambourine signals the "animals" to stop and start. It also sets the rhythm for the animals' realization of each other and themselves.

the action in natural and consistent ways. For example, children moving to a variety of tempos may be signalled to stop with a rapid "one-two-three-freeze" beat. When the same signal is always used the control is not unusual or threatening. It becomes a familiar and well understood signal. Of course each teacher and group of children work out their own signal, and whatever works is suitable. When the signal is understood and agreed upon, it must be consistently used and respected. When the quiet signal is given, the action does not proceed until everyone is quiet. A teacher does not try to shout above the group, and few can do so if they try. Two requisites for successful drama experiences—concentration and involvement—cannot be optimally achieved in a chaotic situation.

Recognizing how children function best also helps to control the group so that opportunities for creative expression are maximized. When children are working hard mentally and emotionally, they also need plenty of opportunities to be physically active. Beginning the drama activities with active warm-up exercises or games contributes to group control. Relaxation exercises should also be built-in—periodically as needed by the group and always at the end of the drama experience. For motivation; to break down inhibitions and tensions; to build in times for sharing, reflection, and evaluation are other reasons for including both vigorous warm-up activities and relaxing quieting ones, but active physical work and relaxing activities are also valuable because they help children to develop and show self-control.

The following movement games illustrate the kind that work especially well as warm-up activities in creative dramatics. They are variations on familiar favorites which serve well to free children to think, feel, and do imaginatively and also allow them to expend energies in constructive and creative ways for better individual and group control. Because many games work best when the rules are followed, even the structure of the activities can be conducive to controlled behaviors.

Movement Games

Variations on Tag

Several variations on the old favorite game of tag make that format useful as a warm-up or beginning activity in creative dramatics. Tag always involves at least one "it" who must catch or "tag" another player. There can be rules about how the players or "it" moves: hopping, heel-toe stepping, skipping, double stepping, slow motion, and so forth. The game may be played using only one mode or several in combination. They are all useful variations to help children develop skill in controlling their movement.

Japanese Tag. The children all begin by finding their own self-spaces. One child is designated "it." When the beat starts, everyone moves. As soon as "it" tags another player, that person becomes "it" but must keep his hand on the spot where he was tagged. The next player does the same thing, and so on, to the end of the game. The players often take on remarkable shapes trying to keep the hand on the tagged spot and must be innovative in their movement to adjust to the new body shape.

"Taper Tom" Tag. This game is named for the folktale hero who carried the golden goose to which anyone who touched it stuck fast until there was a long parade of people following Tom and the goose. It begins the same way as Japanese Tag, but one person remains "it" throughout the game. Each person who is tagged comes along with "it," forming a train. Only "it" is allowed to tag another person, and each new addition goes to the end of the line.

Animal Tag. The players move as whatever animal "it" names. Each new "it" calls out a different animal. Any player whom "it" observes not moving as the animal named automatically becomes "it."

Races

Races done in a variety of ways can also be good beginning movement or warm-up activities. The rules are designed to incorporate creative movement into the races, for example, relay races done as animals. Children who fail to move like the animal named must go back and start again. This puts the emphasis on the creative movement rather than on speed. Children may also have races as other characters. For example, at Halloween, there may be relay races among cats, witches, goblins, and owls.

Other races may be done in slow motion, skipping, hopping on one foot, backwards, and so forth. Team races may be done with each member following the movement of the captain.

Follow-the-leader games

The old favorite game of "Follow the Leader" has many possibilities as a beginning activity in creative dramatics. Players line up behind the leader and follow him as he moves. All of the children try to do whatever the leader does. Pick an imaginative child to be the first leader to inspire the children to try some unusual things, such as playing musical instruments, swimming, skipping while eating an ice-cream cone, jumping rope, tossing a ball, or playing a yo-yo as they move to music. The teacher uses the class signal to signify when it is time to change leader. The person who has been leading then goes to the end of the line, and the next child up becomes the leader. To play until everyone has a turn is generally too long and physically tiring; the teacher and children can take note of who has not as yet had a turn as leader and let those children be at the beginning of the line the next time the game is played. Finding a lively, capricious piece of music to which to move helps to inspire interesting movement ideas.

The "follow-the-leader" format may be used around a theme. If the drama activities are part of a social studies lesson on American Indians, the children may try to show movements that are representative of things Indians did—scouting for game, using bow and arrow, paddling a canoe, grinding corn, and so forth. A piece of Indian music or drum beat makes a good rhythm accompaniment. A circus theme, sports and games, seasonal activities, anything that suggests a variety of actions may be used for follow-the-leader ideas.

Relaxation Ideas

As teacher and children develop experience in creative dramatics, original ideas for warm-up and relaxation exercises begin to flow very naturally from the materials, purposes, concepts, and themes around which the drama activities are developed. Some ideas that have worked for others can help to trigger original ideas in the beginner.

When children are actively thinking and feeling and doing, they can become very involved and very excited. The teacher will not only need to build in controls for communication purposes, she will also want to be able to help the children relax and quiet down at the end of the experiences. The children may also need short relaxing activities within the longer drama experience. Student teachers who may be working with "borrowed" children especially need to be able to get the group down psychologically before returning them to the classroom teacher.

Relaxation activities work best if their primary purpose does not seem too obvious and if they are an integrated and related part of the total experience. All of the following suggestions which have worked with children have been used in drama experiences in ways that related to a particular purposes and theme. (Note that in most of these the children are encouraged to create a physical tension before they begin to relax to increase the feeling of relaxation.)

Candles. The children become firm new candles. If appropriate to the theme, the candles may be a variety of shapes and sizes. The teacher lights the candles which burn brightly and then begin to melt slowly until they are pools of soft wax. The candles may have been on a birthday cake or perhaps lighting a royal banquet room, a pioneer cabin or an old-fashioned Christmas tree. To reinforce the feeling of quietness, the shades may be drawn or the lights turned out as the candles flicker out one by one. We have never seen a child who was frightened about being "lighted"—even nursery children have enjoyed this activity. However, an anxious child is not going to relax, and if a youngster is concerned about being lighted and burning down, he could be a candle in a sunny window who is slowly softened by the sun's warmth.

Flames. Each child is a bright energetic bonfire sending its flames toward the sky. Perhaps cavemen and women or Indians have built the campfires. The sound of the drum can suggest a shower, the lights go out, and rain falls gently on the fires. Soon they are sputtering out until each child is on the floor as the embers and ashes.

Snowmen. After some active movement involved with winter activities (perhaps based on Ezra Jack Keats' book *The Snowy Day*), little children enjoy becoming the snowmen and slowly melting to the ground. The song "Frosty the Snowman" and the short poem "The Snow Man" in Winifred Ward's *Stories to Dramatize* both lead into this quieting activity. Young children, even those who resist resting, delight in becoming mud puddles.

Balls, balloons, and other inflatables. Relaxation ideas involving these materials are appropriate for several age groups. Older children like to be balls used in sports, especially basketballs and footballs, that have developed slow leaks. They have all had experiences with balls that have gone soft. They know that this generally happens very slowly until the ball is totally deflated. Little children may also become balls, especially gaily colored beach balls, but they particularly like pretending that they are balloons. This is fun to be after working with stories like *The Red Balloon* and "Anthony Ant's First Flight" (see Appendix). Encourage the children to deflate slowly rather than pop. Side-coach that there is just a very little hole in the balloon, so small that it is impossible to see, or that the string that tied it shut is becoming undone. Some children may "pop" anyway—no matter, they still end up as a limp balloon. There should always be enough time allowed for actual relaxation to take place before quietly bringing them back to the here and now.

Rag dolls. Modern children still enjoy stories about Raggedy Ann

Creative dramatics is hard work. Relaxation is necessary but it can still be an exercise in imagination, originality, and individuality.

and Andy. Some may have favorite "rag" dolls and stuffed toys that
have fillings that may leak when there is a hole. Stuffing leaks out
slowly, so sufficient time should be allowed. The children enjoy having
the teacher check to see how flat they have become. This can be done
with appropriate sympathy as an arm or leg of "poor old dolly" is
gently lifted and limply falls back.

Sleeping or hibernating animals. Many drama activities are done
with animal stories. If the animals in the story have been involved in
very active and exciting adventures, they will surely need a nap at the
end of the experience. If the story involves animals who hibernate, each
child may find a special cave or nest and curl up for a long winter's nap.

Exhausted humans. Human characters may also need a good rest at
the end of the activity. Perhaps they have walked a very long way,
climbed a mountain, or been shipwrecked. All of these kinds of adventures make people very tired and in need of rest.

The teacher's use of sensory impressions and suggestions can be an
important part of the motivation for relaxation just as it is for stimulating movement. The use of appropriate music softly playing in the
background, dimmed light, and a soft pleasant use of the voice all help
to create an environment conducive to relaxation. It helps if the teacher
makes quiet suggestions about a special environment. Indians may drift
slowly downstream in a birch bark canoe while the teacher describes
the beauty and tranquility of the forest. Adventures that take place in
other times and places may include transportation there and back by a
silently gliding magic carpet. Astronauts may drift to earth inside their
spaceships, carefully suspended from giant parachutes. Nature stories
suggest pastoral music and shady places for resting, perhaps floating
down a stream as a hitchhiking insect on a leaf boat or a stowaway
aboard a huge milkweed puff.

Children may create their own special resting places to which they
always go at the end of a vigorous activity. Such places may be created
from recalled sense impressions of an actual place or experience, or the
children may create them totally with the imagination, incorporating
their own favorite colors, textures, sounds, and scents. The teacher may
invite a few children to describe their favorite resting places each time
until all have had the opportunity to do so. She may need to model this
for some of the low fantasizers by describing for them her mental
picture of an ideal resting place.

In all of the preceding relaxation ideas, recalled and imagined sensory
associations are used to elicit appropriate feelings and physical response. Once children are adequately relaxed both physically and emo-

tionally, they are ready to talk about what has happened, to evaluate and critique their own ideas, and to feel a sense of completeness about the experience. Getting children to relax in drama activities can be as important as getting them to move. Both are important to the quality of drama work; both can challenge the imagination and allow for the expression of individual ideas and feelings; and both can assist the children in developing the kind of self- and group control that is necessary for successful experiences.

Using the Larger Space

Getting children to move in a game of animal tag can be quite different from getting some children to feel free to move about as animals looking for food or trying to find a warm place to escape from a winter storm. In the first, the motivation comes from the competitive nature of a lively game of tag. The introduction of the concept of animal movement is probably only secondary to the challenge of pursuit and escape that is fundamental to the game. Elementary children are generally experienced game players, and they feel comfortable and adequate in that structure.

Participation in other kinds of creative movement activity must be motivated in different ways. When the emphasis is not on competition and winners and losers, but rather on the use of the imagination as it creates certain ideas and feelings which the child interprets and shows through his movement, other kinds of stimulation are necessary. Once children are working well in their own spaces and seem comfortable with movement which is not a part of a game or sport, they are ready to begin utilizing the larger space and sharing it cooperatively. When children first begin to move through the playing space, they continue to work best individually in parallel play. Though the group is working with the same general purposes, each child makes his own interpretations and finds his own ways to express his ideas and feelings.

The teacher may begin an activity in the small space and then enlarge the scope of the action. For example, children may begin by typing on a regular-sized typewriter within their own spaces. (Leroy Anderson's "Typewriter Song" makes an appropriate accompaniment.) The teacher may say a special word or cast a magic spell over their machines which causes them to become larger and larger until each machine almost touches those of the persons nearby. To continue the typing requires that each child enlarge his movements and utilize all of the space available to him. Another time each child may be a painter working at his own easel within his own space. The easel becomes larger and larger until there is one very large easel in the center of the space, and everyone is invited to paint on it. Witches may all stir the brew in their individual pots, and then all contribute to the preparation of a magic potion which is prepared in a large caldron in the center of the space. This technique also works well when the children are dramatizing *Stone Soup* by Marcia Brown. Each child may think of all of the things he can add to his own pot of soup before the scene where all of the people in the village bring their contributions of food to add to the communal pot.

The individualized playing in the self-space encourages each child's involvement and allows for the privacy which is important when children are constructing their own make-believe. Once the ideas begin to develop and the children become involved in the problem, extending the activity into the larger space is natural and comfortable for most.

Some children, particularly older ones, may feel self-conscious at first and need extra encouragement to get them to move into the larger space and still maintain a high level of concentration, involvement, and self-control. The following activity illustrates a successful method to help children move from self-space to the larger space without interrupting involvement. It is a favorite with children near St. Patrick's Day.

The playing begins with all of the "leprechauns" seated in a circle with each person's self-space on the perimeter. Each has a little Irish harp on his lap, and he can play with great dexterity—not only with the fingers but with elbows, nose, even toes. The fairy harps, full of magic, grow larger and larger until the children must move and reach and stretch to reach the strings. Each child is free to continue playing his small harp until he is ready for it to grow. The teacher then suggests that hidden among all of the harps is a pot of gold, and each person is to dance around and play any nearby harp to conceal what he is really doing. When someone "discovers" the pot, he continues to dance in and out, making his way back to his own spot in such a way that he does not reveal where he found the gold. When everyone has returned to his space, the group may share their ideas about the hidden treasure. An appropriate piece of music, particularly harp music, makes this activity more fun and stimulates movement.

There are many many ideas that can work equally well. The point is to present the children with a problem that can be solved only by moving cooperatively in the larger space. Most children are comfortable and eager to move about in the total space, but for those who are hesitant the teacher can help by structuring the activity in ways that encourage the shyer less confident children to get physically involved. If a child still prefers to sit and watch or to continue to work in self-space, he should be allowed to do so. Some children need to be able to

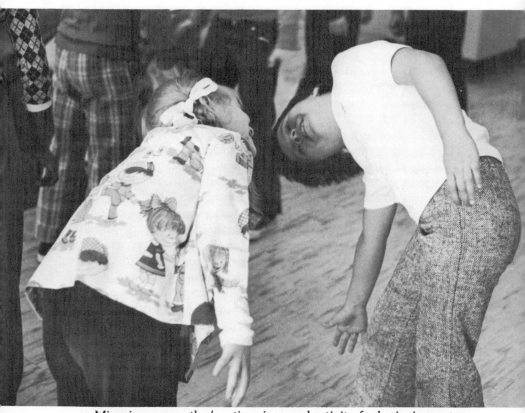

Mirroring one another's actions is a good activity for beginning partner work. Sometimes it is serious but at times it is playful.

participate vicariously at first, and they should never be made to feel inadequate for doing so.

Working in Pairs

At times children will need to work out their own ideas and feelings in parallel activity. However, if the drama is to add significantly to social development, they will need to be involved in cooperative work. The gregarious four year old wants companionship—someone nearby when he is playing. Nevertheless, though several preschoolers may share a sandbox, they may all continue to play quite individually, rarely interacting with one another. The first substantive interaction generally begins in games and make-believe play. The continued use of this kind of play in the classroom affords an opportunity for children to further develop the socialization process. In addition, to dramatize stories, whether from literature or based on the children's own ideas, requires interaction and the development of relationships.

Kindergartners, first graders and older children who are less socially mature than their peers need to learn how to work with others. A logical way to begin is to present ideas and design activities that can be done in pairs. Mirroring one another's actions and the palm-to-palm activity described in the section on Touching are a good beginning activity for partner work. The mirroring may be done with music as the stimulation, or the teacher may narrate a series of activities.

The teacher may begin by sharing Eleanor Farjeon's poem "The Sounds in the Morning," which ends with the lines:

> Till the sun through the slats
> Of my blind shoots his arrows,
> And the world of my ears
> Seems to dwindle in size
> As I jump out of bed
> To the world of my eyes.

In the preplay discussion the children may describe some of the activities they do in the morning as they prepare for the day—washing hands, face, neck, and ears; brushing teeth; combing hair; dressing; and having breakfast. Several of these preparations are often done in front of the mirror so the idea of doing this with a partner as your "reflection"

makes sense. After the discussion everyone finds a par
will have an opportunity both to lead and to follow. T
will be the first leader. The teacher then narrates a seque
based on the earlier discussion. Part way through the pl
are reversed and the play is continued. The children m
this same activity as characters other than self, perhaps as Cinderella
preparing for the ball, a knight putting on his armour, an Indian warrior
applying war paint, or a circus clown putting on his clown make-up and
costume. When the children are familiar with this "game," the teacher
will not need to narrate but only to make suggestions if some of the
initiators seem stumped for movement ideas.

Following the movements of the leader of the action requires concentration, control, and, above all, cooperation. There are many excellent
variations on the Mirror Game particularly for older boys and girls, in
Viola Spolin's *Improvisation for the Theatre*.[1]

Other pair work may grow out of a need for two people to work
cooperatively to accomplish a task. The teacher may narrate an experience in which there are several tasks that require more strength or hands
than an individual has.

The stories by Laura Ingalls Wilder about her own childhood are
enjoyable to children. Both *The Little House on the Prairie* and *Little
House in the Big Woods* have many scenes that are fun to dramatize.
Either may supply the motivation for children to pantomime the building of a pioneer home, which requires hard work and cooperation. In
the discussion the children will talk about the many tasks required to
build a "little house." Some of the work may be done individually,
even with parallel activity; other jobs, such as lifting heavy beams into
place, will require two people working together. The teacher can encourage this kind of cooperative work with a reminder that if a task is
too hard to do alone, find a partner and work it out together. The
children are not required to choose roles and develop characters, though
they may decide to do so. What they will need to decide is what each
will do so that between them they can complete their job.

Many kinds of tasks either require the efforts of two people or are
simply more fun when done with a partner. The following are several
suggestions to illustrate the kinds of activities that are good to do in
pairs:

1. Animals (beavers, birds, squirrels, etc.) building a home
2. Planting a garden
3. Doing the dishes
4. Giving a pet a bath
5. Building a large sand castle

6. Playing with a ball
7. Helping a friend cross a busy street
8. Helping a friend learning to skate
9. Cooking and baking
10. Reaching the cookie jar on the top shelf
11. Decorating the room for a party

Though the preceding may be done by children of all ages, the following are especially appropriate for older boys and girls:

1. Washing a car
2. Rescuing a kitten from a tree
3. Playing games such as tennis, ping-pong, shuffleboard, or horseshoes
4. Building a campfire or putting up a tent
5. Climbing a mountain or rappelling down a cliff
6. Rowing a boat and portaging it around the rapids
7. Boxing, fencing or swordfighting
8. Building a secret clubhouse or treehouse
9. Saving someone from a burning building or from drowning
10. Carrying heavy materials
11. Putting up a tall ladder
12. Piloting a spaceship
13. Exploring a cave
14. Selling and buying

Several of the activities in the sections dealing with sensory stimulation are also useful for work in pairs.

When children are working together, there is often spontaneous speech. This should be allowed as long as there is also action. Cooperative activity may also require conversation in the planning, and this should be encouraged. Talking over the experience with the partner at the end of the activity is also important, and time should be allowed for this kind of interaction as well.

Small-Group Movement and Pantomime Activities

Many of the activities for pairs can also be done by small groups of five or six. This is excellent for giving young children further opportunities to develop ways of working cooperatively and developing interaction and communication skills, but will not work until the children are ready. Some first and second graders are sufficiently mature to work in a group without the constant presence of the teacher; others are not.

They may continue to employ a great deal of parallel play even though they are physically grouped together as a unit. The teacher may divide a class of first graders into groups by category of role or activity. For example, in the playing of "The Three Little Pigs" there may be four groups; "big bad wolves," "first little pigs," "second little pigs," and "third little pigs," All of the children in each group play the role of that group, but each child will play in his own way. This kind of structure can introduce the children to the idea of working cooperatively in small groups even though in the actual playing each child works alone. The idea of sharing the role creates a feeling of "groupness" upon which later activities can be built. It also encourages the children to work cooperatively in the preplay discussion and in the discussion which follows.

Older boys and girls enjoy small-group work and may prefer to play that way. Being a part of a group can reduce feelings of self-consciousness and related anxieties. They are often more comfortable in this structure than in any other, and they enjoy the group interaction in the planning and working out of their ideas together. Working in small groups can encourage more sharing and brainstorming of ideas than might come from the whole class working as a unit. This is particularly true if the children do their own grouping so that they are with others with whom they feel comfortable. Sometimes, however, the teacher will want to divide the class by counting off or other techniques for random selection to encourage children to get to know and be able to work with peers other than special friends.

Particularly in beginning work, the children will look to the teacher for stimulation and guidance; as they gain experience, they will require less stimulation and organization by the teacher and will want to make more decisions for themselves. When the teacher has provided them with satisfying models, the children will be better prepared to discover their own motivational materials and develop their own ideas successfully later on.

The following illustrate the kind of simple easy-to-describe situations that suggest a problem to be solved by a small group working together. They should be presented in ways that stimulate the imagination and suggest action. Because small-group work is more often done with middle- and upper-elementary children, the following situations are geared to older interest levels:

1. Several children are skating on a pond. Though it is bitter cold, the ice is thin. One of the skaters breaks through the ice. The others must decide what to do.

2. A group of fishermen are trying to bring in a large net of fish. They are members of a village of people who depend upon fish for their main food. This is the best catch in a long time. They see a storm approaching.

3. A team of several spelunkers are exploring a cave. They arrive at a ledge. Far below them they discover a chest that is partially covered by an underground stream.

4. You are research scientists working in the laboratory. Something goes wrong during an experiment, and some people feel the building should be evacuated as quickly as possible. There are such noises in the room that you cannot communicate by talking.

5. Several shoppers board an elevator on the ninth floor. The car begins its descent when suddenly it stalls.

6. You are members of a wagon train. You are in the territory of unfriendly Indians when you come to a wide river to be forded.

7. You and several friends are playing in the alley. Suddenly a stranger runs past and hides in the doorway to your building.

8. You are members of a circus troupe. During the show in the main tent, there is a crash of thunder, and lighting strikes the Big Top.

9. You are launching a hot air balloon. Just before the last restraining rope is loosened a very strong wind catches the balloon.

10. You are dock workers unloading a cargo of animals for a zoo. One of the crates breaks open and a lion escapes.

The preceding situations offer children opportunities to develop skill in working together cooperatively in drama. Though the emphasis is on developing group work, some of the situations may be related to subject areas or concepts in curriculum. Additional ideas for small-group work are included in Chapters 3 and 6.

Dramatization of short stories and poems and development of scenes from longer stories and narratives are well done in small groups. The format allows an entire class to work simultaneously on a story or to divide the longer story into scenes, with each group working on a different scene. Individual input that can intensify each child's feeling of importance in the activity is encouraged. With a voice in the planning, it is easier to become more deeply involved. The communication of ideas is easier with only a few people. Younger children, particularly, are often intimidated by large groups and are less willing to try something new. Small groups give more children the opportunity to try a variety of roles as well as the courage to do so. Thus small-group work is conducive to more serious work in characterization. Within their group, the children often decide among themselves what parts they want to try and may experiment with a number of roles during repeated playings.

Dividing the class into small groups makes particularly good sense when dramatizing short stories. There are many excellent stories to dramatize which have five or six interesting roles to play; there are not nearly so many with 25 or 30 interesting roles. Working in small groups allows for multiple casting of the same scenes or several scenes from the same story so that many children have an opportunity to play the favorite characters. The use of pantomime has the additional advantage of allowing children to concentrate on the development of characters without having to supply dialogue. This is important in beginning work, particularly for the less verbal children.

Characterization

If learning in the classroom is to have real significance for humanity it must have an overriding concern with what it means to be human. Children have opportunities to become involved in a variety of human relationships through identification with the thoughts, ideas, feelings, and emotions of others. The portrayal of the human qualities of another is called characterization. Of all the ways in which creative drama can involve children in valuable learning experiences, characterization may be the most meaningful of all. Through the portrayal of many different characters, the child can experience for himself the vast complexities of being human. He may discover new insights about himself as he is encouraged to "try on" the self of another. As he seeks to become someone else, he must also clarify certain things about himself. In the development and playing out of a role, he may find facets of his own personality about which he was unsure or unaware and capacities and abilities he did not know he possessed. To become someone else, the child must decide how that person moves, thinks, speaks, and feels; and he must search for ways within himself to communicate those characteristics to others. In his exploration for the means with which to show his character, he must find ways to utilize his own physical, intellectual, and emotional resources.

In creative drama the process of characterization rather than the quality of the product (how well a character is portrayed technically and aesthetically) makes the experience valuable for children. Recall how the young child, in his own dramatic play, tries out the behaviors of significant people in his life. He "does" them as he perceives them, and in the doing the understanding most clearly takes place. He seems to know intuitively that this kind of identification is important to his own growth and development as a person and to the establishment of valid relationships with others. In the book *Speech and Man* Brown and Van Riper write, "Identification is a man's most significant imaginative act."[2] The make-believe play of young children supports this statement. Though their characterization appears to be imitative in nature (playing Mommy, Daddy, firemen), it is, in fact, more accurately described as being representative of behaviors they have discovered are characteristic of specific others. A further clarification of this aspect of the young child's play is discussed by John L. Phillips, Jr. in *The Origins of Intellect: Piaget's Theory.*[3]

Pantomime and characterization

The use of pantomime for the development of characterization allows children to concentrate on identification with the self of another and to express their perceptions nonverbally, free of anxieties about creating speech. To further reduce self-consciousness the children's first attempts should be with characters quite different from themselves. This is one good reason for beginning with animal characters, for most children can readily distinguish between animal behaviors and their own. Of course they can create such characters only out of their own human ideas and feelings; therefore, the characterization of animals, birds, insects, and other nonhuman things in nature will be each child's presentation of human qualities through animal movements and behaviors. It is not surprising to see ravenous lions nearly faint with hunger, frightened or sad puppies and kittens rub their tearful eyes with their "paws," and gorillas double up with laughter when they have startled a timid human in the jungle. Working with animal characters and other nonhuman roles can allow a child to express some of his own feelings, and he can dramatically portray meanness, silliness, stupidity, or cowardice in characters who are quite far removed from himself without the fear that others may relate those traits to him personally.

Children need to identify with their characters and to clarify their relationships with them. The teacher as guide can help them to do both. Indeed, the teacher's role in character development, as in other aspects of drama, is so important that it is valuable to examine it more closely.

The teacher's role in guiding characterization

When a child is able to imagine how another perceives through the senses and how those perceptions make the other think and feel and do, he is able to both internalize and externalize his character. Initially the children may need considerable guidance from the teacher to help them to imagine how it is to be someone other than oneself. This is particularly true for children who have not had continuing opportunities to engage in make-believe play since early childhood. The use of provocative questions can help them to think imaginatively about themselves, and sensory experiences to stimulate ideas, feelings, and physical response introduced through a series of questions can also direct their thinking in ways that help them to make discoveries about others. The following example illustrates a beginning experience in animal characterization using sensory stimulation and the inquiry approach.

The teacher has shared with the class the story of *Andy and the Lion* by James Daugherty which concludes with a scene at the circus. She then invites everyone to find a comfortable place where they can close their eyes and listen with their imaginations. She chooses a lively piece of circus music, perhaps the "March of the Gladiators" from *Merle Evans Directs the Ringling Brothers and Barnum and Bailey Circus Band* (Decca label). Before the music begins she makes the following suggestions: "Listen to the music and imagine that you are there under the Big Top. Think about what you might see and hear and smell. What do you like best at the circus? What are the most exciting acts, your favorite animals? Watch closely—what are they doing?"

After the children listen to a short selection of the music, the teacher may assume a role to heighten the intensity of the experience. With the voice and posture of a ringmaster she announces, "Ladies and gentlemen, boys and girls, we invite you to direct your attention to the center ring where you are about to witness the greatest lion act on earth." She may add whatever details and embellishments seem appropriate until she feels that she has provided sufficient stimulation and direction. The children remain listening to the music while they create their own scenes with their imaginations. The teacher must remain observant and sensitive to the children's level of involvement so that there is enough but not too much time allowed for them to create their own mental images. When there seems to be an optimal amount of involvement, the music is gradually tuned out, and the children open their eyes and share some of their ideas and feelings. They talk about what they have seen and heard.

Once again the teacher suggests that they close their eyes and remain in their places, but this time they listen to the music as lions, concentrating on being the lions in the circus act. She may direct their thinking about their lions by suggesting that they notice the size and shape of the lion, the suppleness of its body, the glossiness of its coat, and so forth. As she does this she speaks to the children as lions, and makes a subtle shift from directing the children's exploration of lions objectively to subjective involvement with their lions. Time should be allowed for this to happen before she suggests that the lions move about the circus ring, silently and majestically to the music. The children are encouraged through the side-coaching of the teacher to remain in their places until they are ready to move, first in their own spaces and then in the larger space. When there is generally good participation and movement, the teacher may help the children to a satisfying conclusion of that activity by describing how the lions finish the first part of their act by moving slowly about the ring, and with fine leaps, full of power and grace, freeze upon tall stools awaiting the trainer's further directions.

This approach allows children to create some real identification with the lion character. Some may be so eager to move that they find it difficult to remain in place with eyes closed for very long, but the side-coaching from the teacher can encourage the kind of fantasizing that helps most children to build some mental images and to become involved with them before they must move. When the activity is ended, the teacher may suggest that each child think for a short time about his lion, what was special about it and if he would be the same lion or a different lion another time. The activity may be played again, beginning with each lion leaping from the high stool, parading about the ring and moving back to the cage, but this time some of the lions may want to try their special tricks such as freezing on their hind legs or rolling over and over to the music. During the entire experience the play is parallel but with many opportunities for individual interpretations.

Boys and girls usually begin by playing animal characters on all fours; during repeated playings the teacher may suggest that they try moving as their lions but doing so by walking only on their feet. (She may remind them of how this was done by the cowardly lion in the film *The Wizard of Oz.*) The better a child can concentrate on his lion and the closer the identification with it, the easier it becomes for him to be a lion walking on his feet. The upright position is less tiring and prepares the players for easier interaction with others later on.

When there are repeated playings, each child is encouraged to define his character for himself more clearly. Again using the lion to illustrate, typical questions might be: Is your lion young or old? Is he terribly hungry and anxiously looking for food, or is he happy and contented because he just finished a fine meal? Most lions are very brave. Is your lion very brave and adventurous or perhaps a little timid and shy? Does your lion like being in the circus and doing tricks? The teacher's questions and supportive comments can help even the less imaginative or more timid children better to perceive and identify and express someone or something other than self. Indeed, all of the children can benefit from that kind of guidance and support.

The fact that the entire group is working on the same problem at the same time also helps. No one is required to solo, and each child may work in his own place and in his own way for as long as he feels it is necessary. The in-place work is tremendously important. Children who want to move immediately should be gently but strongly urged to concentrate on discovering as much as they can about how their character thinks, feels, and does before attempting to move. Practice in this kind of identification can give character work in drama real significance in helping children to develop understanding and empathy with others. This, rather than the development of "acting" techniques, is what the teacher hopes the children will achieve and she guides them accordingly.

Choosing Stories

The selection of appropriate literature also helps to guide and reinforce successful character development. In choosing stories for dramatization, whether with pantomime or with dialogue, the teacher will look for those with characters who can be clearly defined. Many stories are favorites to dramatize not only because of sufficient action, but also because children can easily distinguish what is unique about most of the characters and can therefore more adequately identify with them. This is true, for example, in "The Story of the Three Little Pigs." Each pig is different from the others in ways that can be physically expressed; each is clearly defined; and all have familiar qualities and characteristics. This makes all of the pigs fun to play and equally appealing—so much so, in fact, that all of the children will enjoy playing each pig, in unison, as the teacher tells the story. The same is true of many favorite tales which are enjoyed by older boys and girls. All of the wonderful characters in *Robin Hood* are excellent examples of well defined distinctive personalities who are exciting to portray.

Generally speaking, nursery and early-elementary children can more closely relate to characters whose ideas, traits, behaviors, and actions are familiar to them in real life, even when the characters are nonhuman. Each of the little pigs represents human characteristics with which young children are familiar—one pig is lazy, one likes to play and have fun, and one is very conscientious and hard-working (and perhaps not so much fun as number two). These are all personality traits and behaviors with which young children can relate, and they are fun to dramatize through pantomime because each pig has characteristics that can be portrayed with the whole body.

In selecting literature for character development using pantomime for older boys and girls, the teacher also looks for clearly defined, true-to-life characters who are involved in situations that have appeal for the players. They like to identify with characters who lead adventurous lives and do exciting things they would like to do. They are suspicious of anyone or anything too perfect, for in their more advanced wisdom they have learned that most creatures who have minds and wills of their own are neither all good nor all bad. Children of this age enjoy developing villains as well as heroes, particularly if the characters can be played with a great deal of action.

Perceptive teachers can help children play out some of their own desires, ideas, and feelings by introducing them to appropriate characters with whom to identify. The regular classroom teacher may be the best person to lead drama in the classroom because she has a greater opportunity to know the children and to use her special awareness of them as people. Her selection of motivational materials, particularly in the choice of literature for use in drama, can take into account the needs of the children in the group. A timid child who is encouraged to identify with a courageous character, and to play that role has also been encouraged to find ways within himself to portray courage. To suggest that he can play that role also suggests that the teacher is confident that the child has the capacity to show courage.

A beautiful example of this was a sensitive junior high teacher who encouraged a physically immature adolescent boy to play an aggressive domineering role in a group-developed pantomime based on a story introduced by the teacher. Some of the other children had been teasing this child about some of his mannerisms and calling him names— "Pansy" was one of the less cruel. This had gone on for a time, and the boy was beginning to accept the others' evaluation of him and began to adopt additional behaviors as a kind of self-fulfilling prophecy. The teacher also recognized that the child was becoming increasingly distressed by what was happening to him. With her support he accepted and developed the aggressive role in the story, played it very well and suprised both both himself and his peers with his portrayal. During the evaluation period, the other children talked about how well he had played the part, how believable he had been, and expressed admiration for his work. For the next several days, those who had worked with him on the pantomime continued to kid him about his "Bogart" role. It was a turning point for the boy and also for those who had given him a very bad time.

The best small-group pantomimes come when the children have already had ample opportunities to try many roles through parallel activities. The smaller group is a more comfortable situation for trying out roles and experimenting with them as each child seeks to translate his perceptions about a character in visible ways. It allows for more

Young minds and bodies are captured by the well-told story. Young listeners may become the heroine or villain or even the wicked witch.

interaction among the children, which can help to strengthen each characterization as the group determines the relationships among the characters in their story. The children may do the casting themselves, but the teacher may also encourage repeated playings with all of the children having a chance to try different roles and to work to more develop a role of their choice. Many children cannot be so free to experiment and try new things when they are part of a large group, and they particularly like to be able to experiment and improve something before sharing it with the teacher and with the rest of the class. And sooner or later, the groups will want to share what they have been working on and to see what others have been doing.

The role of audience

When a class has been working in small groups, freely experimenting and developing their own ideas, some of the children will want to share what they have been doing with others. Or when the teacher sees that children are sincerely involved in their work and seem confident and excited about what they are doing, she may ask if any or all of the groups would like to show their work to the rest of the class. She accepts each group's decision to share or not and helps them to feel that it is alright to decide either way. However, she may want to suggest that they work a bit more so that they can easily communicate their work to the others. She may then allow a stated amount of time for polishing. This is also a logical time to discuss the role of audience, and to discuss with the children the ways in which they can be good audiences for one another.

To be a good audience requires children to show respect by being quiet and attentive. Small-group pantomimes make excellent experiences for children to share with one another. The emphasis on showing rather than on oral communication requires attentive watching, and the activity is a quiet one. The teacher can help by providing a model who shows appreciation and after the presentation asks questions and makes commentary that can lead to constructive evaluation and encourage further development of the work. During the presentation, the teacher's attention and nonverbal approval can influence the children in the audience to give positive feedback. At the conclusion, her attention to the strengths rather than to the weaknesses can serve to direct the children in the audience to an awareness of what was well done and to help the players see how to use their strengths to improve the entire work.

Summary

For the young child, movement and pantomime are important modes of communication, related not only the child's lack of language development and socialized speech, but also to his internal physical and neurological processes. Pantomime with older boys and girls maintains and sharpens their abilities to communicate nonverbally and encourages self-expression without having to speak. Indeed, in early pantomime work any speech is accepted that comes naturally out of the child's internal identification with what he is creating. As the work progresses, the addition of dialogue in creative drama becomes natural, logical, and necessary for the child. As facilitator and guide in the creative process, the teacher provides stimulation through the selection and introduction of motivational materials that encourage physical response, through a sensitivity to the needs of the children so that she creates psychologically reinforcing environments, and by helping children to make identification with the various facets of themselves and with others through role-playing and characterization.

An equally important function of the teacher is to remain attuned to opportunities for encouraging and facilitating oral expression and to respond to them.

Your Turn

1. Develop a lesson plan for use with children of your special age interest which can be done using only the space at or beside the desk for movement and pantomime.
2. Expand on the lesson plan above and incorporate a parallel pantomime activity in which the children can utilize a larger amount of space.
3. Make an annotated bibliography of six poems and six stories that invite action. Design your list for a particular age group according to your special interests or include poems and stories for a variety of ages and designate the approximate interest level for each entry.
4. Find a short story and develop from it a sequential pantomime that tells the story. See "Columbus Discovers the New World" in Chapter 3 for format.
5. Find and read a short story with one main character with appropriate action for use with parallel pantomime. Lead a group of children (or your classmates) through the story as they pantomime the actions of the main character.
6. Find a longer story with one main character with appropriate

action for use with parallel pantomime. Based on the story, develop your own narrative to be used with children playing the main character in unison. Your narration will be told in your own words and is not limited to the activities described in the story but is consistent with the character and theme of the book. Hint: Folk heroes like Robin Hood, William Tell, John Henry, and Daniel Boone offer lots of possibilities.

7. Develop a card file of ideas for small-group pantomimes to use with children. On each card state the who, where, when, and what but leave the solution open to development by the children. Example: You are a group of coal miners working down deep in the mine. It is quitting time and you prepare to leave. One of the group who is leading the way looks back and notices that the timber supports are shifting. In your pantomime show who and where your are, what you are doing, and what happens to you. Create your own ending.

   For your idea file you may want to organize your ideas by theme, seasons, subject area or around certain concepts you desire to reinforce through an experiential activity.

8. In a group, write a cinquain poem that contains the nucleus of a dramatic event: character, action verbs that carry the movement, tension and resolution of conflict, and feelings. (a) Suggest ways to expand each part with children to develop a larger event or short story that can be pantomimed by children, (b) as a group, further develop your ideas contained in the cinquain into a very short story and show it to the rest of your class using pantomime. (See section on "Color," Chapter 3, for cinquain format.)

9. In groups of four or five begin with just a statement of conflict. Decide who you are, where, and when; pantomime your idea. Each group will work from the same conflict. Example: You are lost. Something unknown and mysterious is following you. You are caught in a severe storm. You are trapped. In the follow-up, discuss how the different scenes evolved from the individual ideas in each group.

10. Working in groups of three, explore your immediate environment and discover one sight, one sound, and one texture you can incorporate into a ministory to be shown through creative movement and pantomime.

11. Discuss as a class stereotypes versus unique interesting characterizations. Then begin with a simple character description such as "old man," "a musician," "an oak tree," "fire." Brainstorm all of the words you can think of that could further define each term.

12. Each student takes a generic term such as *man, woman, horse,*

storm, building and so forth. Each one then writes a short biographical paragraph that gives the general term a specific identity. You will want to consider such things as age, sex, size, personal history, personality traits, and anything else that is relevant. State the information briefly; do not elaborate. Divide the class into groups of three or four. Each group will exchange its descriptive paragraph with another group. Each group will create a ministory using only the character descriptions it received. Tell the stories aloud or show them through pantomime to the rest of the class.

5

Exploring with Words

Once speech has begun to appear with some ease and fluency, it can be developed. The possibilities of the dramatic approach for such development are almost limitless.

Arthur Wise

Research indicates that, particularly during the early years, oral language is foundational to the acquisition of the other communication processes. Freeing children to talk as part of the learning program is necessary to the development of both the speaking/listening processes and reading and writing. "The similarities between the spoken and the written word are in many ways the essence of new approaches to teaching the language arts in the elementary school and in even earlier years of schooling," report the authors of *New Horizons in the Language Arts.*[1] Creative dramatics offers many different ways for involving children in oral communication: (1) sharing their ideas and feelings in response to the sensory experiences provided to stimulate awareness and imaginative thinking, (2) providing sounds to enrich a teacher-told story, (3) building stories orally, (4) planning of small-group pantomimes through informal discussions, and (5) evaluating drama work through discussions by both the participants and the audience.

Contemporary research in psycholinguistics supports the premise that there is a relationship between physical activity and speech and

From *Communication in Speech.*

that the clarification of a role through pantomime before adding dialogue is invaluable.[2] The research validates the informal observations of drama specialists, classroom teachers, and speech specialists.

A theoretical basis that supports the use of creative drama with children rather than formal approaches that depend on scripts and memorized lines would also support the contention that children need many many opportunities to engage in a variety of verbalizing activities. This would include time to freely exchange ideas with their peers, particularly within the context of the learning situation; many occasions for informal discussion; both informal and formal reporting to the group; and the kinds of creative oral expression that are involved in storytelling, choral reading, and drama. Indeed, the approach through drama may involve several or all of these language activities, sometimes as the natural outgrowth of physical activity, but not limited to it.

The development of verbal ability from physical activity is only one way drama can be used to encourage speech. Any kind of problem-solving situation can be used, both those that involve identification with another, as in characterization, and a personal identification with the problem as is done in role-playing. In characterization a physical identification precedes the verbalizing; in role-playing there may be relatively little physical activity but a great deal of mental activity as the child explores a specific situation as though he himself were involved in it. Both kinds of experiences may be a part of creative drama, and both can lead to spontaneous and natural oral expression and the further development of oral language skills.

Role-Playing for Oral Language Development

Very young children do not attempt to characterize. The child remains central to his role: "*I'm* being the fireman. *I'm* putting on my boots and hat. *I'm* driving my fire engine" (accompanied by fire engine noises, and until he arrives at his fire, he is both fireman and fire engine). The two year old is more skilled at role-playing than at characterization, and he does not achieve real characterization—identification with another—until three or four.

In many dramatic activities the school child may also play himself involved in a variety of experiences. Teacher-narrated pantomimes in which the children explore a particular environment, mood, or situation may be played with the children being very much themselves. The values to be gained by children imagining exploring a special place such as a factory, the post office, a farm or zoo as themselves, can give children a sense of having personally been there. The same is true of

Very young children do not attempt to characterize. They remain central to their roles. They *are* the mouse or the storekeeper.

involving them in a variety of situations in which they try out through the imagination and physical participation the ideas, emotions, and activities that are a part of that situation. The following example describes this kind of teacher-led drama activity.

Let us assume that a class of children and their teacher are planning a field trip to a museum and that the teacher would like to give them a preview of the experience prior to the actual event. The children have been reading and studying all about prehistoric animals, and the trip to the museum will give them an opportunity to see a collection of bones and skeletons of prehistoric animals. The teacher may narrate their imaginary trip either by side-coaching or by playing the role of a museum guide. She will lead the class through a preplaying discussion about where they are going, what they may expect to see there, how people conduct themselves when they are guests in a museum, and perhaps some of the things that they may wish to do as a result of their trip. Drawings of prehistoric animals and pictures of reconstructed skeletons would give the class an additional sensory experience during the preplay preparation.

The teacher would begin the narrative by having everyone imagine that they have put on their outdoor clothes and are boarding the bus for the trip. They may pantomime these activities, and their desks or chairs may be the bus or they may set up chairs as bus seats in a special part of the room. The imaginary bus ride makes an interesting setting for the preplay discussion to continue. The teacher's excitement and enthusiasm about the trip can help to generate oral response and questions from the children. She may comment about what can be seen out of the window and may direct questions to the children. Questions and comments about the kind of day outside, the traffic, the problems of finding a parking space for the bus can all help to create a mood and atmosphere conducive to involvement and oral expression.

Once the children have arrived at the museum, the teacher may assume the role of the museum guide conducting the class on their tour. She naturally makes comments, asks questions and encourages the children to ask questions both of her and of their classmates and share their ideas and knowledge based on their prior reading and investigation. During the tour the children may actually move about in the room or remain in their seats; either way, the guide will encourage them to use their eyes, ears, and perhaps their sense of touch to explore and discover as much as possible. Questions about feelings are also important. A sample bit of the teacher's questions and comments which deal with ideas, knowledge, and feelings might be as follows:

"How do you feel standing next to the huge skeletons of the dinosaurs? Here is a particularly fierce looking one. Which one of the prehistoric animals we read about do you think he is? (Several answers can be correct.) Who recalls where he lived? What he ate? How do you suppose you would have felt if you had met him in person? Who has made another interesting discovery? Tell us about it."

When the tour is over and the group is back on the bus, the teacher may conclude the experience by playing the role of the bus driver who greets the children and briefly asks about the tour.

This kind of imaginary play can also be an exciting substitute for all of the real and personal experiences which are not possible. A third grade teacher once reported that her children became so involved in several imagined trips to parts of Africa over a period of several days that they continued to discuss the many things they had learned "when we went to Africa" for the rest of the school year.

All of the children work simultaneously but with each child as his unique self and with opportunities to express his own ideas, understanding, and feelings. There are also many situations in which the children work in pairs or small groups, with each unit developing the dialogue as themselves. In beginning oral work the pairs or groups may find appropriate places in which conversations may take place with or without physical activity. Once again the teacher will supply the initial motivation through shared sensory experiences, preplay discussion, and a description of the situation. Setting the scene, creating the atmosphere, describing the "problem" that is central to the individual conversations is always important.

To encourage optimal oral expression the situations and problems must be familiar and interesting to the children. Real-life situations and problems hold the most potential. The following are suggestions for use in pairs.

1. You have been invited to visit your friend's house on Saturday. You need directions, and your friend will need to describe the best route to take.
2. You are a newcomer at our school. You need directions to the library. Ask a classmate to tell you how to get there from your room.
3. You have tickets to sell for a special event. Your friend will want to know about the event and the tickets. One participant can be the seller and the other the potential buyer.
4. You are visiting a friend who is home recovering from an accident. You stop by after school. The shut-in has many questions about what is happening at school. You will try to catch him up on all of the news.

5. One of you has a favorite game you would like to play with a friend. The other has never played that game before. Describe how the game is played to the other person.
6. There is a piece of equipment in the room which one of you knows how to use. The other needs to use it. Decide what you will discuss (record player, pencil sharpener, tape recorder, slide projector perhaps). Without using the actual equipment, describe how it works.
7. You are shopping with a friend. You need to buy a present for a family birthday. You can't decide what to buy, and you ask your friend for advice.
8. You are collecting money to buy a going-away gift for a classmate who is moving to another town. You approach a classmate for a contribution.
9. One of you is new to our school. The other person is a reporter on the class paper. Interview the newcomer.
10. The two of you saw another child in your room appear to take something from the teacher's desk. Talk over what you should do.
11. Explain to another person how to care for the classroom pet.
12. After summer vacation, you and a friend talk about what you did that was the most fun.

Each child is himself or herself in a dyadic situation. The emphasis is on oral communication, but the addition of body movement could be useful. Several of the situations involve a problem to be solved and require little recollection of special information. The teacher will also know many kinds of experiences related to the environment, lifestyles, interests, and needs of her specific group of children.

Exchanging roles allows each child to be the primary initiator of questions or to be the primary respondent. The same or a similar situation or problem may be the focal point of the new conversation.

Some of the activities suggested for oral activities in pairs may also be used with small groups of children. The following can provide a focus for oral interaction for middle- and upper-elementary students.

1. A small group of children on a hike in a wilderness area is separated from the rest of the group. They need to make plans for survival.
2. Some friends walking home from school together are the only witnesses to an accident. They must decide what to do.
3. A group of children decides to form a club. They need to discuss the purpose of their club and the details of organization.
4. Some friends playing together in an abandoned house find a cache of money under a loose floor board and must decide what to do.

5. One of the children in a school club always wants to be the leader. The others have become annoyed and want to find a way to handle the problem. Discuss what might be done.
6. The school is planning a fair to raise money for some new equipment. There will be all kinds of booths, games, and entertainment. A group of friends meets to plan what they will do for the fair.

Generally the pairs or groups work simultaneously. This requires that the children have developed some self-responsibility in independent work. These kinds of activities and structures can give them further experiences for developing responsibility. The teacher will want to remain alert to what is happening in each unit and allow as much freedom as the children can handle. If some of them appear to have difficulties, she may visit that group in a role that complements the purpose of the conversation.

With younger boys and girls, the teacher may role-play similar kinds of situations with the entire class. Though she is working with the entire group at one time, she may relate to each one as though in a dyadic situation. For example, she may play the role of the next-door neighbor who comes to use the phone because hers is out of order. Each child plays the child at home alone who has been cautioned not to let anyone in the house while Mother takes care of an emergency. The "neighbor" speaks to each child on a one-to-one basis.

Other ideas for this kind of oral activity with young children are:

1. The teacher plays the stranger who offers a child a ride home from school.
2. Teacher is the salesperson at the ice-cream store where a child has come to buy a treat and must decide what to buy.
3. Teacher is the librarian in the school library. Each child has come to find a book. She discusses the kinds of stories rather than specific titles.
4. Teacher is the neighbor whose window was just broken by a baseball.
5. A child is lost and teacher plays the policeman on the street.
6. A child is home and Mother has an accident. The teacher is the telephone operator.
7. The children are Brownies or Cub Scouts (or some other organization appropriate to the group) selling tickets to a show. Teacher plays a neighbor at whose home they call.
8. Teacher is a visitor from another country who is visiting their school and is eager to find out all about it.
9. A child has a pet who has dug up the neighbor's flowers.

10. The teacher is a visitor from outer space whose ship has landed near a field where the children are playing games.
11. The seasons and holidays can present exciting possibilities for the teacher to play a role while talking with the children—a witch or goblin who came on the wrong day; a Pilgrim, Indian, or reluctant Thanksgiving turkey; the March wind; the first snowflake of winter or the first robin of spring; a Valentine the sender forgot to address.
12. Dialogue with the children may also be encouraged by the teacher talking with them as a character in a favorite story. Giving children an opportunity to visit with a storybook character can make reading more fun and books more personally meaningful.

The last activity may begin with only the teacher playing a role and the children playing themselves in the presence of the storybook character. This activity may lead very naturally into the children assuming roles of other characters in the story when it is read aloud.

Playing Roles with Language

Any adult who has ever read the story of *The Three Little Pigs* several times to the same audience knows what will happen when they get to "little pig, little pig, let me come in!" Such verbal exchange as that between the wolf and the little pigs is soon "known by heart" because of the repetition and dramatic quality. Short rhythmic passages like the "fie, fi, fo, fum" speeches of the Giant in *Jack and the Beanstalk* also baits the trap for involving children in dialogue as characters other than themselves. The characters and their language are so strong that young children can easily identify with them, even without physical involvement, and children enjoy helping with the storytelling by creating the voice and giving the familiar lines.

Stories that do not have this kind of dialogue appeal may suggest interesting sounds to make as a character in the story. Wind and rain, boats and trains—all kinds of things that blow, whistle, chug, or toot—offer possibilities for little boys and girls to share in the storytelling by adding the sounds of the elements or nonhuman characters. Animal stories and poems may also be shared in this way. For example, the children may supply the "mew, mew, mew" that concludes each verse of Vachael Lindsay's poem about the "proud mysterious cat." Before the poem begins, the teacher may suggest that all of the children can become the cat, and when she gives a signal, each cat can mew in its proudest most mysterious voice.

When the story is familiar, the teacher may also ask questions and make commentary to the children as characters in the story. This kind of interaction works best when the children have had an opportunity to build a character through pantomime and are involved with some physical activity of the character.

For example, let us imagine that the children are all playing the part of the peddler in the story *Caps for Sale.* Each child is pantomiming the peddler packing his bag of caps to take to the village to sell. The teacher may get the action started by side-coaching some of the things the peddler might do as he sets off through the woods carrying his burden of caps. She might then enter the scene as a number of potential buyers, asking first one child and then another about his caps. Are they made well? What styles, colors, and prices are they? The teacher's use of simple direct questions and descriptive commentary can help children to respond with brief direct answers that are appropriate to the character. This kind of dialogue must be kept short and simple so as not to distract from the characterization or stifle the child's involvement with the physical expression and activity. If the teacher tries to develop long segments of dialogue too soon, the child cannot maintain his involvement as he struggles to supply the language for ideas and emotions he has not really developed.

This kind of brief improvisation works best when the children are working with strong and well-defined characters who suggest plenty of things to do physically. During the follow-up discussion the teacher can reinforce all of the good things that were observed and emphasize how interesting and exciting it is to see the many different ways the children played the roles. When the children are working in parallel role development, the teacher has a unique opportunity to reinforce individuality and originality. Her interaction with individual children on a one-to-one basis during the parallel play can provide a structure that supports individuality and personal interpretation so that each child feels successful about his own work. Each child developing a separate character from his peers reduces imitative behavior and better prepares him for handling characterization with dialogue. From this kind of parallel work in which some dialogue is added to the pantomime, the children can comfortably and with some assurance of success, move into small group work.

Developing Dialogue in Small Groups

Repeated opportunities to create characters in parallel play means that all children can move into scene dramatization with experience in characterization. Their one-to-one interaction with the teacher has provided each child with a model for creating dialogue while playing a role. To move from single-character work done in unison to small groups of children who play a scene from a story with several characters who interact is the next logical step. To motivate oral expression every child must have an opportunity to participate in the scene *in a speaking role.* When children understand that everyone plays a role and will have opportunities to develop and play a variety of parts, the casting of a scene by each small group is simplified. Based on her observations and perceptions of the needs of each child, the teacher may make some initial suggestions; however, the children generally decide among themselves who will play each role the first time through.

Working in small groups allows for multiple casting of the same scene. This is important, for one scene often stands out as the one most exciting to play or is most conducive to the spontaneous development of dialogue. Every child may have an opportunity to participate in the favorite scene while preserving for each group the necessary autonomy for creative interpretation, individual input, and originality. The use of small groups also allows a class to develop several scenes from the same story simultaneously. However the play is organized, everyone is invited to participate.

Generally first playings are done for the benefit of the participants rather than planned for an audience. If the children understand this from the beginning the environment encourages natural spontaneous dialogue. This does not detract from the value of sharing later on; it simply keeps the relationship between process and product in proper perspective in terms of each child's growth and development as an expressive creative person. Despite the apparent chaos of initial improvisational work, it is often where the greatest individual creativity is expressed. If later presentations develop, they will probably be more polished, but they may also be more stilted with less participation from some of the children.

When children first begin to add dialogue, there is often either too much or very little, depending upon the age of the group, the kinds of characters they are playing, and their feelings of security about their characters and about the group. Some children may do all or most of the talking without a clear understanding of what and to whom they are trying to communicate. Some of the more verbal children may provide dialogue for their own characters and continually make suggestions about what others "should" be doing and saying. They often talk past one another. Such activity may be especially frustrating to the teacher who may see little relevance between the scene to be played and what seems to be happening. The apparent confusion may not bother the children, but those with a high sense of order or leadership may be

Puppets offer a vehicle through which the child can express his views and live out his fantasies. It's right in his reach.

disturbed by what they perceive to be a lack of initiative or direction on the part of others. When this happens, the group can play the scene through using only pantomime until the relationships among the characters become more clearly defined. Removing the need for dialogue for a brief time may allow everyone to become more comfortable and secure about what they are trying to do and say.

Repeated playings of scenes from literature which involve the development and portrayal of strong and interesting characters can lay a foundation for the development of stories and scenes created by the children from their own ideas. The teacher should not be surprised or distressed to see characters, dialogue, and plots generously borrowed from favorite stories, poems, movies, and television shows. These sources provide children with ways to begin, with ideas and models, and with a certain kind of security which comes from working with the tried and familiar. Recognizing how children use such sources, the teacher will want to provide them with ample exposure to well-written literature and well-rounded multidimensional characters that beg physical and verbal portrayal. In addition to the stories suggested throughout the text, an annotated listing of stories to use in creative drama is included in the Appendix.

As the children develop their roles and create dialogue, the portrayals may become a composite of the storybook characters and significant others in the children's own lives. A group of children will often continue a scene from a story in their own way so that an entirely new situation and set of characters evolve which are of their own creation. Such drama is generally marked by a high degree of involvement, well-defined characters, and spontaneous dialogue which is both appropriate and authentic. These behaviors indicate that the drama is indeed contributing to each child's growth and development as a thinking, feeling, creating, and achieving human being!

Puppets

Puppets are naturals as a delightful means for encouraging verbal interaction and communication with and among children. They can be especially useful with special children, particularly the mentally retarded and emotionally impaired and those with certain kinds of speech problems. Insecure and shy children gain confidence when a friendly puppet helps them with their oral communication, and they can feel more mature and self-confident because the puppet needs their special assistance. Anxieties about sharing ideas and feelings are reduced, and if the puppet makes a mistake, says something silly, or has ideas that are in conflict with others, it was the puppet speaking. Puppets can do and say things the child may be afraid to try and allow for a safe way for children to do considerable trying out.

Of course when we think of puppets we think of plays and puppet theatres, but they have other uses as well. When children are first getting involved with puppets, the teacher may find that their greatest value is in helping each child's self-expression. The teacher may also speak through a puppet to encourage free and comfortable interaction with a child. Being corrected by a puppet is not nearly so threatening as being corrected by the teacher. The teacher's puppet may conduct an oral spelling review or other language arts activity, showing disappointment when a wrong answer is given, a mistake in grammar is made, a word is mispronounced, and so on. It can empathize and sympathize with the child who is struggling for the right answer and be enthusiastic when the child succeeds. Children may use their puppets to give answers to math problems, in spelling and language lessons, and especially when reading aloud. Both the teacher and the child can help the puppet to correct his errors and to show improvement. They can help the puppet to overcome a bad day by showing it how to modify its behaviors and express more positive attitudes. After all, what can a puppet know without a helping friend or two?

If the class is working with puppets, it will also want to interact with one another through their puppets. Working in pairs, the children may role-play any number of interpersonal relationships. Many of the ideas suggested for verbalizing in pairs may be used with puppets. Children can use their puppets to help them develop stories and plays in small groups. Boys and girls who are reticent can gain experience and confidence by first working in puppetry.

Once children are enjoying work with puppets, they will want to develop and present puppet plays. They will need a special space where the puppeteers can remain behind in the scenes—at least most of the time. Puppet theatres can be extremely simple (a work table turned on the side in a corner of the room) or elaborately constructed with an act curtain and special lighting. The children can make their own from large cartons, adding whatever embellishments the group wishes. The construction of the threatre makes a good group project, and if large and sturdy enough, it can be used for other kinds of presentations as well.

Puppet plays should be kept short and simple, and only three to five children should participate in each one. Too many hands, arms, and bodies trying to function cooperatively in a small space can invite problems behind the scenes. Small groups also allow each child to make important contributions to the play. There are many excellent sources for ideas for puppet plays. They can be created from real-life experiences, including actual social problems with which the children are dealing in their own lives. Plays based on poems and short stories, or scenes from longer ones encourage improvised dialogue. If the children are using basal readers, the stories and characters can be brought to life through the puppets. The children can read aloud from the text, with the puppets providing additional motivation to read with clarity, fluency, and animation. With the puppet serving as an extension of the child's own vocal resources, he may find the courage to experiment with vocal range and rhythms. Children who speak with monopitch, insufficient volume, too much rapidity, and other common speech problems that are deviations within normal speech can be urged to develop a variety of voices and speech patterns for puppet characters and consequently work on breaking their own habits.

Working with simple hand or stick puppets offers young children work in small muscle control and coordination. Presenting and exiting a puppet at the right time also means keeping alert to what others are doing, being aware and responsive to all of the other puppeteers, and maintaining a high level of concentration. Cooperation is required, both in the planning and in the performance of the play.

Puppets offer exciting ways for integrating the arts, working with different materials and techniques, developing skills with equipment, creating stories and dialogue, and using music and songs. Sometimes they are introduced into the classroom as an art activity, and the initial involvement is with the construction of the puppets. Once created, children enjoy giving names and personalities to their puppets, and to incorporate them into a story idea gives them even greater value.

When puppets are constructed primarily to be used in oral communication activities and puppet plays, simple easy-to-make puppets are best. Marionettes are complicated to make and to use and may, therefore, depreciate their usefulness as children concentrate on the mechanics of making the puppets work. The following are some ways for making simple, easy-to-manipulate puppets.

Bag puppets can be made from a variety of sizes of brown bags. The size used for school lunches are just right for inserting a hand and using the fold between the bottom of the bag and the side as the mouth. The face is drawn or painted on the bottom of the bag; and buttons, felt, and colored yarn may be used for eyes, ears, and hair. Little children enjoy making these simple puppets to represent themselves, animals and pets, and other characters suggested by stories and poems. Older boys and girls often name their puppets after their heroes, and favorite sports and television personalities. They also love to create weird and "far out" characters. The older children may prefer working with larger bags, the kind groceries are packed in from the supermarket. They make fine puppets when stuffed with crushed paper and the open end twisted shut with a sufficient handle for easy gripping.

Rod puppets are made by fastening faces cut from cardboard or heavy construction paper to flat sticks (stir sticks for house paint are excellent), or ½-inch dowel rods with white glue. Gathered cloth can be used to cover the rod below the face to suggest clothing or fur, and the fabric covers the child's hand when the puppet is used. Styrofoam balls may also be used for heads for rod puppets, and round dowels may be inserted into the plastic. Colored paper or felt features and yarn hair are held in place with common pins. The plastic balls are more expensive than the cardboard, but they can be changed into new characters several times if the features are carefully pinned on and removed when making a change.

Wooden spoon puppets are interesting rod-type puppets. Faces are painted or glued on the backs of inexpensive wooden spoons and the handle is used for holding and moving. Rod and spoon puppets lack versatility of movement but are rugged and easy to handle.

Sock puppets made from knee sox or men's sox, are easy to make and to use. The hand and arm are inserted into the sock with the sole section covering the back of the hand and the leg of the sock drawn up over the arm. They are excellent for making snakes, worms, caterpillars, eels and fishes, and the heads and necks of giraffes and dinosaurs. They afford much flexibility of movement, and the knitted material allows for a variety of facial expression.

Mitt puppets may be made from oven or bath mitts or cut from a pattern and sewn. Like sock puppets, they are quite easy to make and use and are more permanent than paper bag puppets. Terry cloth, flannel, felt, and fake-fur materials all work well; they have sufficient body and do not fray so easily as some other materials.

Often these kind of puppets can be made and used the same day. However, older boys and girls, or the teacher, may want to try more elaborate puppets made from papier maché or the plaster-over-styrofoam method using the following procedures.

Initial materials: One styrofoam egg and a variety of styrofoam scraps, toothpicks, and one styrofoam dowel 1-½ by 2 inches, sandpaper, and a dull knife.

Procedure: Time required is two class periods of forty-five minutes each. Making the puppet heads is the most time consuming.

The styrofoam can be cut or pressed. (1) Depress the eye sockets; (2) Cut and attach nose; (3) Cut and attach the ears; (4) Cut and attach the mouth; (5) Shape cheeks, etc. During the second session the completed styrofoam head must be plastered. Because plaster hardens very quickly, have the students get in a line, and the teacher dips each puppet head in a bucket of plaster. Materials needed are plaster of paris, a large mixing bowl, paper towels, water, large bucket for dipping the puppet heads, spray paint or tempera, yarns or old wigs, scraps of materials. After each head dries the face is painted, and some kind of hair is constructed from yarn or pieces of wig.

Insert something into the bottom of the puppet head to hold it upright. A toilet paper roll will work well. The puppet is then ready to be dressed. If the heads are to be used for hand puppets, a simple pattern can be sewn by the children. The "body" section may also include arms made as part of the shirt or dress with felt hands fastened at the ends of short sleeves. This kind of head can also be used on string puppets.

Bailey Films offers two ten-minute films on puppet making. The films are in color and are geared for primary and intermediate boys and girls. *ABC of Puppet-Making—Part One* demonstrates the procedures for making and dressing very simple hand puppets; *ABC of Puppet-Making—Part Two* shows how to make puppet heads from picture wire and papier maché and how to hold and use the puppet.

The following stories and poems are suggested for puppet plays with early elementary children and are arranged in alphabetical order according to title. Many more stories and poems are equally suitable; this list is only representative of the kinds of stories and poems that work well with puppets.

Andy and the Lion, James Daughterty. Viking, 1966. Andy reads a book about lions and imagines an adventure with one similar to Androcles in the classic *Androcles and the Lion.* The book is divided into three parts which can be done as separate scenes. The last part is about Andy's visit to the circus. Lots of action and good chase scenes.

Ask Mr. Bear, Marjorie Flack. Macmillan, 1958. Involves several animal characters from whom Danny asks help when he can't decide what to give his mother for her birthday. The number of animals can be reduced or increased to accommodate the children's own ideas.

"Boa Constrictor," Shel Silverstein. *Oh, What Nonsense!* Viking, 1966. Short poem with a funny ending. Good for use with sock puppets.

"The Caterpillar," Christina Rossetti. *Sing-Song and Other Poems for Children,* Macmillan, 1924. A caterpillar is threatened by a toad and a bird before it becomes a butterfly. Further story ideas could be built from the poem. Also good for use with sock puppet.

Henny-Penny (English Fairy Tale). Another version of this cumulative tale is *Chicken-Licken.* Can use several animal puppets to tell this story. Ample space is needed if all of the characters are represented in the final parade.

Jack and the Beanstalk (English folk tale). Strong conflict and repetition makes this a favorite for dramatizing; telling with puppets would add new possibilities.

Little Red Riding Hood, Charles Perrault. There are several versions of this French fairy tale. The reference here is to the version in the Johnson, Sickles, and Sayers *Anthology* and ends with Riding Hood being devoured by the wolf. Children find this ending logical and do not seem distressed by the violence. However, a less violent and dramatic ending can be substituted. Characters can be done with hand and rod puppets.

Millions of Cats, Wanda Gag. Coward-McCann, 1928. A little old man goes in search of a cat for his wife and comes home with "hundreds of cats, thousands of cats, millions and billions and trillions of cats." Everyone's stick puppet cat can be used to create the crowd scene.

The Story of the Three Bears (English Fairy Tale). Hand or rod puppets to suggest the characters can be made by young children. The familiar story includes repetition and makes dialogue easy to improvise.

The Story of the Three Pigs (English Fairy Tale). Like "Three Bears," children like this exciting tale which has good conflict and an exciting ending. Characters would be suitable for hand or stick puppets.

Three Billy Goats Gruff (Norse folk tale). This story has strong characters to create with puppets. Cumulative tale has repetitive dialogue. Fun to create simple setting for this story.

Where the Wild Things Are, Maurice Sendak. Harper and Row, 1963 (also available in paperback from Scholastic Book Services). Max is sent to bed without his supper for acting like a "wild thing." He imagines sailing to where the wild things are and that he is made king of all wild things. Children can let their imaginations go in creating wild-thing puppets.

Your Turn

1. Select a story or poem on which you could base a creative dramatics activity (you need not further develop the drama activity but rather have in mind how you would proceed). Develop a number

of questions that could be used during the preplay preparation to stimulate involvement and engage the children in oral communication.

2. Begin a collection of provocative beginning lines that could be used to stimulate oral storybuilding.
3. Working from a set of three or four pictures you have collected to stimulate imaginative thinking, develop a series of questions related to each one that is designed to encourage verbalization. You may also do this with other kinds of sensory materials you have collected or created (sound tapes, environment boxes, touch boxes).
4. Make a card file of ideas that could be used with an age group of your choice to stimulate role-playing in pairs. Try for 10 stimulating ideas.
5. Find a story with which you can create several opportunities to interact orally with the children as the story is told.
6. Find a story for children to do as parallel pantomime and develop several questions you may use with them on a one-to-one basis as they work.
7. Write a short original story that provides opportunities for children to make sounds and add brief passages of dialogue as the story is shared. Keep in mind how bits of rhyme and repetition may be used in this way.
8. Find a story in which you could assume a role as the story is told and can use that role to engage children briefly in oral expression. Work in pairs and share a representative portion of the story with your partner. After each person has done the presentation, discuss and evaluate what happened from the point of view of the storyteller and the listener. Did this approach make the story more interesting? Was the listener more involved? Did the interaction increase or decrease the dramatic impact of the story?
9. Working from a basal reader, identify several scenes that could be done with puppets.
10. Using characters from a reading text or other literature being used in a classroom, create a list of questions that would help children develop ideas for original scenes utilizing the familiar characters. Such scenes might be dramatized by the children working in small groups or with puppets.
11. Make a bibliography of stories to dramatize which have the kinds of characters and conflicts that should encourage the development of improvised dialogue. Identify the most appropriate scenes to develop with language.
12. Create at least two simple puppet characters that could be used to

stimulate oral language with children at a grade level of your choice. You may wish to build a simple easy-to-use puppet stage as part of a larger project.

6

Drama in Curriculum

Creative drama offers to the teacher approaches that, using the materials and the environment already present, may engage students in experiences which prepare them for a world that is changing so rapidly that no one is certain what tomorrow may hold.

Charles R. Duke

"I hear and I forget. I see and I remember. I do and I understand." These observations were made by the writers of the Nuffield Mathematics Project.[1] Children come to school to gain understanding, and learning for understanding is to be achieved through a program of study educators call "the curriculum." A great deal of time, money, and professional expertise is devoted to developing a curriculum that may or may not result in children learning with understanding. How a program is implemented in the classroom is what gives it value.

Recognizing this, creative teachers are always searching for ways to breathe life into the program of study so that it comes alive for children, reaches out to them; captures their minds, bodies, and emotions in ways that generate the kind of involvement that leads to understanding. Drama means doing, and when it is integrated into the curriculum, it can provide one way to involve children in experiences that foster understanding. The use of drama in curriculum also means that no teacher need bemoan a lack of time to "do all of those beautiful,

From: *Creative Dramatics and English Teaching.*

innovative, fun things with children because there is no time to do both 'the curriculum' and creative activities as well." Through the preceding sections are examples and suggestions of ways to develop creative dramatics in the elementary classroom; many of the activities are also related to subject areas and concept development and are most relevant when integrated into curriculum.

Once children and teachers discover how naturally exciting learning through drama can be, the possibilities are almost unlimited. The suggestions, examples, and illustrations described in this text are only the "aperitif" intended to sharpen the appetites of those who have enjoyed a taste through experiences described here. As an additional stimulus for integrating drama into the curriculum, the following suggestions are arranged by subject area. Again, these are not intended to cover all of the ways drama may be used in curriculum but are representative of what has been done that works!

Language Arts

Creative dramatics depends on the integration of the language processes, most especially speaking, listening, and reading, and, to a somewhat lesser extent, writing. The best of contemporary research indicates that integration is the way in which children best learn the language arts. The National Council of Teachers of English has reported: "Mastery of the arts of communication occurs in situations in which several or all of the phases of language are present. For this reason, the curriculum in the language arts should be so organized as to provide experiences which involve all facets of language in their normal relationships."[2] Educators whose field of expertise is the teaching of reading concur. "The relationship of reading to the other language arts—oral language, literature, spelling, writing—is especially close, and these several phases of language must be organized as an integrated, mutually facilitating, program," states Henry B. Nelson, editor of *Reading in the Elementary School*.[3]

In their drama children use their communication skills and gain additional practice with them to improve those skills. The listening activities suggested in Chapter 3 are not only useful for stimulating drama activities, but also give children experiences and practice in developing the listening process. Oral storybuilding, storytelling, role-playing, and the development of dialogue in drama give children practice in developing speech in ways that are relevant to their oral language needs in everyday life. The many verbal activities that are a part of drama can be used to aid language acquisition and growth. Children involved in drama are introduced to new words and can use their enriched and expanded vocabulary in simulated real-life situations so that the meaning of language can be more easily assimilated. The exploration of literature, particularly the best of children's literature, is necessary and important to the development of creative drama. To dramatize a poem or story requires children to internalize the meaning of the literature and to make the literary and human ideas, concepts, and values presented in the literature meaningful to themselves.

Many of the ideas used for oral storybuilding can be used with equal success in stimulating creative writing. As children work to develop their ideas into original stories to dramatize, they continually reinforce an understanding of the components of a story. The development of interesting characters engaged in the resolution of some kind of conflict which results in a climax and ending which gives the drama a plot is the same kind of structure used to develop a written story.

Several of the movement activities involve the kind of physical coordination required for reading, and those activities have a value in the preschool and early elementary grades as a part of the reading-readiness preparation. Mirroring and shadow activities, creative movement games, and pantomime may require hand-eye coordination and large- and small-muscle control. In addition to the activities that have been more fully described elsewhere in the text, the following creative drama activities may be used in some special concept or skill development in the language arts.

Moving as verbs. The children may pantomime the action suggested by the verb to reinforce meaning and to better understand the function of verbs in the language. More specialized learning about verbs may also be done with pantomime. For example the leader presents a short sentence to the class in which the verb is in either the active or passive voice. If the verb is active, the children pantomime an action suggested by the meaning of the verb; if the verb voice is passive, everyone freezes. Children who move when the verb is passive are "caught" and must make up a new sentence in which the passive voice of the verb is used. Children working in pairs can do similar activity with transitive and intransitive verbs. If the verb is transitive, one child pantomimes the action of the verb and the other becomes the direct object. If the verb is intransitive, both children do the verb action.

Adding adverbs. This is fun to do as an add-on pantomime. One child begins by presenting an action, perhaps skipping. When another child thinks of an adverb that could be used to modify the verb *skipping,* he pantomimes the verb as modified. As many children as can supply additional adverbs that could reasonably modify the verb may add on. When there are no more additions, someone who has not participated in the pantomime and who thinks he can identify the verb and all of the modifiers, writes the answer on the board. If it is correct, he may pantomime the next verb.

Spelling. Young children may enjoy practicing spelling words by printing the letters in the air with various body parts—fingers, hands, elbows, feet, and legs. A group of children may form the letters of a word with their bodies. When they have spelled the word as they think it should be, the group freezes in order.

Pantomime may be used to give a silent spelling quiz. The first child pulls a word from the spelling list from a hat and pantomimes an activity that suggests the word. The other children each write down the word on their spelling papers. Children volunteer to do the pantomime, and over a period of repeated practice, all of the children should have an opportunity to present a word. The words on the quiz are numbered, and when a child has shown a word, he puts a star opposite that number rather than the word.

New vocabulary words. "Living Dictionary" is a good name for this game. The class is divided into several small groups of three or four. Each group, in turn, is given a new vocabulary word—perhaps taken from reading, science, mathematics, or social studies. Each group looks up their word in the dictionary. Before each group pantomimes its word, the word is written on the board. The observers discuss in their small groups what they think the word means. The first group to arrive at a consensus of meaning reports. The "showing" group then confirms the meaning or looks to another group for the correct answer. If no group gives a correct response, the demonstrating group tells the meaning to the rest of the class.

Antonym and homonym games. The children work in pairs or small groups. Half of each pair is presented with a word that has an antonym. The partner guesses the word. If it is correct, that child is allowed to pantomime the antonym. If the class is divided into small groups, the first group is given a word to pantomime that has an antonym. The first group of observers who think they know the word, pantomimes its antonym. If they are correct, they begin the next round; if not, another group may respond with their pantomime.

A similar game may be played with homonyms. The class is divided into small groups. The first group is given a word that has one or more homonyms (words which are pronounced the same but have different meanings, origins, and usually different spellings). The demonstration group pantomimes one meaning of the word. When another group thinks that it has a homonym, they pantomime their word. If the homonym(s) is spelled differently, each group will give the correct spelling of their word after it has been identified.

Science

The use of creative dramatics can create experiential activities to stimulate involvement, interest, and understanding in the various branches of science. Teacher-narrated pantomime experiences can give children opportunities to "visit" and "explore" through their imaginations and with the use of pantomime a number of environments related to science areas and concepts—farms, marshes and ponds, lakes and streams, forests, power plants, an aerospace center, and so forth.

Children are always interested in growth, and demonstrating life cycles of living things is fun. Growing from a baby to maturity (perhaps as animals or insects, especially those which dramatically change form such as caterpillars, larvae, and tadpoles) is exciting to do. The doing reinforces both understanding and remembering. Sequential pantomime games may be used in this way to show growth, change, and development as something lives, grows and matures, becomes old, and dies.

There are several excellent books and stores about ecology and preservation of the environment which are fun to dramatize. Little children enjoy *Litterbugs Come in Every Size* by Charles Bracke and *The Wump World* by Bill Peet; older children may create their own problem-solving improvisations based on Rachael Carson's *The Silent Spring*.

Energy has become an important concern of contemporary society both in terms of the environment and the availability of necessary energy to support our needs. Children need to know about energy as part of the physical sciences, the ecology, and its importance to society. Sources of energy and different kinds of energy production may be demonstrated through movement and pantomime. Energy problems may be demonstrated through group pantomimes and improvisations.

Dramatizing stories about the behaviors and habits of animals, insects, and other nonhuman living things such as the planting and care of plants may all be integrated into the elementary science program.

The use of creative movement and pantomime can also be used to demonstrate other science concepts: kinds and uses of magnets, properties of materials (showing through pantomime whether a material is heavy, light, hard, soft, flexible, rigid, and so forth), mirror and shadow games that show science concepts such as reflectional symmetry, demonstrating relationships and grouping according to similar properties or function, demonstrating velocity and rhythm—fast, slow, regular, or erratic movement.

Children may also become interested in the lives of scientists and inventors and enjoy dramatizing significant events from their lives. Stories about Louis Pasteur, George Washington Carver, Madame Marie Curie, Isaac Newton, Benjamin Franklin, Thomas A. Edison, Dr. Jonas Salk, and many others all have those moments of great discovery which are exciting to dramatize. Correct scientific procedures including research and laboratory procedures and techniques can be pantomimed.

Since science and drama are both involved with exploration, invention, and discovery, they are natural allies. Whether it is little children dramatizing a thunderstorm or older ones demonstrating a rather sophisticated scientic procedure through pantomime, science concepts can supply a wide range of ideas for drama.

Social Studies

Next to the language arts, there are probably more ways to integrate drama into social studies than into any one other curricular area. Dramatizing stories related to history, including actual historical events, is always an excellent source of materials for pantomimes and other forms of improvisational drama. The two sequential pantomime games included in the text as examples are based on historical events. Sequential pantomime and listening games make excellent ways to introduce and review all kinds of materials, but especially historical events since both the game format and the subject matter are concerned with an ordering of things.

Children love the idea of going back in time (time machines, time tunnels, magic potions—the group may get there through whatever fantasy device interests them). They also like to "visit" other places and peoples and dramatize events from their history or show aspects of their culture such as occupations, lifestyles, traditions, and customs. Getting there can be part of the fun, and the mode of transportation can be related to the people and culture (camel trains, reed rafts, dug-out canoes, perhaps) or can be a creation of the imagination such as riding the jet stream or a super-sized magic carpet with room for everyone.

Pantomiming a variety of occupations may be part of the social studies curriculum for both young children and upper elementary boys and girls. For the little ones, pantomiming a variety of work activities helps them to identify the duties and responsibilities associated with them; older boys and girls may do role-playing as a part of the career-education program. They may also enjoy dramatizing stories that show people engaged in various occupations.

Planning and evaluation in the social sciences can involve students as much as a storybook. Studies of society encourage discussion and openness.

The behavioral sciences are introduced at the elementary level in several ways but particularly through those concepts that deal with human relationships. The whole process of identification with another through characterization previously discussed can make important contributions to growth in understanding about self and others. Several of the verbal activities suggest ways to solve human problems through role-playing in pairs and small groups. Cooperation, friendship, kindness, compassion, generosity, brotherhood, self-worth, truthfulness, democracy, interdependence, freedom, privacy, courtesy, and forgiveness are some of the concepts teachers wish to reinforce. They are all suitable for exploring through drama, both through role-playing and characterization. The children may create their own situations around human problems to be resolved, and there are many fine stories to dramatize that illustrate these and similar concepts.

Mathematics

Some children have difficulties using mathematic facts and concepts, though they can correctly work their math problems. The application of math in real-life situations is important. Many story problems are suitable for dramatizing and allow children to see how math is used. Buying and selling situations, planning enough food for a party or picnic, serving a giant birthday cake to the class, deciding how many days it will take for the wagon train or space ship to arrive at its destination if it travels so many miles per day are situations that might be dramatized and which require the application of specific math skills. Counting games and songs can also be dramatized, and movement and pantomime activities may be used to involve children in learning geometric shapes, number sequencing, and working with sets and subsets. Mathematics, like language, deals with symbols and abstract ideas.

Whenever children can make relationships between the abstract and the concrete through a subjective experience, the more understanding is possible so that learning has meaning and can be assimilated and utilized in real life. It is exciting that this translation and application from the abstract to the real can often be assisted and reinforced through the use of make-believe and "let's pretend." It can happen in any classroom through the use of creative dramatics.

An Integrated Arts Activity

The following is a sample creative drama lesson for upper-elementary and middle-school children which draws upon other art forms such as working with clay, form and line, colors and painting. The lesson can also incorporate music to accompany movement and pantomime activities and may conclude with both real art work and descriptive writing.

The idea of an art display can be introduced by a visit to an art gallery or an outdoor art show where children can have real and personal experiences with a variety of art and craft displays. If such an experience is not possible, the teacher may bring a variety of art and craft items to be examined by the children. Original paintings or prints, pieces of pottery, tapestries, copper work, and wood carvings would give a variety of sensory experiences. The poem "Art Fair in the Park" (see Appendix) could be used to stimulate ideas and imaginative thinking through the sensory experiences suggested.

The drama activities would begin with simple, in-place art work done in unison with each child working independently in his own space. This is followed with work in pairs, and finally with some small-group pantomimes. The emphasis in these activities is on the nonverbal expression through movement and pantomime rather than on characterization.

Parallel activities

After the motivational materials have been introduced and discussed, the children begin with parallel activities (weaving, carving, and other arts and crafts may be easily substituted for those suggested here).

Working with imaginary clay, each student in his own space, mixes and molds something of his own design from clay. The teacher may move quietly among the artisans chatting briefly with them about their work.

Each student, in his own space, creates a scene to paint. "Imagine your own outdoor scene—landscape, seascape, mountains, skyline of city or country—create it in your mind with colors, textures, shapes, and perspectives. Decide what part of your scene you wish to paint. Set up your easel, get comfortable, and begin to paint." For continued stimulation, accompany this activity with soft background music such as the theme from "Elvira Madigan" played by the Mantovani orchestra (London label).

Activities for pairs

Sculptors and Statues. Choose a partner. One person from each team will be the sculptor and one the material to be made into a statue. Each artist will decide how he wants to use his material and, working carefully, arranges his partner into a statue. Some children may prefer to create abstract pieces with the emphasis on form and line; other will want to create a specific character such as a soldier, ballerina, an animal statue, or famous character from real life or literature. Tell the class how long they will have to complete their work. On a signal the statues will be considered completed and will "freeze." Since some of the poses will be difficult to maintain for long, allow just a short time for the sculptors to look about and see the other statues. "On the stroke of midnight" the statues will come to life and briefly move while maintaining their basic forms. Roles may be reversed and the activity repeated.

After the first statues are completed and while they are "frozen," the sculptors will move among them. Each sculptor will choose a statue made by another artist and assume a mirror image of that statue. On signal, all of the statues will come to life. The mirror pairs move, first in place, then about the space together. This activity may also be done to music. A selection from "Pictures at an Exhibition" would complement the theme.

Statues and sculptors may again reverse roles, but with the new partners with whom they have been mirroring.

Small-group pantomimes

The class is divided into four or five small groups. Designate an open space on the floor as the work space. Allow groups a brief planning time to coordinate each part of the activity.

Group I: Build an imaginary frame using the work space well. As a group, carry a large roll of canvas to the work space and stretch and tack the canvas to the frame.

Group II: With buckets and brushes, size the piece of canvas in preparation for painting.

Group III: Working as a group, paint a picture on the canvas. Use all of your space.

Group IV: Within the frame area, create a "living picture," using the space in an interesting way. When everyone is in position, freeze to a count of ten.

Group V: (optional, depending on size of class) You are a group of art critics. Look at the painting and pantomime how you evaluate the work.

Or, when the picture is complete, all of the previous workers observe the finished painting. Show with faces and body posture how they feel about the painting.

As a follow-up activity, each student will write a short descriptive

Group imagination and perceptions come to life as pantomime machines begin to work. Perhaps they offer a means of silent communication.

paragraph telling his individual perceptions of the picture. Include the imagined colors, shapes, perspectives, and subject matter. Give the picture you perceived a title. Share your perceptions.

Other writing activities based on the picture might include developing a story from your perceived picture, writing a poem or song. In addition, real art experiences would follow these imaginary ones, perhaps in preparation for a class art fair.

Your Turn

1. Design a unit plan for some area in curriculum for a period of time each day for one week. Your entire unit need not be thoroughly developed but should include an overview with goals and objectives for the unit and more detailed development of the drama activities. See how many ways you can integrate creative drama activities into your unit both to "teach" and to enrich the total experience.

2. Choose a concept that is appropriate to a designated grade level. Develop three drama activities that could be used to teach this concept. (Your concept may be related to a subject area—democracy as it might relate to social studies—or it might be a concept that is related to self-identify, behaviors and attitudes—kindness, for example.)

3. Begin a creative drama activities file for use in the major areas of curriculum. You will want to include titles of stories to dramatize that relate to a subject area, poems and work cards that suggest drama activities for working independently or in small groups.

Storytelling with Young Children

The role of the storyteller is of such value in the development of creative drama with any age group that the adult who intends to integrate drama into any educational program will want to develop his or her own abilities as a storyteller. The well-chosen and superbly told story, whether from literature, created by the teller, or developed as a shared experience with the children can be a delightful and exciting experience for everyone involved. Some excellent helps are available, and a short bibliography of books and articles to aid and encourage the novice storyteller is included in the Appendix. The following brief guidelines can get anyone started, but the real pleasure is in the sharing. Storytelling, like any creative art form, requires both preparation and practice and happily eager young listeners are always available.

The sharing of real and imagined wishes, dreams, experiences, ideas and feelings should begin with the infant and continue throughout a child's education. People of all ages enjoy a well-told story, and it is unfortunate that the oral sharing of stories is often discontinued beyond the middle school years. No matter how well the older child reads, a story that is shared aloud with the group is special. Oral storytelling with the preschool and elementary child is of such value that its use is of paramount importance (1) to assist in the acquisition and development of language, including the development of an appreciation for language; (2) to stimulate and enrich each child's imagination, including the ability to use the imagination for problem-solving and pleasure; (3) to create commonalities of interest among children and with adults; (4) to share with children the experiences, thoughts, and feelings of others, particularly as these span cultures and periods in history; (5) to stimulate interest in the language processes—speaking, listening, writing, and reading; and (6) to acquaint children with good books, stories, and poems of human and literary value.

Choosing the story material

In selecting story material for a specific time, place, and set of listeners, it is generally necessary to identify the purpose or purposes for which the story is to be told. Our particular concern here is to present stories to stimulate the imagination and to foster dramatic play in preschool and elementary children. All material to be used for storytelling should meet the children's interest level and be of an appropriate length. Little boys and girls have short attention spans, and some stories may need editing to hold the attention of the listeners. Young children like stories about characters and events with which they can identify, but they also like their world to be expanded. If they are not challenged to deal with new concepts, feelings, places, peoples, and situations, how can their imaginations be truly stimulated?

Shared stories offer the parent or teacher an excellent opportunity to present positive values. Stories that present people of other races, cultures, and social status in constructive and accurate ways foster respect, understanding, and admiration for humanity in its beautiful diversity. The same is true of stories that break down sex-role stereotyping; both boys and girls need to hear stories in which girls and women are problem-solvers and do exciting things and stories in which boys and men show qualities of gentleness and compassion. Children of all ages love animal tales and can learn concern for all of the nonhuman in nature from well-selected stories. The positive values presented are particularly enhanced when the stories can lead into dramatic play.

Early childhood is the time when repetition, rhythm, alliteration, and rhyme are especially enjoyed, and stories and poems that utilize such conventions invite children to join in the storytelling and can be useful when adding language to any make-believe play stimulated by the story. In addition, materials for stimulating make-believe with young children should have a simple plot and a distinct climax with sufficient conflict to create action. Though nursery-aged children seldom act out their make-believe with any regard for the beginning, middle, climax, ending sequence, they are sensitive to what constitutes the dramatic. The instances of conflict often trigger the imagination and become the basis for the dramatic play.

The many delightful picture books with colorful and appealing illustrations can be used to tempt the young child's imagination. However, the continuity of the story should not be broken to show illustrations unless the pictures are large and clear enough to be seen easily by all. It is also not necessary to show all accompanying illustrations, even in a picture book, when the emphasis is on the storytelling. If the storyteller is sharing an original story or recreating a personal experience in story form, a few appropriate pictures may heighten the involvement or help to "set the stage." But a suitably chosen story of good quality well told, does not rely on illustrations, but on the mental images created in each child's mind. The teller of the tale may decide that pictures may limit the imaginative response in the listeners and not show them at all or save them for a quieting activity later on.

Preschoolers and kindergartners like stories about animals, children like themselves, and other real-life characters to which they can relate from their own experiences. They are still learning about their own world, and their abilities to abstract from it are limited and immature. But first and second graders love stories that are pure fantasy. Six and seven are the years when stories about fairies, elves, witches, and goblins are most enjoyed. Most early-elementary youngsters have an active fantasy life and rich imaginations with which they can participate in the adventures of purely imaginary characters, places, and situations.

Middle- and upper-elementary children have expanded mobility and broader horizons. They like to imagine themselves involved in exciting escapades and delight in stories about real and fictional characters who solve challenging problems and lead adventurous lives. Boys and girls of this age enjoy the exploits of characters who do things on a grand scale: folk heroes, explorers, knights and warriors, and boys and girls of their own age who overcome obstacles, outwit villains, and do all of the exciting things they imagine themselves doing in their fantasies. Stories about other lands and peoples are also good choices for these children who are developing increased social consciousness and more global interests.

Telling the story

The storyteller may read a story aloud just as it appears in literature, paraphrase a story from its written source, tell about one's own experience in either the first or third person, or create an original story.

Particularly for the beginning storyteller, one method may not be superior to the others. A story that is well read from the manuscript is certainly preferable to a poorly told story, and an exciting personal experience is more rewarding for the listeners than a dull or inappropriate selection from literature. In choosing the most rewarding and suitable method, the storyteller will want to examine several variables—the content of the materials and resources available in terms of the storyteller's objectives, the way in which the ideas are presented, the length of the story, the storyteller's abilities, and the maturity and interests of the listeners. All of the methods may allow the storyteller to model an ability to think and use language imaginatively and to use the story to stimulate the imaginations of the listeners.

When the storyteller uses a piece of literature written by someone else, the material may be either read or paraphrased, depending upon the objectives, the material, and the storyteller's capabilities. One excellent reason for reading a story as it is written is to share the ideas in the exact language of the author. The delight of children in the stories of Dr. Seuss is based, in part, on the way in which the author plays with language. To paraphrase such stories would depreciate their charm and decrease their impact on the listeners' imaginations. However, in some stories the ideas are appropriate for the listeners, but the language is too sophisticated, the story too long, or the plot too involved. The storyteller may wisely choose to tell the story in his or her own words, using more suitable language, carefully editing to a more desirable length, or simplifying the plot. However, even the storyteller in the nursery room should give due credit to the creator of a story and present the ideas of the author with integrity. Young children learn by the teacher's example that the ideas of others are to be treated with respect, including the recognition of authorship.

Perhaps the most important reason for paraphrasing a piece of literature is to create a more intimate experience between the storyteller and the listeners. Putting a story into one's own words allows the teller to infuse the story with a personal involvement and an immediacy that is not otherwise possible. This kind of storytelling passes on to children an oral tradition that has its roots in the very beginnings of civilization. It allows for the kind of rapport that makes the listener feel that the story is being told just for him.

All storytelling requires careful preparation, especially when the story is to be told rather than read. In selecting the story the storyteller will be wise to choose material that she enjoys, for to become properly prepared requires a thorough familiarity with the story and plenty of rehearsing. The material is not memorized, but the chronological order of events and a knowledge of the characters are completely assimilated by the storyteller. To accomplish this, two techniques are extremely useful: (1) the preparation of an outline indicating the significant events, which can be used for rehearsal, and (2) the creation in the mind of mental pictures of the characters, setting, and events. If a story is to "come alive" for the listeners, it must first come alive for the storyteller.

The idea of personal involvement suggests another excellent source for storytelling material: one's own experiences. As mentioned in Chapter 1, little boys and girls love to hear about the childhood experiences of those adults who are important to them. There is a special mystique about "what it was like when I was just your age" (which they may equate with the dawn of history). Any adult seems old to little children, and they are intrigued with learning about things as they were before they were born. They may also enjoy hearing about real-life experiences of the teacher's adult life as long as those experiences meet their interest levels. Because little boys and girls are very real-life oriented, stories based in reality may stimulate their imaginations even more than fictional ones. A personal experience, well told with clarity, adequate fluency, and enough richness of language to engage the imaginations of young listeners may be an excellent way for an adult to model oral storybuilding.

Of all the kinds of storytelling, telling of an original story cannot be surpassed as a means of modeling for children the way the adult feels about imagination. Whether based on one's personal experience or created solely from the imagination, children are delighted when an adult shares a story made especially for them. Sometimes just the right material cannot be found for a special story. The creation of an original story or story poem can supply the desired resource. The teacher's own story can be designed toward meeting specific learning objectives. For example, the children in the class may become characters in the story who have lively adventures, successfully handle problems and conflicts, and show the kinds of resourcefulness and attitudes the teacher wishes to foster. Children who appear to be low fantasizers may be named as characters who have exciting ideas and vivid imaginations, and so forth. The identification of a specific purpose for which a story is needed can create just the right impetus to hatch an idea for a very good original story.

Read or told, borrowed or original, the storyteller should be seated so that all of the listeners can see and be seen at a comfortable eye level. A storyteller is not primarily an entertainer and certainly not an actor, but a sharer who creates a feeling of mutual interaction between self and each of the listeners. Any well-shared story makes each listener feel that the story is being told especially for him. This means that there is actual eye contact with each child from time to time. The language should be descriptive yet simple, appropriate for the group, the occasion, the purpose, the material, and the style of the storyteller. Too much detail detracts from the action and may curtail the child's own imaginative involvement. Though some small gestures may add vividness, interest is best created and maintained by vocal flexibility and facial expression. The material and the feedback from the listeners will help to dictate pacing and timing. Until the storyteller has developed a great deal of skill with a particular piece of material, she will want to continue rehearsing and polishing it each time it is used.

In all of the preceding discussion of storytelling, the teacher is the chief storyteller. However, one of the most exciting ways of interacting with young children to both model the use of the imagination while stimulating the children's own creativity is the shared experience of creating a story orally together. Initially, the teacher may find that she is doing most of the creating, but as she encourages participation through her questions and comments and her interest in the children's ideas, her listeners will become more responsive and involved. Children can be storytellers too; exposure to well-told stories and participation in the creation of oral stories can help them to preserve the old and noble tradition of the storyteller. It can be a wonderful experience for our media-bound children.

Art Fair in the Park

Where yesterday was only grass,
A miracle has come to pass.
Along the walks, beneath the shade,
The artists show the things they've made.

Ceramic pots all bright with glazes
For holding fruit—to use as vases.
Beneath a tree one artist sits
And cuts black paper silhouettes.

Abstract paintings aglow with color—
Oh, there is one to please my mother.
Sculptured figures made from clay
In this art-gallery-for-a-day.

Seascapes, landscapes, portraits done in oils.
Copper work, macrame, mobiles made from coils.

Woven shawls and leather goods,
Platters carved from native woods,
Silver jewelry set with jade,
A chess board done with woods inlaid.

A handhooked rug all worked in blues.
So many things I cannot choose.
A drop of rain—oh how tragic!
The booths soon disappear like magic.

The gentle rain soon paints new scenes
In soft pastels of greys and greens.
No gilted frames nor marble floors—
I like this gallery out-of-doors.

*Using movement and sound to create all kinds of machines is great fun,
especially when one of the machines turns out the most wonderful toys
in the world. A holiday story for middle- and upper-elementary children to dramatize.*

Alfred Bean and the Perfect Machine

Alfred Bean was quite an ordinary looking fellow—well, maybe his
legs were a bit bowed and his ears a bit more pointy than most folks.
When Alf was a young boy, his mother always dressed him in a peculiar shade of green. Not that she planned it that way. She would set out
to buy him a nice red plaid shirt or a pair of blue-striped pants, but
somehow it just never worked out. All the red shirts would be too large
or too small—and the blue shorts had all the stripes going the wrong
way. Finally the saleslady would find an outfit in just that certain shade
of green, and it would fit him just right.

While the other boys and girls played with their toys, climbed trees
or went swimming, Alf would build something. In fact, Alf would
build anything! He borrowed any bit of materials he needed for his
latest invention. Odds and ends, he called them. He borrowed the key
from Sister's skates, Mother's best lace tablecloth, and the lawn mower
wheels. Once he took the left lens out of Grandfather's reading glasses.
When he needed some tough twine, he helped himself to all the strings
from his big Brother's violin.

Alf made things that galumped, and things that blippered, and horrid
smelly things that gologgeled and falopped.

"Oh my," cried his Mother, "will that boy ever grow up and stop
making such a mess?"

And he did grow up, indeed he did. But his ears looked just as pointy
and his legs seemed even a bit more bowed. When Alf went shopping
for a brown suit or a grey hat, the salesman never could seem to fit him
in anything but green—a rather peculiar shade of green. And he kept
right on inventing the strangest things that anyone had ever seen. The
more people complained, the more he built—a gigantic whoosher that
created such a wind that when Alf tested it one day in July it blew all
the leaves off an oak tree. He used his odds and ends to build a high-

speed cholocker that ground up four blocks of sidewalk before he could turn it off. Though each new machine turned out to be more terrible than the last, Alf didn't plan it that way. Secretly he dreamed of building the perfect machine, one that would make people feel good all over. He simply had to keep trying.

After awhile when he walked down the street, the neighbor children would chant:

> Alfred Bean
> Dressed in green
> Move away
> And take your machine.

Of course, all the mothers told the children that it was very rude to say such things, but when the wind was in a certain direction and the mothers were hanging out nice clean sheets on the clothesline, they could be heard saying softly to themselves:

> Alfred Bean
> Dressed in green
> Move away
> And take your machine—please.

When the tired fathers tried to read their evening papers, their heads throbbed from the calunking, pissinging, berwooping of Alf's latest invention. Guess what they were thinking to themselves?

"They just don't understand," sighed Alf, "building a perfect machine isn't easy, not even for Alfred Bean."

So he kept on planning and building and dreaming of the perfect machine. Instead of black, greasy smoke it would send forth wonderful odors like lilacs and hot dogs and peppermint candies. The perfect machine would make beautiful sounds like spring breezes and crystal waterfalls and sleigh bells. It would saw and mold and plane and drill and polish with the touch of a finger. Everytime he thought he almost had it, someone would pass by whispering or shouting or even singing:

> Alfred Bean
> Dressed in green
> Move away
> And take your machine.

"Alright," thought Alfred to himself one day, "I will—I will—I'll move away where I can work in peace and quiet."

So he bought an old house on wheels, packed up his odds and ends and moved out into the country. With a goat to help him tidy up his place, he kept on building his machine.

Things were going along quite well until one day he looked out his window and saw a new highway being built. Soon hundreds of people were driving past, holding their noses and shouting:

> Alfred Bean
> Dressed in green
> MOVE AWAY
> AND TAKE YOUR MACHINE!

"That does it," said Alf. "I'll move someplace where there are no cities, no freeways, and no neighbors—where I can work in peace and quiet."

He got out a large globe of the world and looked it over very carefully. There seemed to be towns and cities and highways just about everywhere. Just then the goat bumped the globe with one of his horns and it rolled over on its side. When Alf reached over to set it straight, he made a great discovery.

"I've found it! I've found it," he cried, "the perfect place. No cities, no highways and no neighbors—not a one."

So he took his goat, packed his house on wheels full of odds and ends and moved to the North Pole. And there were no cities and no highways and no. . . .

Then Alf saw it—a cozy little house with a large workshop behind and a mailbox out in front that said: Mr. and Mrs. S. Claus.

"Oh my," moaned Alfred. "I forgot all about them. I'll just have to go someplace else."

Alf began to repack his odds and ends when he discovered his goat was missing. The poor thing had gone looking for a bit of grass or a nice bramble bush for lunch, but everyplace he looked there was nothing but ice and snow.

Poor Alf set off following the goat's footprints in the snow. They led straight to the large workshop behind the little house. The door stood open and Alf walked in. HORRORS! There was the goat having a tasty lunch of the blueprints for all of the new Christmas toys.

Just then Alf heard the tramp of feet—many feet—and in came a dozen little men all dressed in green, a familiar, peculiar shade of green. Their legs were a bit bowed and their ears just a bit more pointy than most folks. They looked just like someone Alf had seen before, but he was much too embarrassed to remember where.

While Alf stared at the little men, *they* stared at the goat who was now enjoying a fine variety of nails and hammers and saws for his dessert. Suddenly they all began to shout and chase the goat around the workshop. The poor goat was terrified and leaped from workbench to workbench and from shelf to shelf breaking all of the finished toys and destroying the tools for making more. As the goat ran past the doorway, Alf grabbed him by the tail and hung on. IT WAS A WILD RIDE! Then suddenly, the goat tired of the chase and stopped.

Now the little men stared at Alf.

"Look what you and that goat have done," they cried in a chorus.

"Oh dear me," said Alf, "I guess the poor thing was very hungry. You see, we just arrived and with all the bother of finding a suitable place to begin my work, I quite forgot to give him his lunch."

"Well, he certainly ate us out of hammers and saws," said one of the little men.

"And all the children out of Christmas toys," said another.

"Now, if you had only listened to me," said a third, "and set up a modern production line and modern machines, this couldn't have happened."

"Machines!" exclaimed Alf. "I have probably built more machines than anyone else in the world. I'm a machine specialist. Of course, my latest one still needs a little work, but building a perfect machine isn't easy—not even for Alfred Bean. It takes peace and quiet—or another pair of hands," sighed Alf.

"We have lots of hands," cried one of the little men, "two apiece."

"Oh yes," said another, "we're very handy."

So Alf and the little men went right to work—after giving the goat something for his stomachache and putting him out with the reindeer.

In no time at all, the most beautiful machine was whirring and buzzing and bleeping and bopping. It sent forth wonderful odors. It sawed, hammered, molded, drilled, and polished with the touch of a finger—even an elf finger.

But best of all it turned out the most beautiful, remarkable, stupendous, tremendous toys like nothing the children had ever found on a Christmas morning before.

Overnight Alf was famous. His picture was in every newspaper and even on TV. Soon carloads, busloads, truckloads, planeloads, and sledloads of happy boys and girls came all the way to the North Pole just to shake the hand of Alfred Bean.

When the children headed home, leaving Alf to work in peace and quiet, their singing echoed over the ice and snow:

Alfred Bean
Dressed in green
Three cheers for you
And your perfect machine.

And Alf decided his life at the North Pole was just perfect too, and he hummed a familiar tune as he went about his work.

Imaginary balloon rides, magic carpet trips, and sailing aloft on the tail of a kite are all ways for giving children "out-of-this world" make-believe experiences. This is the story of an ant who has an adventure when he stows away aboard a red balloon. It is written for dramatization by early elementary children with everyone playing Anthony.

Anthony Ant's First Flight

Anthony Ant went for his first flight the day that little Tobi Miller had his fifth birthday party in the park. Now when most folks take a trip, they plan ahead for days. They make arrangements with the neighbors to water the roses and feed their hamsters. They read travel folders and decide just what they want to do. Then they pack a suitcase and buy a ticket and do things in a proper way.

That's what most folks do, but Anthony Ant was never one to plan ahead. While all of the other busy little ants were storing up food for the winter, he would lie on his back in the shade or go wading in a dewdrop or try a few bounces on a maple leaf trampoline. Then, he would rush around like a whirlwind just before the first snow to gather enough food to see him through the winter. So what happened to him at the birthday picnic in the park was not too suprising!

It was a nice warm fall day and Tobi Miller and his friends had been having a wonderful time playing games. They had races and played tag until everyone was tired and hungry. Then they chose a table under a shady tree and began to eat their lunch. Of course, Anthony Ant and his friends just happened to be in the neighborhood. All of the ants, except Anthony, were soon busy gathering crumbs from hot dogs and hamburgers and potato chips. Anthony was busy, too. He pretended he was a mountain climber as he crawled over an empty pop bottle. He played hide-and-seek in and out of Janie Jones' bare toes. Then he spied something red and flat laying on the ground. He crawled over to take a better look and then he saw a little tunnel at one end. In went Anthony Ant.

Just then Sandy Simpson picked up his red balloon and began to blow. Poor Anthony was blown deeper and deeper inside until he bounced against the end of a long red tunnel. He thought he had been caught in a hurricane. Sandy blew and blew. Over and over tumbled Anthony Ant. Then, just as suddenly as the windstorm inside the ballon had started, it stopped. What a relief for Anthony! He could not see that at that same moment, Sandy was tying a nice long string to one end of the long red ballon.

All of the children began running through the park with their balloons held high. Anthony settled down to enjoy the ride for he did like a little excitement now and then. Suddenly Sandy Simpson sneezed a giant sneeze. For just that second he forgot to hold tight to the red balloon and away it went sailing through the air. Higher, higher, and higher it went. Up, up, and up went Anthony.

"Bring me down. Bring me down!" shouted Anthony Ant in his biggest voice.

But, of course, no one on the ground could hear him—they didn't even know that Sandy's balloon was carrying a stowaway.

"Oh dear me," moaned Anthony who was feeling just a bit funny in his tummy, "I'll bump my head against a star if I don't come down soon."

But the balloon kept going higher until it was just a red speck high above the pine woods. This way and that way the wind tossed the balloon. Suddenly a friendly downwind shot it straight into the top of a prickly pine tree. POP! Spzzzzzzz . . . and there was Anthony sitting on a pine cone, a shiny green pine cone. Now Anthony Ant had seen pine cones before. There were always fat, brown cones on the ground beneath the trees in the park. But he had never seen one still too green to fall from the tree.

"I must have landed on the moon," said Anthony to no one in particular. He looked down through the tree, and there, way below, was his old neighborhood.

"Oh, well," said Anthony to himself, I'll just sit here for awhile and climb down to earth later."

To tell the truth, he was quite out of breath from all of that shouting and bumping about inside the balloon. And before you could whistle two bars of "Rock-A-Bye-Baby," Anthony Ant was sound asleep.

And that is how it happened that just before dark on the day that Tobi Miller and his friends had a picnic in the park, Anthony Ant came walking slowly back to the picnic grounds from his first flight. All of the ants had just finished a feast of chocolate cake crumbs.

"Well, well," said Edgar Ant in a very stuffy manner, "late again, Anthony. Too bad, the dessert was delicious. And your favorite, chocolate cake with fudge nut icing."

Now Anthony was so tired and hungry that at least four of his six legs were dragging, but he would never let stuffy old Edgar get the better of him.

"Perfectly alright," replied Anthony as cheerfully as he could, "I'm so full of green cheese I couldn't eat a bite. Had a wonderful dinner on the moon. It's a fantastic place; you should go there sometime. Why, from up there everything on earth looked like ants!"

But that night, Anthony Ant hardly slept a wink for his tummy was as empty as the hollow log where he lived, and the very next day when Susie Thompson and her friends had a picnic in the park to celebrate Susie's sixth birthday, Anthony Ant came early and stayed late, and didn't miss a crumb on a paper plate.

How the Touch-Me-Nots
Got Their Name

Long, long ago when many things upon the earth were still waiting to be named, the flowers were having a hard time trying to decide what to call one another. Of course, they knew that someday they would all be given important-sounding Latin names by which they could be listed in encyclopedias and scientific books. But in the meantime, they all needed common, everyday names with which they could greet each other on a fine summer morning or call out quickly in case some danger threatened.

Finding just the right names for some of the flowers was very simple indeed. Who would have dared to suggest that the tall, golden flower that stretched up higher and higher each day be called anything but Sunflower? Or that the pure white blossoms that looked like miniature moons aglow in the night garden be named anything but Moonflower. Just one look was enough to find the perfect names for Rose and Violet and Buttercup. One whiff of Skunk Cabbage and it was named, but it took ever so long to find Petunia, Zinnia, and Gladiola. (Discovering just the right name of each of them is a separate story in itself!)

At last most of the flowers were named, and even Skunk Cabbage had to admit that all of the names were just right—though he preferred to be called "SC." Still there were, here and there, in the garden, some varieties of flowers for whom no one could come up with a name that seemed at all fitting. In one corner grew a row of fragile pastel blooms upon straight green stalks. Despite their small size and charming appearance, these flowers were very proud and uppity. Since they were so hard to get to know, none of the other flowers had ever thought of a suitable name for them. The tulips referred to them as "the proud ones" and decided not to bloom while the proud ones were also blooming. But the little plants didn't mind; they only wanted to to be left alone.

When a friendly blue Morning Glory crept over one summer day, the proud little flowers all whispered, "Go away. Don't bother us, we're still resting."

The poor Morning Glory quietly crept back the way she had come. Not long after that, a yellow and white Field Daisy, smiling a wide daisy smile, leaned over to ask the proud little flowers a riddle. A few sprinkles of pollen (which looked just like gold dust) fell from the Daisy's smile.

"Don't touch us, you're such a common thing, and don't tell us your silly old riddles," said the proud little flowers.

The Daisy kept right on smiling, but forever after, she wouldn't tell another riddle to anyone.

Some of the bolder flowers, like Marigold and Foxglove tried for a long time to be neighborly. But every time a blossom came close in a friendly way, the proud flowers all called out in a chorus, "Don't touch us, we don't like to be bothered."

Most every day the sun shone and a gentle breeze helped the flowers to send their perfumes through the air. Sometimes a soft, kind rain fell and all of the garden would have a cool drink of water and take a bath. After such showers, a brisk breeze would blow to dry their petals and all of the flowers would have a lovely time dancing and playing games with one another. All except the row of proud little flowers; they would stand just as straight as little tin soldiers and wait for the warmth of the summer day to dry their blossoms.

One day, toward the end of summer, the sun disappeared behind a huge dark cloud. For a few moments it was very dark and still; then the wind began to blow harder and harder. All of the flowers began to huddle together to keep safe and warm. All except the row of proud little flowers. They stood as always, haughty and stiff. Sunflower, seeing how fragile they looked standing all alone, tried to bend down and cover them with his wide blossom and big leaves.

"Leave us alone. You frighten us leaning over that way," the flowers shouted up to Sunflower.

Blue Morning Glory, afraid to look when it was so dark and stormy, stretched out her vines to feel the other plants nearby.

"Don't touch us, Morning Glory. Stay in your own part of the garden," shouted the silly, proud flowers in their loudest voices so as to be heard above the wind and thunder.

All that day and night the wind blew and blew. The rain beat down upon all of the flowers in the garden. But the next morning the sun was there as usual, shining brightly in the deep blue sky. All of the flowers opened their blossoms to the lovely day. Blue Morning Glory stretched her vines in the sunshine. The tall Sunflower stood even taller; the Marigolds made merry and the Daisy faces all wore smiles. The flowers could talk of nothing except the Big Storm. Just then, a little green Hummingbird flew into the garden to check up on all of his flower friends. He was so happy to see them looking gay and cheerful after the storm.

"Good morning, Sunflower," said the tiny bird, "you are looking wonderfully tall and important today. How about asking me to lunch?"

"Be my guest," laughed Sunflower, though he knew that Humming-bird really preferred to dine elsewhere.

"That was a terrible storm," hummed the bird, "Morning Glory, I imagine you just slept through the whole thing."

All of the flowers laughed. The Hummingbird was such a tease, always making jokes and flitting from bloom to bloom. They enjoyed having fun with the tiny green bird, all except the row of proud little flowers who stood, as usual, stiff and still wet from the rain.

"And how are all of our little touch-me-nots today?" ask the Hum-mingbird as he hovered just above the little flowers' straight green stalks. The little flowers pretended he wasn't even there.

But the Daisies began to smile harder and harder, the Marigolds giggled and giggled, and tall Sunflower laughed right out loud. Then Blue Morning Glory, who was a quiet, thinking flower said, "I think that is the perfect name for our proud little friends. They are certainly Touch-Me-Nots!"

All of the other flowers in the garden agreed that the name was just right. And from that day until this, the proud little flowers with the stiff, green stems, prefer to live in a shady part of the garden, away from the smiling Daisies, the merry Marigolds, and tall Sunflowers, and are known to one and all as the Touch-Me-Nots.

This short story for young children is fun to do as both a movement story and as a sound story. If the class is quite large, it is good to divide the group into two parts, with half of the children moving and half supplying the sounds. On a second playing, the roles can be reversed.

Merlin the Curious Mouse

Merlin was a curious mouse. He lived with his mother and father and sisters and brothers in an old boot. Merlin had been a curious mouse from the first moment he had opened his eyes, wiggled his two pink ears, and stretched his tiny legs. In no time at all, Merlin began making short trips to explore the world outside his boot home.

Now the mouse family's boot was in the far corner of a closet under the stairs. The closet was full of all kinds of things—an old army coat with shiny brass buttons and deep, deep pockets just right for a mouse game of hide-and-seek. There were flat boxes and square boxes and even a round box that held a straw hat covered with daisies. Merlin poked his whiskers into everything!

One night, while all the other little mice were sound asleep, Curious Merlin heard Mother and Father leave to look for food. This was just the moment he had been waiting for. Carefully he climbed out of the boot house, quickly slid from top to bottom and landed with a soft bump on the boot's toe. Quietly he tiptoed across the closet floor, squeezed under the door, and there he was all alone in the Big World. Now, some little mice would have been very frightened, but not nosy Merlin. He thought it was a wonderful place—so many things to see and hear—so many places into which he could poke his nose—just right for a curious mouse!

Merlin stood very still for just a moment wondering what he should do first. Then he saw the stairway. Up and up, higher and higher it went until it disappeared from sight. Of course, Curious Merlin just had to know where the wonderful stairway led, so right then he started off to see for himself. He ran past the Grandfather clock just as it struck three; he scampered past the open window where the wind was blowing the curtain so it looked like a white ghost. Outside, a big truck rumbled down the dark street. Each new sound made Merlin's heart beat faster and faster. At the top of the stairs was a door, and it was open just a crack!

Curious Merlin crept to the door just as quietly and slowly as he could creep. He looked to his left and he looked to his right. Then he scampered through the crack. Outside, a dog barked and a tomcat began to howl. That frightened Merlin so much that he jumped on the rocker of an old wooden horse. Back and forth and back and forth rocked the horse. Merlin closed his eyes as tightly as he could and jumped off. He landed on the soft tummy of an old rubber doll. The doll squeaked.

Poor Merlin raced around and around the room trying to find the door. He knocked over a wind-up train. Its key bumped the floor with a terrible whirring sound. Down crashed a box of wooden soldiers! What a racket!

Just in time, Curious Merlin saw the door that was open just a crack. He dashed through and down the dark stairway—past the window with the wind blowing the curtain, past the old dog snoring softly, past the Grandfather clock with its big tick-tock. The tomcat on the back-yard fence howled again. Curious Merlin was running so fast he almost didn't see the closet door, but there it was straight ahead. The little mouse made himself just as flat as he could and slipped under the door. Back into his cozy boot house he jumped and landed right next to his mother.

It was lovely and quiet as he snuggled down in his own soft bed, and all Merlin could hear were the tiny snores of his sleeping family and the pitter-patter of his own little heart. From that night on, he would be known as Merlin the *Careful* Mouse.

With a little help from her new pajamas, Peggy Pringle takes a quick trip to India, the home of the Bengal tiger. All children like to play animals, and here is a story with a somewhat different cast of animal characters to play and a little girl as the main character.

A Night in a Tiger Suit

No one in the whole family had ever seen it happen before. The very first time that Mother said "bedtime," Peggy Pringle trotted straight off to bed. Dad raised an eyebrow to show his surprise and Mother wondered if Peggy were coming down with a virus. Even brother Larry looked up from his homework.

"Whatever got into Pokey Peggy?" he asked.

But Grandma just rocked and smiled as she darned a big hole in the toe of a sock.

Jumbo, a large, shaggy dog of unspecified origins, followed Peggy down the hall to her room. Peggy went to her dresser and opened the top drawer. Carefully she took out her brand-new pajamas and put them on the bed. Around the corner to the bathroom she ran. Suds, splash, swipe! Peggy gave her hands and face what Grandma called "a lick and a promise." Squirt, scrub, scrub, scrub. She knew Mother would never settle for a once-over-lightly job on her teeth.

Back in her bedroom, Peggy tossed her sneakers in a corner and left her clothes tumbled in a heap. Then she carefully pulled on her new pajamas. She was just climbing into bed when someone rapped on the door and in came Mother.

"Peggy," she said, "those certainly are the cat's pajamas."

Peggy laughed. Well, there are cats and then again, there are CATS. Grandma had made the pajamas for Peggy as a birthday surprise out of soft, cuddly flannel that looked exactly like a tiger's fur.

"My, my," said Mother, "I've never tucked a tiger into bed before."

As Mother left, Dad stuck his head in the doorway. "Goodnight, Tiger," he called and Peggy answered with her best tiger growl. Under the covers she stretched her legs like a big cat and practiced her growl very softly. Jumbo, half asleep in his bed in the corner of the room, cocked an ear, opened one eye, and went back to sleep. Peggy tried her tiger growl again.

"Oh, no," said a deep voice at the foot of the bed, "that's not right at all."

"This cub really needs training," said a second voice, "but it does have pearly, clean teeth."

Peggy peeked out over the covers. Two beautiful Bengal tigers were gazing down at her.

"Perhaps we'd better take the cub with us," said the first tiger. "She seems big enough."

Peggy thought that she would rather stay all curled up in the nice warm bed, but the big tigers gently nudged her with their soft, black noses.

"I'm not a cub," she said, "I'm a child—I'm Peggy."

But the tigers only nudged a little harder, and Peggy decided she'd better go along. The big tigers seemed friendly enough, but everyone knows you don't talk back to tigers.

"What a pokey little cub this is," said one of the tigers. "She had better hurry if we are going to get to the water hole before the sun goes down."

So Peggy stretched her legs again and tried to spring like a proper tiger. She thought she had done it quite well, but the big tigers just laughed.

"Cubs are so clumsy," said the bigger of the two tigers. "Hurry up little Pokey."

Off they moved with every muscle rippling and their soft paws making no sounds at all. Out into the lush forest they moved. Bright sunshine penetrated the trees making it a world of light and shadow. The big tigers blended in so well that Peggy was afraid she would lose them. She hurried to keep up.

"Coming, Pokey?" called the tigers to Peggy.

It would be easy for a little cub to get lost in the dense underbrush. Peggy would have liked to investigate the beautiful, bright red flowers that hung from the vines, but out of one blossom buzzed a fat bumblebee which nearly stung her on the end of her nose.

Suddenly the tigers broke through the trees and into the open clearing around a pool. The big tigers glided toward the water's edge, but Peggy stopped so fast she tumbled end over end. All around the water hole were birds and waterfowl, and animals of every shape and size having their last drink of the day. A small herd of four-horned antelope stood carefully on dainty hoofs. Nearby, a spotted deer, startled by the sudden appearance of the tigers, moved cautiously back from the water's edge. A shaggy, bad-tempered sloth bear, looking like an unmade bed, moved so slowly toward the trees that Peggy couldn't decide whether he was coming or going. She hoped that he was going, for he looked rather crabby.

Peggy noticed that the deer and the four-horned antelope moved away, and gave the tigers a special place of their own at the edge of the pool. They must be very polite as well as very beautiful, she thought to herself. Just then all of the animals, even the big tigers, froze in their places. Peggy listened but she didn't hear a thing. Instantly, the deer and the antelope bounded off on long, stiff legs, disappearing into the tall grasses. Some of the waterfowl flew off at low altitudes and hid themselves in the bushes. Even the sloth bear hastened his pace. The two big tigers flattened into crouching positions and drew back from the water. They almost flowed into the tall grasses where the last golden rays of the setting sun made them invisible. Peggy stayed close to the side of the bigger tiger.

Then Peggy heard something. She felt the ground vibrate beneath her body. Peeking through the grasses, Peggy saw what all of the animals and birds had sensed earlier. A huge, grey elephant moved slowly toward the shore. Atop the big beast's head rode a small boy about Peggy's age, with jet black hair and eyes and dressed entirely in white. The elephant, sensing the other animals nearby, raised his trunk and sent forth an ear-splitting bellow. Then he immersed his trunk in the water and took a long drink. As he swung his head toward the tall grasses where the tigers were crouching, several drops of water from his dripping trunk sprinkled right over Peggy. For just a second, she thought that the small, bright eye of the elephant had caught her own and she closed her eyes tightly. Slowly she counted to ten.

Peggy opened her eyes. There beside her, sound asleep, was Jumbo, big and shaggy and very damp. Peggy heard the rain beating gently on the roof, and she remembered her open window.

"Oh Jumbo, you disgusting dog," she scolded, but Jumbo didn't even open an eye.

"You're as rumpled and shaggy as a sloth bear, but much nicer," said Peggy as she gave the sleeping dog a hug and jumped out of bed.

"A sloth bear?" she said out loud to herself.

Then Peggy remembered her adventure in the forest, and all of the strange animals at the water hole, and the two beautiful tigers. Peggy, who usually needed three calls to breakfast, washed and dressed in record time. She ran to the kitchen where Mother and Grandma were just starting breakfast.

"Did you sleep well in the new pajamas, dear?" asked Grandma as she handed Peggy some orange juice.

Instead of saying "thank-you," Peggy tried her tiger growl. "Oh, Grandma," laughed Peggy, "I hardly slept a wink. It was too exciting exploring the forest and going to the water hole with the big tigers—

who said I have pearly clean teeth—and seeing all of the strange animals, and watching the elephant with the boy rider take a drink from the pool with his trunk, and . . ."

Peggy stopped for breath, and Mother and Grandma began to laugh. "Oh, Peggy," said Mother, "such an imagination."

Just then Dad and Larry arrived for breakfast. They were both surprised to see Peggy already at the table.

"Whatever happened to our Pokey Peggy," asked Dad, "it must have been the new pajamas, don't you think?"

"Well," said Mother, "I don't know about that, but they certainly had a fantastic effect on her imagination. Wait until you hear about the elephant, and the water hole, and . . ."

But just then, Peggy remembered that she had left that big, wet Jumbo asleep in her bed where Mother did not like to find him.

"May I please be excused," interrupted Peggy, "I forgot something in my room."

"And I bet I know what it is," said Larry who had noticed the telltale mound under Peggy's covers as he had passed her door. "I suppose while you were out in the bush, roaming around with tigers, you captured an elephant and brought him home with you?"

"Don't be silly," called Peggy from the hallway, "elephants are grey and leathery. Old you-know-who is brown and shaggy like a sloth bear."

"A sloth bear?" laughed Dad almost spilling his coffee. "A sloth bear! Grandma, don't ever make that child a pair of space-suit pajamas. Our Pokey Peggy might spend her nights zipping around the galaxies."

"And bring us back a little green man with red eyes that lives on nothing but sloth bears," added Larry.

But Peggy didn't hear a word they were saying. The rain had stopped, and she and a rumpled Jumbo were watching a fat bumblebee climb in and out of a bright red flower that grew on a vine just outside the bedroom window.

A Tall Tale Told under the Woofle Tree

On a hot, lazy afternoon in midsummer, some friends and I had climbed to the top of a small, grassy hill to eat our sack lunches and watch some giant dragonflies who were practicing for the World Insect and Bug Olympics do takeoffs and landings on the river below. Soon, comfortably full of lunch and lulled half asleep from watching the graceful glides and rolls of the dragonflies, we stretched out upon our backs among the tall grasses. Big, fluffy clouds cruised slowly overhead, bumping, joining and breaking apart in a game of slow-motion tag.

"See that cloud up there," said one of the gang pointing skyward, "it looks just like a playful poodle pup."

"Oh no," said another, "it looks like exactly like a bad-tempered old dragon who once owned a summer cottage next door to my great, great uncle Caswell."

Soon everyone joined in and each one was positive that the cloud looked like whatever his own imagination saw. Even as the arguments grew, a sudden breeze scattered our cloud across the sultry sky leaving us each still defending our own point of view. Being old and good friends, and generally tolerant of one another's ideas, we fell to talking about how much more interesting life is because each one of us sees things in our own special way. Such a discussion reminded me at once of a wonderful story I had heard from a mouse I met upon the road one day. Urged on by my friends, I did my best to retell the mouse's story just as he had told it to me.

Actually I met this mouse under a large woofle tree where I had sat down to rest my feet and eat my horseradish sandwich and drink my thermos of cucumber milk. Feeling a little drowsy from my walk in the sun, I leaned back against the smooth purple bark of the woofle tree to take a bit of a nap. Just as I was nodding off, I heard a voice at my elbow cry out.

"Help! Help! I'm on fire! Put me out! Put me out!" a strange voice pleaded.

Since I thought I was all alone under the woofle tree, you can imagine my surprise when I saw a small, grey mouse, neatly dressed in a plaid coat and wearing hiking boots, clutching his throat and jumping up and down.

"Good grief, my friend," I said (though I thought him quite rude), "however can you be on fire sitting on a piece of blue-star moss under a woofle tree?"

"See here," he gasped, "it is really quite shocking to bite into what looks for all the world like a piece of lovely Swiss cheese and discover it is a horseradish sandwich."

"But you should never eat horseradish sandwiches without washing the whole thing down with cucumber milk," I hastened to say, feeling quite sorry for the mouse. I poured the last drop from my thermos into a woofle nut cup and held it for the mouse who greedily drank every drop.

"Ah, much better," said the mouse most politely and he leaned back against the tree trunk as though he wished to sit and chat.

It was then that I noticed that despite his respectable attire for a traveling mouse, he was wearing the most ridiculous eyeglass. I did not realize that I was staring at him until he took off his eyeglass and began carefully polishing it with a clean white handkerchief which he had taken from his jacket pocket.

"You noticed my eyeglass," he said proudly while squinting at me over his whiskers.

"Well," said I, "I'm sorry if I appeared to stare, but I've never seen quite that style before." (And I must tell you that I have never seen such an eyeglass since. The eyeglass had but one lens with a black horn rim all around and bows on either side.)

"For your kindness with the cucumber milk," replied the mouse settling back and lighting his pipe, "I shall tell you how I came by this remarkable equipment."

And this, as closely as I can recall his exact words, is the mouse's story.

"I was born an ordinary mouse of quite ordinary parents in an everyday, ordinary barn. I had no more than seen the light of day until quite extraordinary things began to happen to me. While still a fat, pink infant, I was suddenly scooped up with a pile of straw and tossed in a most frightening manner into the back of a truck which immediately headed for the highway and bumped and rumbled along for hours. When this torture chamber on wheels finally stopped, I was dumped with a thud and a bump and a great deal of straw.

"Being a bright and curious youngster, I quickly scampered out to see where I had landed, but before I could get my bearings, I heard a terrible roar. It seemed to come from an angry brown mountain with a dense forest near the top. Straight up and down over the mountain I ran as fast as my young legs would carry me. Wham! Bang! I crashed into a towering skyscraper that went up and up and up as far as the eye could see. While looking for a door through which to make a hasty exit, I noticed that the skyscraper had begun to shake and rumble as if an earthquake were rocking it. From overhead came a frightful sound and a piece of the building came whipping past me. I closed my eyes and dashed past the grey wall and into an open field and up a hill. Up and up and up the hill I ran until I was standing at its very top and clutching a low stump growing there. Just then my hill came down—another victim of the earthquake I decided—and I was thrown into an ocean where I had to swim for my life."

"Oh, how awful," I interrupted.

"Ah-hum," said the mouse clearing his throat and going right on with his story. "While I was still swimming about in the ocean, a terrible storm came up. The sounds were positively horrifying, and great waves went crashing toward the shore with such force that I was sent flying into space where I collided with an invisible wall. Such wonderful luck!"

"Oh, that was surely more bad luck," I said thinking that the crash must have damaged his brain.

"Not at all," the mouse hastened to say, "for the wall was none other than my remarkable eyeglass! Before my adventure I was not aware that the only reason that everything in the world looked so big to me was that I needed glasses. Indeed, when I had blinked the water out of my eyes, I looked back toward the ocean through my beautiful glass. I chuckled out loud to discover that in my fright, I had nearly drowned in a body of water not much larger than a teacup."

"Amazing," I added and I thought how much I should like to have a look through that eyeglass myself.

"Yes, yes, amazing," said the mouse, "and you recall the hill that went up and up and up? Nothing more than a little animal like myself with a long neck and two stumpy horns on top of its head. A timid creature I have since learned is named Giraffe. And the skyscraper, I know now, is a little fellow called Elephant who seldom seems to know which way he is going since he has a tail both front and behind."

"And your angry brown mountain?" I interrupted to ask.

"I blush to remember how that frightened me—a funny little fellow called Lion who suffers so from the cold that he must wear a muffler around his throat on even the hottest days. This remarkable glass gave me a whole new way of looking at things."

Having told his tale, the mouse leaned back against the smooth bark of the purple woofle tree and appeared to doze. I must admit I took advantage of his closed eyes to stare once again at his eyeglass.

"Would you care to have a look?" he suddenly asked. And before I could again apologize for appearing to stare, he removed his glass, gave it an extra polish and handed it to me.

Carefully closing one eye, I peeked through and looked at the mouse. He immediately became no more than a speck. His remarkable eyeglass was—no more—no less—than the lens from a telescope, wrong side out!

"Your glass is truly remarkable," I said returning it to the mouse. "I should take excellent care of it if I were you."

"Indeed I do," he replied, "for it has made me my fortune. For some time I have been a Very Special Guide at the very zoo where it all began. And if a child gets a crick in his neck while looking at the giraffe, or can't see around the elephant, or is afraid he will fall down the lion's throat when it roars—I just let him take a good look through my wonderful eyeglass."

With that the mouse straightened his lens, bid me goodbye, and walked off down the road as if he were seven feet tall.

"Next time," he called over his shoulder, "try a dash of nutmeg in your cucumber milk."

"Sounds perfectly awful," I thought to myself, but I had to admit, it's probably all in how you look at things.

And having shared the mouse's story with my friends, we soon fell into a lively discussion about which of the dragonflies showed the best gliding form. We each picked our favorite, and do you know, that depending on where we each of us sat, every dragonfly looked a winner.

Appendix and Additional Source Materials

Chapter References

NOTE: Children's books, stories and poems mentioned in the text appear in the bibliography of "Stories to Dramatize." Books on creative dramatics cited in Chapter 2 appear, with others in "Some Additional Readings in Creative Dramatics" in the Appendix.

Chapter 1

1. Joyce McLellan, *The Question of Play* (Oxford, New York: Pergamon Press, 1970), p. 4.
2. Peter Slade, *Child Drama* (London: University of London Press, Ltd., 1954), p. 89.
3. A. R. Luria, F. Ia. Yudovich, Joan Simon, eds., *Speech and the Development of Mental Processes in the Child* (London: Staples Press, 1959), p. 20.
4. Ibid., p. 19.
5. Jean Piaget, *The Language and Thought of the Child* (New York: Meridian Books, 1955), p. 33.
6. Jerome Singer, *The Child's World of Make-Believe: Experimental Studies of Imaginative Play* (New York: Academic, 1973).

7. Mary Ann Spencer Pulaski, "The Rich Rewards of Make Believe," *Psychology Today* (January 1974), p. 70.
8. Ruth E. Hartley, Lawrence K. Frank, and Robert M. Goldenson, *Understanding Children's Play* (New York: Columbia Univ. Press, 1952), pp. 40–41.
9. Margaret Mead, "The Neighborhoods We Need for Growing," *Twentieth Century Faith* (New York: Harper & Row, 1972).
10. Hartley et al., loc. cit.
11. Luria et al., p. 16.
12. Ibid., p. 12.

Chapter 2

1. Sr. Rosemary Winkeljohann, "ERIC/RCS Report: Jean's Influence on Dick and Jane," *Elementary English* (September 1974), p. 877.
2. Clark Moustakas, *The Authentic Teacher* (Cambridge: Howard A. Doyle Publishing Company, 1966), p. 7.
3. Brian Way, *Development Through Drama* (London: Longman Group, 1967).
4. Geraldine Brain Siks, *Creative Dramatics: An Art for Children* (New York: Harper Brothers, 1958).
5. Slade, *op. cit.*
6. Harold H. Anderson, "Meaning of Creativity," *Creativity in Childhood and Adolescence* (Palo Alto, California: Science and Behavior Books, 1965), p. 21.
7. Robert F. Mager, *Preparing Instructional Objectives* (Belmont, California: Fearon Publishers, 1962).
8. Robert J. Armstrong, Terry D. Cornell, Robert E. Kraner, E. Wayne Roberson, *The Development and Evaluation of Behavioral Objectives*. (Worthington, Ohio: Charles A. Jones Publishing Co., 1970).

Chapter 3

1. Mead, op. cit., p. 59.
2. Ibid.
3. Charlotte Selves, "Report on Work in Sensory Awareness and Total Functioning," in Herbert Otto, ed., *Explorations in Human Potentialities* (Springfield, Ill.: Charles C. Thomas, Publisher, 1966), pp. 487–88.
4. Eleanor Craig, *P.S. You're Not Listening* (New York: Richard W. Baron Publishing Co., Inc., 1972).
5. Piaget, op. cit., pp. 34–35.
6. Rachael Carson, *The Sense of Wonder* (New York: Harper & Row, 1956), p. 45.
7. Frank Barron, "The Creative Personality," *Psychology Today* (July 1972), p. 85.

Chapter 4

1. Viola Spolin, *Improvisation for the Theatre* (Evanston, Illinois: North-western University Press, 1963), p. 60.
2. Charles T. Brown, Charles Van Riper, *Speech and Man* (Englewood Cliffs, New Jersey: Prentice-Hall, Inc., 1966), p. 57.
3. John L. Phillips, Jr., *The Origins of Intellect: Piaget's Theory* (San Francisco: W. H. Freeman and Company, 1969).

Chapter 5

1. Alvina T. Burrows, Dianne L. Monson, and Russell G. Stauffer, *New Horizons in the Language Arts* (New York: Harper & Row, 1972), p. 1.
2. Burrows, et al., p. 35.

Chapter 6

1. Nuffield Mathematics Project, *I Do and I Understand* (New York: John Wiley and Sons, 1967).
2. National Council of Teachers of English, *The English Language Arts* (New York: Appleton-Century-Crofts, Inc., 1952), p. 196.
3. Nelson B. Henry, ed., *Reading in the Elementary School, the Forty-eighth Yearbook of the National Society for the Study of Education,* Part II (Chicago: University of Chicago Press, 1949).

Some Additional Readings in Creative Dramatics

Borton, Terry. *Reach, Touch, and Teach.* New York: McGraw-Hill, 1970.
This is not a book about creative drama, but rather about some children who needed help. Drama is only one of the ways through which several were reached.

Burger, Isabel B. *Creative Play Acting.* New York: Ronald Press, 1966.
The second part of the book deals with more formal play production.

Courtney, Richard. *Play, Drama and Thought.* N.Y. Drama Book Specialists (revised), 1974.
A comprehensive book on play, drama, psychodrama, social origins, thought and language.

Crosscup, Richard. *Children and Dramatics.* New York: Charles Scribner's Sons, 1966.
An autobiographical account of the author's work with drama and children over a period of years.

Bruford, Rose. *Teaching Mime.* London: Methuen and Co., 1969.
An English text which concentrates primarily on the use of mime. There is some attention to the addition of speech.

Haggerty, Joan. *Please, Can I Play God?* New York: Bobbs-Merrill, 1966.
A delightful firsthand account with which beginning teachers can identify.

Heinig, Ruth Beall, and Lyda Stillwell. *Creative Dramatics for the Classroom Teacher.* Englewood Cliffs, New Jersey: Prentice-Hall, 1974.
A carefully developed, step-by-step approach to creative dramatics.

Lease, Ruth, and Geraldine Brain Siks. *Creative Dramatics in Home, School and Community.* New York: Harper Brothers, 1952.
Describes the development and use of creative dramatics in several settings.

Mearns, Hughes. *Creative Power.* New York: Dover Publications, 1958.
Deals with several of the creative arts, including drama.

McCaslin, Nellie, *Creative Dramatics in the Classroom.* New York: David McKay, 1968.
A practical text written especially for the classroom teacher.

Pemberton-Billing, R. N., and J. D. Clegg. *Teaching Drama.* London: University of London Press, 1965.
An English text devoted primarily to the description of activities in an easy-to-follow outline form.

Rowen, Betty. *The Children We See.* New York: Holt, Rinehart and Winston, Inc., 1973.
A book which describes how teachers can develop useful observation skills, and includes short sections on the use of creative dramatics and puppetry in relation to the observation of language development in young children.

Siks, Geraldine Brain. *Creative Dramatics: An Art for Children.* New York: Harper Brothers, 1958.
Describes creative dramatics in relation to the stages of child development. Brief sections deal with creative drama in settings other than the classroom.

_____, Hazel Brain Dunnington, (eds.). *Children's Theatre and Creative Dramatics.* Seattle: University of Washington Press, 1961.

A collection of readings by leaders in the field.

Slade, Peter. *Child Drama.* London: University of London Press, 1954.

A philosophical and theoretical approach to child drama is described by a pioneer in Britain.

_____. *An Introduction to Child Drama.* London: University of London Press, 1958.

A condensation of the longer work.

_____. *Experience in Spontaneity.* London: Longman Group, 1969.

A deeply personal account of the author's love affair with children and drama.

Spolin, Viola. *Improvisation for the Theatre.* Evanston: Northwestern University Press, 1963.

The author's own techniques for stimulating improvisation with children and adults are clearly described in her numerous theatre games.

Tyas, Bill. *Child Drama in Action.* New York: Drama Book Specialists, 1969.

Drama experiences with children are described in terms of the teacher's stated purposes and interaction with the children.

Ward, Winifred. *Playmaking with Children.* New York: Appleton-Century-Crofts, 1957.

A widely used text by a pioneer in Creative Dramatics.

Way, Brian. *Development Through Drama.* London: Longman Group, 1967.

Discusses the relationship between creative drama and the development of the whole child.

Wise, Arthur. *Communication in Speech.* London: Longmans, Green and Company, 1967.

A British book on speech communication in the primary school devotes a section to the approach through drama.

Additional Readings for the Creative Teacher

Amidon, Edmund, and Elizabeth Hunter. *Improving Teaching.* New York: Holt, Rinehart and Winston, Inc., 1966.

_____, and Ned A. Flanders. *The Role of the Teacher in the Classroom.* Minneapolis: Paul S. Amidon and Associates, 1963.

Anderson, Harold H., ed. *Creativity and Its Cultivation.* New York: Harper & Row, 1959.

_____, ed. *Creativity in Childhood and Adolescence.* Palo Alto, California: Science and Behavior Books, 1965.

Ashton-Warner, Sylvia. *Spearpoint; Teacher in America.* New York: Knopf, 1972.

Barron, Frank. "The Psychology of Imagination." *Scientific American,* 199 (September 1958), 151–66.

Berger, Terry. *I Have Feelings.* New York: Behavioral Publications, 1971.

Borton, Terry. *Reach, Touch, and Teach.* New York: McGraw-Hill, 1970.

Bruner, Jerome S. *Toward a Theory of Instruction.* Cambridge: Belknap Press, 1966.

Collum, Albert. *Push Back the Desks.* New York: Citation Press, 1967.

Furlong, E. J. *Imagination.* New York: The Macmillan Company, 1961.

Greenbert, Herbert M. *Teaching With Feeling.* New York: The Macmillan Company, 1969.

Groch, Judith, *The Right to Create.* Boston: Little, Brown and Company, 1969.

Hartley, Ruth E., Lawrence K. Frank, and Robert M. Goldenson. *Understanding Children's Play.* New York and London: Columbia University Press, 1952.

Jones, Richard M. *Fantasy and Feeling in Education.* New York: New York University Press, 1968.

Lyon, Harold C., Jr. *Learning to Feel and Feeling to Learn.* Columbus, Ohio: Charles E. Merrill, 1971.

Maslow, Abraham. *Toward a Psychology of Being.* Princeton: D. Van Nostrand Company, 1967.

McLellan, Joyce. *The Question of Play.* Oxford, New York: Pergamon Press, 1970.

Mearns, Hughes. *Creative Power.* New York: Dover Press, 1958.

Moustakas, Clark. *Creativity and Conformity.* Princeton: D. Van Nostrand Company, 1967.

———. *The Authentic Teacher: Sensitivity and Awareness in the Classroom.* Cambridge, Mass.: Doyle, 1966.

Parnes, Sidney J., and Harold, F. Harding, eds. *A Source Book for Creative Thinking.* New York: Charles Scribner's Sons, 1962.

Rogers, Carl R. *On Becoming a Person.* Boston: Houghton Mifflin, 1961.

Taylor, Calvin W. *Climate for Creativity.* New York: Pergamon Press, 1972.

Yardley, Alice. *Discovering the Physical World.* New York: Citation Press, 1973.

———. *Reaching Out.* New York: Citation Press, 1973.

———. *Senses and Sensitivity.* New York: Citation Press, 1973.

Readings on Listening

Anderson, Harold A. "Teaching the Art of Listening," *School Review.* 57:63–67 (February 1949).

Applegate, Mauree. "To Listen Imaginatively," *Grade Teacher.* 74(4):38 (December 1956).

Barbe, Walter B., and Robert M. Meyers. "Developing Listening Ability In Children," *Elementary English.* 31:82–84 (February, 1954).

Berarducci, Joanne. "Original Stories for Teaching the Vocal Skills of Speaking and Listening." Master's thesis. Boston: Boston University, 1956.

Brown, Charles T., and Paul W. Keller. "Three Studies of the Listening of Children," *Speech Monographs.* 32:129–38 (June 1965).

Clark, Genevieve. *It's Fun to Listen* (listening to sounds in nature). New York: Vantage, 1953.

Dills, Eva L. "Listening the Key to Learning, Including the Results of Listening Projects Carried out in the Alfred I. DuPont and Faulk Road Schools, Wilmington, Delaware" (includes work in Sociodrama). Master's thesis. Newark, New Jersey: New Jersey State Teacher's College at Newark, 1955.

Duker, Sam. *Teaching Listening in the Elementary School: Readings*. Metuchen, New Jersey: Scarecrow Press, 1971.

Eastman, Milton. "Listen!" *Grade Teacher*, 81(1):56 (September 1963).

Haun, Ruth. *"Creative Listening,"* *Today's Speech* (October 1953).

Kellogg, Ralph Edward. "A Study of the Effect of a First-grade Listening Instructional Program upon Achievement in Listening and Reading." San Diego: San Diego County Department of Education, 1966.

Lundsteen, Sara W. "Listening: Its Impact on Reading and the Other Language Arts." Urbana, Illinois: National Council of Teachers of English (NCTE/ERIC studies) 1971.

Russell, David H., and Elizabeth F. Russell. *Listening Aids through the Grades*. New York: Bureau of Publications, Teacher's College, Columbia University, 1959.

Taylor, Calvin W. "Listening Creatively," *Instructor* (February 1964).

Taylor, Sanford Earl. *Listening*. Washington, D.C.: NEA, 1973.

Wagner, Guy, Mildred Alexander, and Max Hosier, *Strengthening Fundamental Skills with Instructional Games*. Cedar Falls, Iowa: J. S. Latta and Son, 1959.

Weaver, Carl H. *Human Listening: Processes and Behavior*. Indianapolis: Bobbs-Merrill, 1972.

Films for Use in Creative Dramatics

The following list of films is representative of the kinds that are useful in creative dramatics. They are arranged alphabetically by title, and for each there is a brief description that shows how the film can relate to the development and classroom use of creative dramatics. Where there are two names listed following the description, the first is the producer and second, the film distributor.

ABC of Puppet-Making—Part one
A ten-minute color film that illustrates ways to make and dress simple hand puppets. Bailey Films, 1955.

ABC of Puppet-Making—Part two
Shows how to make and use puppets with molded heads. Bailey Films, 1955.

Adventures of Baby Fox
A delightful film that uses music and rhyme to tell about the habits of a baby fox. Good portrayal of a young animal and nice sensory stimulation. Thirteen minutes long. Encyclopedia Britannica Films, Encyclopedia Britannica Educational Corporation, 1955.

Animals at Work in Nature
Ten-minute color film that shows close-ups of animals at work. Encyclopedia Britannica Films, Encyclopedia Britannica Educational Corporation, 1956.

Arrow to the Sun
An animated tale of a Pueblo Indian boy who has an exciting adventure while looking for his father. Excellent for use in drama work on American Indians; the colors and designs can be used to stimulate the imagination. Texture Films, 1973.

Big Green Caterpillar
A color film showing the life of a caterpillar from birth to maturity. Excellent for insect movement and to illustrate growth. 11 minutes. Stanton, 1962.

Children Discover the World, The Time of Discovery
A 21 minute, color film showing children from three to twelve from the Idyllwild School of Music and the Arts exploring the use of various art forms for self-expression. Idyllwild Arts Foundation, 1967.

Children in Winter
Fun to use with Ezra Jack Keats book *The Snowy Day*. Shows children playing in the snow. Especially useful in climates where children rarely see snow or have an opportunity to experience it. Encyclopedia Britannica Films, Encyclopedia Britannica Education Corporation, 1957.

Fable
A beautiful color film starring Marcel Marceau. Excellent example of the art of mime done by a master. Photographed in an Italian village, the cast includes several children. Xerox, 1973.

Fantasy of Feet
Delightful film showing feet doing a variety of movements and wearing many kinds of shoes and no shoes at all. Good to stimulate the imagination and creative movement. Encyclopedia Britannica Films, Encyclopedia Britannica Educational Corporation, 1972.

Follow Me
A five-minute film of children playing follow-the-leader along the streets of their neighborhood and through a playground. Useful for stimulating story ideas or to use with movement activities. Encyclopedia Britannica Films, Encyclopedia Britannica Educational Corporation, 1969.

Grand Canyon
A feast for the eyes and ears. There is no narration, just beautiful scenes of the Grand Canyon during all seasons set to Ferde Grofes' "Grand Canyon Suite." Walt Disney Productions, 1961.

I Have an Egg
Blind children discover all about an egg through their sense of touch. Celebrity Holdings, Inc., McGraw-Hill Text Films, 1969.

Impressions of a City
A 15-minute tour of London which reveals the contrasts of a big city. Excellent for story ideas and sensory stimulation. G. B. Instructional Films, 1965.

Incredible Wilderness
Short color film showing the remote areas of Olympic National Park. Beautiful vistas and close-ups to stimulate the imagination. Harper's Ferry Historical Association (no date).

Land of the Long Day
Gives children an excellent introduction to the land and life of the Eskimos. In color, 38 minutes. Suggests several ideas creating improvisational scenes. Encyclopedia Britannica Films, Encyclopedia Britannica Educational Corporation, 1952.

Learning through Movement
An excellent film for preservice and inservice teachers on teaching through creative movement. S-L Film, 1968.

Lion Has Escaped, The
A delightful film with the animation created from children's drawings. Featurette Film Studio, Poland, McGraw-Hill Text Films, 1972.

Little Red Hen
Live animals are used to tell this old favorite story. Many uses in the language arts program, and especially fun for young children to dramatize. Coronet Films, 1950.

Medieval Manor
The setting is a 13th-century castle in France. The story contrasts the lives of those who live in the manor with one of the serf families. Provides good background for drama work placed in that period. Encyclopedia Britannica Films, Encyclopedia Britannica Educational Corporation, 1956.

Mr. Shepard and Mr. Milne
A film visit with the creators of Christopher Robin and Winnie-the-Pooh. A treat for teachers and children who love the Pooh stories. Weston Wood, 1972.

Movement Exploration
Demonstrates a wide variety of movement activities for children K-6. 22 minutes, in color. Documentary Films, 1967.

Movement in Time and Space
Using drama, dance, dialogue and characterization, children explore through fantasy to make intellectual discoveries. 30 minutes, color. BBC Television, Time-Life, 1967.

Organizing Free Play
Of special value to nursery and kindergarten teachers, the film deals with the use and organization of free play in early childhood education. U. S. Office of Education, U. S. National Audiovisual Center (no date).

Pioneer Home
A ten-minute film for elementary children that offers a visual introduction to the life and environment of a pioneer family. Can provide a useful background for drama activities related to pioneer times. Coronet Films, 1948.

Puss-in-Boots
The well known fairy tale told with animated puppets. A delightful film which may be used to stimulate language activities and an interest in puppetry. Encyclopedia Britannica Films, Encyclopedia Britannica Corporation, 1951.

Rainshower

The changing moods of a day are captured with sight and sound. A photographer takes his camera to farm and city on a rainy day. A 15-minute color film that brings to the classroom a rich experience in listening and looking. Dimension Films, Churchill Films, 1964.

Red Balloon, The

A lovely fantasy about a boy and his red balloon. The film offers children a visual introduction to Paris. An excellent film for stimulating story ideas for dramatization or creative writing. Albert Lamorisse, Com Films, Inc., 1956.

Rock-A-Bye Baby

An examination of mothering practices around the world with an emphasis on the need of children to be touched and held. 30 minutes, color. Time-Life, 1971.

Searching Eye, The

A ten year old boy's visual adventures at the beach can stimulate looking activities for children. 18-minute color film. Saul Bass and Associates, 1964.

Show Me

The film shows children with physical impairments participating in a variety of movement activities developed for such purposes as body image, coordination and partner work. This is of particular value to the teacher of special children. Bowling Green State University, Universal Education and Visual Arts, 1967.

Stone Soup

Uses the illustrations from Marcia Brown's book, *Stone Soup.* Story is an excellent one to use for small group pantomime and improvisational work. Weston Studios, 1955.

Study in Wet

A seven-minute color film all about water. The sound track is entirely created from water sounds. A fine film for looking and listening activities to stimulate the imagination. Groening, 1964.

Textures of the Great Lakes

A six-minute color film showing the textural qualities inherent in the waters, beaches, dune, and land areas around the Great Lakes. The visual images are accompanied by a beautiful score done on the harp. Karl B. Lohman Jr., Thorne, 1966.

Toes Tell

Another excellent film dealing with textures and movement. Encyclopedia Britannica Films, Encyclopedia Britannica Educational Corporation, 1972.

Up is Down

A film for older boys and girls done in both animation and with actual film clips. A little boy who walks on his hands see things differently than they really are. Morton Goldscholl Design Association, Inc., Pyramid Film Producers, 1970.

What's in A Play
A 17-minute color film that analyzes a simple scene, showing conflict, beginning, climax, and ending. Film Associates, 1967.

What's in a Story
Using James Thurber's *The Unicorn in the Garden,* the film explores the structure of a story. Film Associates of California, 1963.

Zoo, The
Presents a film "field trip" to the Brookfield Zoo. Provides an excellent background for drama activities about animals, their habits and characteristics. Encyclopedia Britannica Films, Encyclopedia Britannica Educational Corporation, 1961.

Collections and Anthologies for Use in Creative Dramatics

Andersen, Hans Christian. There are several excellent volumes of Andersen's Fairy Tales (in translation). Two rather recent ones are: *Fairy Tales,* trans. by L. W. Kingsland. New York: Henry Z. Walck, 1962. *Seven Tales,* trans. from the Danish by Eva Le Gallienne, illustrated by Maurice Sendak. New York: Harper & Row, 1959.

Arbuthnot, May Hill. *The Arbuthnot Anthology.* Glenview, Illinois: Scott, Foresman, 1961.

Johnson, Edna, Evelyn R. Sickels, Frances Clarke Sayers. *Anthology of Children's Literature.* Boston: Houghton Mifflin, 1970.

Kipling, Rudyard. *Just So Stories.* Garden City, New York: Doubleday, 1912.

Ross, Eulalie Steinmetz, ed. *The Lost Half-Hour: a Collection of Stories with a Chapter on How to Tell a Story.* New York: Harcourt, Brace and World, 1963.

Sandberg, Carl, illustrated by Maud and Miska Petersham. *Rootabaga Stories.* New York: Harcourt, Brace, 1936.

Siks, Geraldine Brain, *Children's Literature for Dramatization.* New York: Harper & Row, 1964.

Thorne-Thomsen, Gudrun, ed. *East o' the Sun and West o' the Moon and Other Norwegian Folk Tales,* rev. ed., New York: Harper & Row, 1946.

Uchida, Yoshiko. *The Magic Listening Cap.* New York: Harcourt, Brace and Company, 1955.

Ward, Winifred. *Stories to Dramatize.* Anchorage, Kentucky: The Children's Theatre Press, 1952.

Stories to Dramatize for Younger Boys and Girls

Several of the following stories also appear in anthologies; however, the versions briefly described here refer to separate volumes.

Alan, Sandy. *The Plaid Peacock.* New York: Pantheon Books Division, Random House, 1965.
Told in the style of a storyteller, this tale takes place in the India of Queen Victoria's reign. A "different" peacock and a regiment of Her Majesty's Scottish Fusiliers join forces to their mutual advantage. An exciting climax and roles for everyone.

Asch, Frank. *George's Store.* New York: McGraw-Hill Book Company, 1969.
A man named George and his dog with the same name run a grocery store. Interesting folk come to shop and the two Georges always try to guess what each will buy. Hilarious black and white illustrations by the author. Children may play the characters described and create more.

Barton, Byron. *Where's Al.* New York: Seabury Press, 1972.

Done in comic strip format, the story is about a lost dog whose owner asks many people, "Where's Al?" Excellent to encourage verbalizing.

Asbjornsen, P. C., and J. E. Moe, illustrated by Marcia Brown, *The Three Billy Goats Gruff*. New York: Harcourt, Brace and World, 1957.

A delightful version of a favorite story to dramatize. The end is violent as the troll is destroyed and tossed into the river, but this is logical and satisfying for most children.

Bowen, Elizabeth. *The Good Tiger*. New York: Alfred A. Knopf, 1965.

Sarah and Bob make friends with a "good" tiger and invite him home to tea. The tiger's adventure is fun for all to play in unison.

Brennen, Anita. *A Hero by Mistake*. New York: Wm. R. Scott, 1953.

Dionoso, a Mexican Indian boy, has many frightening adventures before he catches a bandit. Much to his own surprise, he becomes a hero.

Brown, Marcia. *Once a Mouse*. New York: Charles Scribner's Sons, 1961. (Caldecott winner)

A mouse in India is befriended by a hermit who can work magic. The Hermit changes the mouse into a series of animals and finally into a haughty tiger whose arrogance leads to his downfall. Everyone can begin as the mouse and proceed to develop several characters.

_____. *Stone Soup*. New York: Charles Scribner's Sons, 1947.

Soldiers use their wits instead of force to get a reluctant village to feed them. "Playing a trick" has child appeal and is exciting to dramatize.

Burn, Doris. *Andrew Henry's Meadow*. New York: Coward-McConn, Inc.

Andrew Henry is the child in the middle who seems to be left out of the activities of his brothers and sisters. He likes to build things and gets into trouble for his efforts. He moves his projects to a meadow where he is soon joined by other children who need a private place. There is a great crowd scene to play at the end.

Burningham, John. *Mr. Grumpy's Outing*. London: Jonathan Cape, 1970.

A cumulative tale for nursery and kindergarten children to dramatize. An exciting climax results when all of the animals who go with Mr. Grumpy on his outing misbehave in the boat.

Carle, Eric. *Do You Want to be My Friend?* New York: Thomas Y. Crowell, 1971.

A picture book for little children. Valuable for encouraging oral language.

Carrick, Carol. *The Dragon of Santa Lalia*. Indianapolis: Bobbs-Merrill, 1971.

A grandmother who tends the island goats braves the fury of a cry-baby dragon to look for grass for the goats. She takes food to the hungry dragon until there are only dried kernels of corn to bring. The corn and a fiery dragon result in a shower of popcorn on the village.

Carrick, Carol, and Donald Carrick. *The Pond*. New York: The Macmillan Company, 1970.

Beautiful pictures and descriptive language to stimulate interest in pond life, the imagination, and creative movement.

Coombs, Patricia. *Dorrie and the Goblin*. New York: Lothrop, Lee and Shepard Company, 1972.

A little witch named Dorrie babysits a small goblin while her mother enter-
tains at a Tea and Magic Show. One of several books about Dorrie; especially
fun to play at Halloween.

Craig, M. Jean. *The Dragon in the Clock Box.* New York: W. W. Norton, 1962.
A lovely story about small Joshua and his imagination which supplies him
with a dragon egg and finally a dragon "big enough to fly away." Children
can identify with Joshua's need for his very own companion which is his
private responsibility. Perfect to introduce young children to the fun of
having an imaginary visitor.

Daugherty, James. *Andy and the Lion.* New York: Viking Press, 1966.
Andy reads about lions, dreams about lions until he finally has an adventure
with a lion and becomes a hero. A modern tale of Androcles which ends with
a circus scene that is great fun to dramatize.

deRegniers, Beatrice S. *Red Riding Hood.* New York: Atheneum, 1972.
Familiar favorite in verse form, with a happy ending for everyone but the
Wolf.

_____ *May I Bring a Friend.* New York: Atheneum, 1965. (Caldecott winner)
A little child is invited to have tea with the King and Queen. He brings his
animal friends and everyone has a grand time.

DuBois, William Pene. *Bear Circus.* New York: Viking Press, 1971.
These "bears" are koalas, and the circus guests are kangaroos who have
befriended the koalas after grasshoppers steal all of their food. The koalas
thank their benefactors by performing for them at a "bear circus." Many
opportunities for action.

Fenton, Edward. *Fierce John.* New York: Doubleday, 1969.
A delightful story about a boy who makes believe he is a lion. Deals with
self-identity.

Fern, Eugene. *The Most Frightened Hero.* New York: Coward-McCann, 1961.
A beautifully illustrated story about courage, both in the face of physical
danger and moral courage in response to disappointment.

Freeman, Don. *Penquins of All People!* New York: Viking Press, 1971.
Peary Byrd Penquin is invited to the UN to explain how penquins live
together so peacefully.

Gag, Wanda. *Gone is Gone.* New York: Coward-McCann, 1935.
Fritzl assumes that his work is harder than that of this wife. They exchange
roles and after a hectic time of it, Fritzl is happy to return to his fields. Many
ludicrous situations make this fun to play.

_____. *Millions of Cats.* New York: Coward-McCann, 1928.
An old lady wants a cat, and her obliging husband goes to find one for her.
He returns with more than enough! Children are challenged to develop
unique cat characters, all interesting and appealing.

Hayes, Wilma P. *Christmas on the Mayflower.* New York: Coward-McCann,
1956.
The crew of the Mayflower is eager to return to England. This would leave
the new settlers without the ship's support during the first long winter in the

New World. Presents another Pilgrim story to play besides the familiar Thanksgiving episode.

Johnson, Crockett. *Harold and the Purple Crayon.* New York: Harper & Row, 1955.

A little boy creates his very own world with a little help from a purple crayon.

Keats, Ezra Jack. *The Snowy Day.* New York: Viking Press, 1962. (Caldecott Award)

A little boy goes out on a snowy day and plays in the snow. Excellent for parallel pantomime play and early small-group work as children create their own snowy-day activities.

Lamorisse, Albert. *The Red Balloon.* Garden City, New York: Doubleday, 1957.

A provocative story of a boy and a red balloon on an adventure in the colorful Montmartre district of Paris. Before sharing the end of the story, it is fun to stop and have the children create their own endings.

Lawrence, John. *The Giant of Grabbist.* New York: David White, 1969.

A friendly giant from Cornwall comes to live on a hill in Exmoor. When he rescues a leaky fishing boat during a storm he becomes a hero to the town.

Ness, Evaline. *Sam, Bangs, and Moonshine.* New York: Holt, Rinehart and Winston, 1966. (Caldecott Award)

Sam, "named Samantha but always called Sam" and her cat, Bangs, have some wild times until Sam discovers that there are times to talk "moonshine" and times to talk about things as they really are.

NicLeodas, Sorche, and illustrated by Evaline Ness. *All in the Morning Early.* New York: Holt, Rinehart and Winston, 1963.

Partly told in rhyme, here is an easy to dramatize tale about a boy from Perthshire who takes his grain to the mill and meets interesting human and animal characters who join him on his way. An adaptation of a Scottish folktale retold for American children.

Payne, Emmy. *Katy No-Pocket.* Boston: Houghton Mifflin, 1944.

A story enhanced by large colorful illustrations, shows how many animals carry their young. Excellent for helping children to develop animal characters.

Peet, Bill. *The Wump World.* Boston: Houghton-Mifflin Company, 1970.

"Man" finally succeeds in paving the entire planet and forces all of the Wump society to take refuge underground. A charming ecological story for young children who can develop a great empathy for the plight of the delightfully ridiculous-looking Wumps.

Petersham, Maud and Miska. *The Box with Red Wheels.* New York: Macmillan, 1949.

A group of barnyard animals discover a cart with a baby in it. Great for animal movement and sounds.

Peterson, Hans, and Harold Wiberg. *When Peter Was Lost in the Forest.* New York: Coward-McCann, 1970.

This is a story that talks about fear and loneliness in a new and refreshing way. Peter finds out that being alone in the beautiful winter woodlands can be an exciting experience if he remains calm. After playing Peter, children may enjoy creating their own incidents about fear and loneliness to play out.

Piatti, Celestino. *The Happy Owls.* New York: Atheneum, 1964.

Picture book which illustrates the futility of quarreling and the pleasure and happiness which results when we try to get along with others.

Politi, Leo. *Lito and The Clown.* New York: Charles Scribner's Sons, 1964.

This heartwarming story of a boy who lost his little grey kitten will delight all children who love pets. It stimulates creative expression of both sadness and joy. The setting is a Mexican town at Carnival time.

Preston, E. M. *Monkey in the Jungle.* New York: Viking Press, 1968.

A small monkey decides that he will not go to sleep. Children will delight in becoming the monkey and pantomiming his adventures. Excellent for parallel pantomime. During the preplay discussion, children will want to create a jungle setting in their imaginations.

Rand, Ann. *Umbrellas, Hats, and Wheels.* New York: Harcourt, Brace and World, 1961.

No two things and no two people are ever exactly alike. This simple idea told in a delightful story makes the world much more fun to live in. In addition to possibilities for creative movement and pantomime, this story can lead into role-playing.

_____ and Paul Rand. *Listen! Listen!* New York: Harcourt, Brace and World, 1970.

Listening becomes fun in a book full of the sounds children like to hear, and such sounds are equally fun to make. The prose is both perceptive and rhythmic.

Reesink, Maryke, and Georgette Apol, *The Two Windmills.* New York: Harcourt, Brace and World, 1967.

An easy-to-understand and moving story which explains the happiness of working together, sharing talents, and being friends. The full-page illustrations are colorful and make the book easy to share with an entire class.

Reit, Seymour. *Animals Around my Block.* New York: McGraw-Hill Book Company, 1970.

An excellent introductory book for involving children in animal movement and characterization. Illustrated with photographs of animals.

Sendak, Maurice. *Where the Wild Things Are.* New York: Harper & Row, 1963. (Caldecott Award)

Every child can identify with Max who made mischief and is sent to his room without his supper. To cope with his punishment, Max creates a wonderful adventure for himself to "where the wild things are." Everyone can play Max, and then, for the wild rumpus, create fantastic wild things.

Showers, Paul. *Find Out by Touching.* New York: Thomas Y. Crowell, 1961.

A delightful book which can help children explore and make exciting discoveries all through the sense of touch.

Slobodkina, Esphry. *Caps for Sale.* New York: William R. Scott, 1947.

A peddler sets out to sell his caps. He falls asleep and some mischievous monkeys steal his caps. The peddler plays a clever trick on the monkeys and fools them into returning his caps. Children who enjoy the mirror activities will love the final scene.

Stewart, Robert. *The Daddy Book*. New York: American Heritage Press, 1972. Especially suitable for preschool and kindergarten children. All kinds of daddies do all kinds of things. Lots of ideas about occupations and recreation activities to help children be fathers in their dramatic play.

Uchida, Yoskiko. *Sumi's Prize*. New York: Charles Scribner's Sons, 1964. A little Japanese girl dares to enter the kite-flying contest as the only girl. Boys as well as girls will want to play Sumi.

Udrey, Janice May. *Mary Jo's Grandmother*. Chicago: Albert Whitmas, 1970. A beautiful story about an independent Grandmother who preferred to live alone on her isolated farm. Her small granddaughter, Mary Jo, comes to visit during a winter storm. When Grandmother has an accident, Mary Jo is resourceful and competent.

Zion, Gene. *Harry the Dirty Dog*. New York: Harper & Row, 1956. Harry refuses to take a bath until even his family no longer recognize him. Children can relate to all of Harry's frustrations.

Zolotow, Charlotte. *William's Doll*. New York: Harper & Row, 1972. A lovely story about a little boy who wants a doll so that he may practice being a Daddy.

Stories to Dramatize for Middle- and Upper-Elementary Children

Individual children and specific groups of children vary widely in maturity, needs and interests. Many of the stories from the preceding list for younger children may also hold the interest of boys and girls in the middle grades, particularly when the story is used as a basis for drama. Children may feel most comfortable and free to experiment when working with thoroughly familiar materials. This is often true for older children who have had little previous experience in creative dramatics.

The following list, for middle- and upper-elementary children, has been selected to represent the most useful types of literature for dramatization and to expose children to ideas, traditions, and environments that may be new to them.

Aesop. *The Fables of Aesop*, retold by Joseph Jacobs. New York: Macmillan, 1964. An excellent retelling of the famous fables of Aesop. Strong characters, conflict, and the brevity of the tales make them particularly suitable for small-group improvisation, with or without dialogue.

Alexander, Lloyd. *The Book of Three*. New York: Holt, Rinehart and Winston, 1964. Also: *The Black Cauldron* (1965), *The Castle of Llyr* (1966), *Taran Wanderer* (1967), and *The High King* (1968). These five books, set in an imaginary land of Prydain, have been evolved by the author from a wealth of Welsh legends and mythology.

Bishop, Claire Hutchet, illustrated by William Pene DuBois. *Twenty and Ten.* New York: Viking Press, 1953.
Twenty French children help to hide ten Jewish children from Nazi soldiers who have come to their mountain retreat in search of Jews.

Bond, Michael, *A Bear Called Paddington.* Boston: Houghton Mifflin, 1968.
When a London family adopts an almost-human bear, their lives become a series of crises. Lovable Paddington and his near disastrous adventures are great fun to play.

Brown, Marcia, *Dick Whittington and His Cat.* New York: Charles Scribner's Sons, 1950.
Poor Dick Whittington must part with his only possession, a cat named Puss, when his master insists that all of the servants must send something to be traded during a voyage of the master's ship. Later the cat is sold to a King of Barbary for a handsome price and Dick becomes a wealthy man. An old tale retold in words and prints by a superb storyteller.

Buck, Pearl S. *The Big Wave.* New York: The John Day Company, 1948.
A story of Japan told by a woman who lived there for many years. Young boys who live in a fishing village show great courage and compassion when a great tidal wave radically changes their lives. The book is illustrated with beautiful 18th-century Japanese prints.

Buff, Mary, illustrated by Conrad Buff. *The Apple and the Arrow.* Boston: Houghton Mifflin, 1951.
An exceptionally well told and illustrated story of the Swiss hero William Tell.

Clemens, Samuel L. (pseud., Mark Twain). *The Adventures of Huckleberry Finn.* New York: Heritage Press, 1940. Illustrations by Norman Rockwell.
_____ *The Adventures of Tom Sawyer.* New York: Dodd, Mead, 1958.
Biographical information and drawings from early editions. Many scenes from both of these beloved books are fun to dramatize. Excellent for small group work.

Clymer, Eleanor. *How I Went Shopping and What I Got.* New York: Holt, Rinehart and Winston, 1972.
Thirteen-year-old Debbie feels left out in her family. She disobeys her mother and follows the advice of some friends instead and takes her little sister Judy shopping. Judy gets lost and Debbie must muster all of her courage to handle the problem.

Dahl, Roald. *Charlie and the Chocolate Factory.* New York: Alfred A. Knopf, 1964.
Charlie, a poor boy who lives with his parents and ailing grandparents, wins a chance to visit a fantastic candy factory. There is tremendous sensory stimulation from beginning to end.
_____. *James and the Giant Peach.* New York: Alfred A. Knopf, 1961.
When young James is suddenly orphaned, he goes to live with two dreadful aunts. He escapes from their tyrannical rule when he enters a giant peach and shares an amazing flight across the Atlantic with several super-sized insects.

Dalgliesh, Alice. *The Courage of Sarah Noble.* New York: Charles Scribner's Sons, 1954.

Set in the Connecticut territory of the early 1700s, this true story shows how little girls can cope with danger with resolution and courage.

DeJong, Meindart, illustrated by Maurice Sendak. *The House of Sixty Fathers,* New York: Harper, 1956.

A young Chinese boy becomes separated from his family and finds himself stranded in Japanese-occupied China.

Dodge, Mary Mapes. *Hans Brinker.* New York: Charles Scribner's Sons, 1915.

A story full of suspense, human dilemmas, and action; particularly fun to use during the ice-skating season or with a unit on the Netherlands. Many fine scenes to dramatize.

Forbes, Esther. *Johnny Tremain.* Boston: Houghton Mifflin, 1943. (Newbery Award)

The setting is pre-Revolution Boston. Johnny Tremain yearns to become a fine silversmith, but an accident to his hand forces him to leave his apprenticeship. Later, as a messenger for the Sons of Liberty, he becomes deeply involved in the colonies' fight for freedom.

Hamilton, Virginia. *Zeely.* New York: Macmillan, 1967.

On her way to spend the summer with her Uncle Ross on his farm, Elizabeth Perry decides that for the vacation she will be a girl named Geeder. Her fantasizing takes on new dimensions when she meets Zeely Tayber who is six-and-a-half feet tall and the color of ebony. Geeder decides Zeely is really a Watusi queen.

Held, Kurt, trans. by Lynn Aubry. *The Outsiders of Uskoken Castle.* Garden City, N.Y.: Doubleday and Company, Inc., 1967.

The story is set in the ruins of an old castle on the Adriatic coast in Yugoslavia where a group of children without homes have taken refuge. Their leader is a spirited red-haired girl named Zora, and the gang's exploits are based on fact. There is lots of action in the tradition of Robin Hood.

Konigsburg, E. L. *From the Mixed-Up Files of Mrs. Basil E. Frankweiler.* New York: Atheneum, 1967. (Newbery Award)

Claudia and Jamie run away from home and hide in the New York Metropolitan Museum of Art. They have many adventures and solve a mystery. Many excellent scenes to dramatize, several especially suitable for work in pairs.

Krumgold, Joseph. *And Now Miguel.* New York: Thomas Y. Crowell, 1954. (Newbery Award)

Miguel finally is old enough to help with the summer pasturing of the family sheep high in the mountain meadows. Several scenes to play about the trials and triumphs of growing up.

Lawson, Robert. *Ben and Me.* Boston: Little, Brown and Company, 1939.

The story of Benjamin Franklin told by a very talented and self-important mouse. Fun to dramatize some of the famous discoveries and inventions.

_____. *Rabbit Hill.* New York: Viking Press, 1944. (Newbery Award)

The "natives" of Rabbit Hill are worried when new folks move into the people house. Animal characters that are best played with strong human qualities.

Lewis, C. S. The seven books known as "The Chronicles of Narnia." New York: The Macmillan Company.

The Magician's Nephew (1955); *The Lion, the Witch and the Wardrobe* (1950); *The Horse and His Boy* (1954); *Prince Caspian* (1951); *The Voyage of the Dawntreader* (1952); *The Silver Chair* (1953); *The Last Battle* (1956). A master writer of fantasy created these books for all lovers of "other world" stories; they are full of fantastic characters, both human and nonhuman caught in moments of great conflict. This list is arranged in the order recommended by the author, and can provide months of fantasy reading and dramatizing for older boys and girls.

Malory, Sir Thomas. *King Arthur,* retold by Mary MacLeod. New York: Macmillan, 1963.

All of the favorite adventures of King Arthur and his knights and ladies.

McCloskey, Robert. *Homer Price.* New York: Viking Press, 1943.

When young Homer helps out in the doughnut shop, he is plagued by near disaster from a lost diamond and a contrary machine that will not quit making doughnuts. Great fun to build machines with body movements and sounds.

Norton, Mary. *The Borrowers* (and subsequent adventures of the borrowers) New York: Harcourt, Brace, 1953.

Children delight in the adventures of the tiny folk who live parallel lives to full-sized humans but do so tucked away in the recesses of old houses and rely on what can be "borrowed."

Rostron, Richard. *The Sorcerer's Apprentice.* New York: Wm. Morrow, 1941.

A contemporary version of an old tale about a sorcerer's apprentice who discovers that a little knowledge is truly a dangerous thing. Doubly exciting when played with the Paul Dukas music of the same name.

Seredy, Kate. *The Good Master.* New York: Viking Press, 1935.

An autobiographical story of life in Hungary prior to World War I. The round-up scene is exciting to play, particularly for children who only equate round-ups and stampedes with the American West.

Sherlock, Philip M. *Anansi, the Spider Man: Jamaican Folk Tales.* New York: Thomas Y. Crowell, 1954.

Folk tales of the West Indies based on older African stories. The animal characters are especially intriguing to play.

Speare, Elizabeth George. *The Witch of Blackbird Pond.* Boston: Houghton Mifflin, 1958. (Newbery Award)

An historical novel for young people about a young girl who leaves her home and comes to the Connecticut Colony where she is confronted with attitudes and beliefs new to her. Like the old woman of Blackbird Pond who becomes her friend, young Kit Tyler is accused of witchcraft.

White, E. B. *Charlotte's Web.* New York: Harper, 1952.

A favorite story about a spider and her friends, especially Wilbur the pig. The story deals sensitively with death, and there are many fine scenes to dramatize.

Wilder, Laura Ingalls. *Little House in the Big Woods, Little House on the Prairie* (and others). New York: Harper, 1953.

The author tells of her own childhood and growing-up years which began just after the Civil War. She has described everyday events with such clarity that contemporary children can identify with the Ingall's family and its way of life.

Resource Books and Articles for the Storyteller

Colwell, Eileen, ed. *A Storyteller's Choice: A Selection of Stories, with Notes on How to Tell Them.* New York: Henry Z. Walck, 1964.

Laughton, Charles. *Tell Me a Story.* Chicago: McGraw-Hill, 1957.

Sawyer, Ruth. *The Way of the Storyteller.* New York: Viking Press, 1942.

Shedlock, Marie L. *The Art of the Story-Teller.* New York: Dover Publications, 1951.

Spain, Frances Lander, ed. "A Storyteller's Approach to Children's Books," *The Contents of the Basket.* New York Public Library, 1960, pp. 51-59.

Tashjian, Virginia A. *With a Deep Sea Smile.* Boston: Little, Brown , 1974.

Tooze, Ruth. *Storytelling.* Englewood Cliffs: Prentice-Hall, 1959.

Viguers, Ruth Hill. "Over the Drawbridge and Into the Castle," *The Horn Book Magazine,* Vol. 27, (January 1951), pp. 54–62.

Index of Ideas and Activities

Several of the foregoing activities are useful for two or more purposes, and, therefore, appear under all appropriate categories.

Character development activities

Development through pantomime.
Development of dialogue as characters—teacher led.
Development of dialogue as characters—small groups.

Listening activities

Games:
Can you Ride the Pony, John?
Elephants Fly
Getting to Know You
Give and Take—two variations
I Packed my Bag
Sequential Listening Game—"Early Life of George Washington"
Statues
The Beat Goes On
Variation on "Simon Says"
Other Listening Activities:
Creating sounds for storybuilding
In-space movement—imagined sound stimuli
Listening to actual sounds
Listening to actual sounds—on tape
Listening to imagined sounds—teacher led narrative
Listening to music to create moods and emotions
Rhyming games
Sound stories
Storybuilding from sounds

Looking activities

Games:
Black Magic
Detective (Indian Chief)
Second Look
Sequential Looking Game—"Columbus Discovers America"
Other Looking Activities
Activities with colored scarves
Cinquain poems on color
In-space movement—visual stimuli
Pair work with pictures

Storybuilding from props
Using visual media

Movement and pantomime activities

Active Movement Games:
  Follow-the-Leader
  Races
  Variations on tag
Creative Movement and Pantomime Games:
  Antonym/homonym games
  Can You Ride the Pony, John?
  Detective
  Elephants Fly
  Getting to Know You
  Sequential Looking Game—"Columbus Discovers America"
  Statues
  The Beat Goes on
  Variation on "Simon Says"
Other Creative Movement and Pantomime Activities:
  Activities with colored scarves
  Character development through pantomime—circus theme
  In pairs tasks to pantomime
  In-space movement
    Imagined sensory stimuli
    Seasonal activities
  Integrated Arts Activity—"Art Fair in the Park"
  "Living Dictionary"—new vocabulary words
  Math concepts to pantomime
  Mirror activities
  Moving as verbs
  Moving as verbs—adding adverbs
  Palm-to-palm activities
  Responding to imaginary odors
  Science concepts to pantomime
  "See How Many Ways You Can Say Hello!"
  Silent Spelling Quiz
  Small group pantomimes—problem solving
  Social studies concepts to pantomime
  Tasting imaginary foods
  Using the larger space—ideas

Multisensory activities

Examining objects using two or more senses
Storybuilding from multi-sensory stimuli

Oral storybuilding

Small group pantomime—problem solving
Storybuilding from props
From sounds
From tactile experiences
From multisensory stimuli
Using visual media

Pair activities

In pairs—tasks to pantomime
Integrated Arts Activities—"Art Fair in the Park"
Mirror activities
Pair work with pictures
Palm-to-palm activity
Role-playing in pairs—verbalizing
Sharing space in pairs

Relaxation activities

Small group activities

Antonym-homonym games
Developing dialogue as characters—small groups
Integrated Arts Activities—"Art Fair in the Park"
Math concepts to pantomime
Planning an imaginary feast
Role-playing in small groups—verbalizing
Science concepts to pantomime
Sharing space—small groups
Small group pantomimes—problem solving
Social studies concepts to pantomime

Spatial activities

Exploring self-space in unison
Sharing space in pairs
Sharing space—small groups

Tasting/smelling activities

Describing favorite foods
In-space movement—taste/smell stimuli
Planning an imaginary feast
Responding to imaginary odors
Tasting imaginary foods

Touch activities

Handling imaginary objects
In-space movement—tactile stimuli
Palm-to-palm activity
Passing real objects
"See How Many Ways You Can Say Hello!"
Storybuilding from tactile experiences
Using the Touch Box

Verbalizing activities

Cinquain poems on color
Describing favorite foods
Developing dialogue through puppetry
Developing dialogue as characters—small groups
Developing dialogue as characters—teacher led
Evaluating group work
Role-playing in pairs
Role-playing in small groups
Role-playing—teacher led
Sound stories

NTC DEBATE AND SPEECH BOOKS

Debate
Basic Debate. *Fryar and Thomas*
Strategic Debate. *Wood and Goodnight*
Advanced Debate. *ed. Thomas*
Modern Debate Case Techniques. *Terry, et al.*
Cross-Examination in Debate, *Copeland*
Student Congress & Lincoln-Douglas Debate. *Fryar and Thomas*

Forensics
Creative Speaking, *Buys, et al.*
Creative Speaking Series:
   Oratory. *Scott*
   Oral Interpretation. *Hunsinger*
   Extemporaneous Speaking. *Buys*
   Serious Dramatic Interpretation. *Cobin*
   Humorous Dramatic Interpretation. *Cobin*
   Special Occasion Speeches. *Miller*
   Group Reading: Readers Theatre. *Beck*
   Radio Speaking. *Beck*
Coaching and Directing Forensics. *Klopf*
Forensic Tournaments: Planning and Administration.
   Goodnight and Zarefsky
Forensics as Communication. *ed. McBath*

Speech Communication
Person to Person. *Galvin and Book*
Person to Person Workbook. *Galvin and Book*
Literature Alive! *Gamble and Gamble*
Speaking By Doing. *Buys*
Contemporary Speech. *Hopkins and Whitaker*
Self-Awareness. *Ratliffe and Herman*
Working in Groups. *Stech and Ratliffe*

Resource Materials
A Guide for Teaching Speech Today. *ed. Halliday*
New Horizons for Teacher Education in Speech
   Communication. *eds. Newcombe and Allen*
Speech Communication, *Galvin and Book*
Teaching With Creative Dramatics. *Cottrell*
Speech Activities in the High School. *Buys and Copeland*
Speech in the Jr. High School. *Herman and Ratliffe*

 For further information or a current catalog, write:
National Textbook Company
4255 West Touhy Avenue
Lincolnwood, Illinois 60646-1975 U.S.A.